Canto is an imprint offering a range of
titles, classic and more recent, across a
broad spectrum of subject areas and
interests. History, literature, biography,
archaeology, politics, religion, psychology,
philosophy and science are all represented
in Canto's specially selected list of titles,
which now offers some of the best and
most accessible of Cambridge publishing to
a wider readership.

In this book John Bowker shows something of what has emerged out of religious interpretations of death, not as a comprehensive history of death but as an indication of what lies at the root of the major religious traditions, lending to each its characteristic style. Bowker shows how the accounts of the origin of religion, as a denial of death through the offer of eternal life, are false, and surveys those themes in eastern and western traditions which indicate the original significance of death in the world's religions. It thereby becomes clear (with particular reference to contemporary physics and biology) how religious and secular attitudes to death might be unified in a manner that could support pastoral involvement in hospice and hospital work.

THE MEANINGS OF DEATH

THE
MEANINGS OF DEATH

JOHN BOWKER

Adjunct Professor, University of Pennsylvania
Adjunct Professor, North Carolina State University
Fellow of Trinity College, Cambridge

CAMBRIDGE
UNIVERSITY PRESS

Published by the Press Syndicate of the University of Cambridge
The Pitt Building, Trumpington Street, Cambridge CB2 1RP
40 West 20th Street, New York, NY 10011–4211, USA
10 Stamford Road, Oakleigh, Victoria 3166, Australia

First published 1991
Canto edition 1993

Printed in Great Britain at the University Press, Cambridge

British Library cataloguing in publication data

Bowker, John 1935–
The meanings of death.
1. Death. Attitudes of religions
I. Title
291.23

Library of Congress cataloguing in publication data

Bowker, John Westerdale.
The meanings of death / John Bowker.
p.   cm.
Includes index.
ISBN 0-521-39117-2
1. Death – Religious aspects – Comparative studies. I. Title
BL504.B6 1991   90-41518
291.2′3 – dc20   CIP

ISBN 0 521 39117 2 hardback
ISBN 0 521 44773 9 paperback

WG

For Margaret
Beneficiorum gratia sempiterna est

Contents

Acknowledgements

The author and publisher gratefully acknowledge the following for permission to reproduce copyright material: Harcourt Brace Jovanovich Inc. and Faber and Faber Ltd, excerpts from *Collected Poems 1909–1962* by T. S. Eliot; Random House, Inc., excerpt from *The Immense Journey* by Loren Eiseley; Harvard University Press, excerpt from *The Practice of Chinese Buddhism* by Holmes Welch; Grove Press Inc. and Faber and Faber Ltd, excerpts from *Waiting for Godot* by Samuel Beckett; Orbis Books and Darton Longman and Todd Ltd, excerpt from *Summoned by Love* by C. Carretto; William Collins and Sons Ltd, excerpts from *Part of a Journey* by P. Toynbee and *Incognito* by Petru Dumitriu; Alfred A. Knopf Inc., excerpt from *Death Customs: An Analytical Study of Burial Rites* by E. Bendann; Century Hutchinson Publishing Group Ltd, excerpt from *The Psychological Attitude of Early Buddhist Philosophy* by Govinda; Duckworth and Co. Ltd, excerpt from *Awakenings* by Oliver Sacks; Hodder and Stoughton Ltd, *Christian Words and Christian Meanings* by John Burnaby; Russell and Volkening Inc., excerpts from *Hasidic Tales of the Holocaust* by Yaffa Eliach; Oxford University Press, excerpts from *An Introduction to the Study of Man* by J. Z. Young and the *Bhagavad-Gita*, trans. R. C. Zaehner; BBC Enterprises Ltd, excerpts from *Worlds of Faith* by John Bowker.

Every attempt has been made to contact the owners of copyright material. However, should there appear material which appears without acknowledgement, the publisher will be glad to provide full acknowledgement in any reprints or future editions of this work.

Abbreviations

Ait. Br.	Aitareya Brahmana
Ang. Nik.	Anguttara Nikaya
Ant.	Antiquities
AV	Atharva Veda
B.	Babli [Babylonian]
Brh.	Brihadaranyaka
Chan.	Chandogya
Chron.	Chronicles
Cor.	Corinthians
Dan.	Daniel
De Cher.	De Cherubim
De Gig.	De Gigantibus
De Post.	De Posteritate Caini
Deut.	Deuteronomy
Dial.	Dialogues
Dig. N.	Digha Nikaya
Eph.	Ephesians
Ezek.	Ezekiel
Gen.	Genesis
Hab.	Habakkuk
Is.	Isaiah
J.	Jerushalmi [Jerusalem]
Ket.	Ketuboth
Kgs.	Kings
Lev.	Leviticus
Macc.	Maccabees
Mahabh.	Mahabharata
Majj. Nik.	Majjhima Nikaya

Matt. (Mt.)	Matthew
Mund.	Mundaka
N.	Nikaya
Neh.	Nehemiah
Num.	Numbers
P.	Pitaka
Ps.	Psalms
Quis Rerum	Quis Rerum Divinarum Heres
RV	Rg Veda
Rom.	Romans
S.	Sura
Sam.	Samuel
Sam. Nik.	Samyutta Nikaya
Sata. Br.	Satapatha Brahmana
Svet.	Svetasvatara
Tait. Br.	Taittiriya Brahmana
Tim.	Timothy
Up.	Upanishad
Vin. P.	Vinaya Pitaka

For references which are not given in full in the text, the reader should refer to the bibliography.

I

Introduction

CHAPTER I

Death and the origins of religion

Early in 1981 a memorial plaque, from a rather unusual funeral home, was submitted in evidence to a Los Angeles court. The inscription read:

Today is the first day of your life: Mildred A. Harris ... entered into suspended animation, Sept. 1970.

The body of Mrs Harris had been entrusted to the Cryonics Society of California whose founder, Mr Robert Nelson, had read a book which suggested that bodies could be kept at sub-zero temperatures until a way could be found to revive them. When the family went to check their deep-frozen parents less than five years later they found that the company had been insufficiently funded to pay the fuel bills for what might, after all, have turned out to be eternity. Consequently, the nitrogen supply had been cut off. The bodies had defrosted and were already in an advanced stage of decomposition.

They (and two other families) duly sued Mr Nelson for $10.5 million damages, including half a million dollars for emotional suffering: in 1981 they were awarded $1 million. As the saying goes, you haven't lived until you've died in California. But the award was a feather in the scales when weighed against the destruction of yet another human hope of immortality. Not that the hope was totally irrational: 'suspended animation', via the deep-freeze, had its own anticipations. The science of cryogenics (from the Greek *kruos*, 'frost') has already enabled the freezing of embryos with a subsequent, successful, implanting in the womb. Even at the time of the freezing of the body of Mrs Harris, it was well-known that some living organisms can recover after

3

being subjected to the low temperatures of such liquefied gases as nitrogen, hydrogen and helium. The theoretical implications of this had already been spelled out by the biologist, Hudson Hoagland, in 1968. He had argued that for such organisms, at those very low tempertures, with metabolism virtually stopped, time, as a reciprocal of the rate of metabolism, must pass very rapidly as far as the organism is concerned. Thus in effect such organisms are projected forward into the future at those low temperatures. A stay of a century at $-270C$ (the temperature of liquid helium) with subsequent warming and recovery would, if it were possible to effect, be precisely equivalent to projecting the organism forward a century into the future; and he regarded that as 'a sort of Wellsian time-machine idea' (p. 326).

What, of course, the short-lived cryonics boom ignored was the clause 'if it were possible to effect'. The problems of resuscitation seemed soluble because it was believed that they would mimic the natural processes of hibernation. The fact that hibernation is not resuscitation did not, at the time, affect the argument. What seemed more impressive was the kind of observation which Loren Eiseley once made, when he cut a block of ice out of a frozen river in which a catfish had been imprisoned. When he took it home and allowed the ice to thaw, 'a vast pouting mouth ringed with sensitive feelers confronted me, and the creature's gills laboured slowly' (p. 23).

Cryonics, reinforced by anecdotes of that kind, produced an optimism about immortality which culminated in a book by Ettinger (*The Prospect of Immortality*), which appeared in 1967 and became a Scientific Bookclub selection. It began with the forth-right words: 'Most of us now breathing have a good chance of physical life after death – a sober, scientific probability of revival and rejuvenation of our frozen bodies' (p. xxi); and it ended with an appeal to the readers to get involved in the deep-freeze programme, if not for themselves, at least for those whom they love: 'With your active co-operation, the next death in your family need not be permanent' (p. 194).

In this way, the appeal of the Cryonics Society is very easy to understand. It resembles many other human hopes of defeating death (Ettinger put the matter more pungently by claiming that we no longer need to take death lying down), and it does so in two ways: it evokes the human feeling of wanting to do the best we can for those we love, especially in the circumstance of death where there is so little else that we *can* do for them (with all the tangled legacies of guilt and untransacted business which necessarily accompany death); and it catches at clues in nature (albeit nature imperfectly understood) which suggest, by analogy, ways in which we (or some aspect of ourselves) may continue through and beyond death.

In that way, the human imagination has been prolific. To give some examples (all of which occur in at least one religious imagination of how life beyond death may be possible): if the seed falls to the ground and is born again into more abundant life, perhaps also the body will do the same; if the very same breath (which returns finally to the air in death) is the air which, when I have breathed it, you can inhale in your turn, perhaps also what I have been when alive can be breathed into another life; if the smoke of a fire can be carried beyond discernment into the sky, perhaps also the smoke of the burned body will carry the reality of that person beyond our present discernment; if salt dissolved in water disappears and yet, if the water is tasted, the salt is still undoubtedly present, perhaps we also will be dissolved in earth or fire or water, and yet still be discernibly present; if the snake sloughs its skin and lives on with its dead and useless coverings left behind, perhaps we also will shed this body and live in a new realisation.

Like the transaction underlying those analogies, the hopes of immortality based on suspended animation are equally unlikely to be realised as events in which you or I will be involved. Their importance as analogies may remain. But if they are offered as a prospectus of a future event, then they clearly fail. Yet many people buy these stories as literal truth; and the verb 'buy' is itself literal, since the death business is a major industry – as Jessica Mitford's *The American Way of Death*, Harmer's *The High Cost of Dying*, and Evelyn Waugh's *The Loved One* made abundantly clear.

All this, according to many, is both the power and the origin of the whole religious enterprise: religion offers compensating paradises to those who cannot face the realities of death and oblivion. It feeds on futile hope, and offers, to follow the title of a Victorian tract, *The Traveller's Guide from Death to Life*. Throughout their history, all religions have described what Zaleski calls 'otherworld journeys'. But is there any such journey to be made? Would it not be a great deal more realistic to accept, as did Othello, that, at death, we reach journey's end? Where, anyway, *could* he go – 'Where should Othello go'? Khrushchev took great delight in making this comment on Gagarin's first flight into space, in 1961:

As to paradise in heaven, we heard about it from the priests. But we wanted to see for ourselves what it is like, so we sent our scout there, Yuri Gagarin. He circled the globe and found nothing in outer space – just complete darkness, he said, and no garden at all, nothing that looked like paradise. We thought the matter over and decided to send up another scout. We sent Herman Titov and told him to fly around a bit longer this time and to take a good look – Gagarin was only up there for an hour and a half, and he might have missed it. He took off, came back and confirmed Gagarin's conclusion. There's nothing up there, he reported.

Or as the writer of the First Letter of John put it more succinctly, 'No man has seen God at any time.'

So what is religion doing? Offering (on this view) the colloquial 'pie in the sky'; or in Ambrose Bierce's definition, in *The Devil's Dictionary*: 'Extinction, n. The raw material out of which theology created the future state.' This is a view of religion which locates it firmly in the ignorance of the human race. It argues that our ancestors, who were unfortunately but unavoidably ignorant, looked for the best explanations they could find for the events and the feelings which they experienced. Having no 'true' explanations, they attributed the unknown to the agency of unseen but powerful beings. Such beings would have to live somewhere, and the obvious locations would clearly be above or below the earth; and heaven and hell were thus invented.

An account of that kind sounds like a travesty, but it was extensively held in the nineteenth century (and it remains a widespread popular assumption). Thus Winwood Reade wrote in his bleak history of human martyrdom:

The savage lives in a strange world, a world of special providences and divine interpositions, not happening at long intervals and for some great end, but every day and at almost every hour ... Death itself is not a natural event. Sooner or later men make the gods angry and are killed. It is difficult for those who have not lived among savages perfectly to realise their faith. When told that his gods do not exist the savage merely laughs in mild wonder at such an extraordinary observation being made ... His creed is in harmony with his intellect, and cannot be changed until his intellect is changed. (pp. 136f.)

It then becomes simple for the slightly more wise, or at least for the more powerful among them, to exploit these beliefs for the purposes of political and economic control – an argument that is at least as old as Polybius (see my *Licensed Insanities*, p. 85). If you take off the shelf volume I of *The Great Soviet Encyclopedia* (admittedly no easy task since each volume weighs in at 4 lb. 4 oz.) you will find the following entry:

Hell: according to the majority of religious teachings, the abode of the souls of sinners supposedly doomed to eternal suffering ... Theologians and clergymen use the concept of hell, which they contrast with paradise, to influence the conscience and feelings of believers.

On this view (by no means confined to Leninist orthodoxy) it is not surprising to find the use and abuse of death pushed back to account for the origin of religion itself. 'Of all sources of religion,' proclaimed the anthropologist, Malinowski, in 1925, 'the supreme and final crisis of life – death – is of greatest importance' (p. 46). In maintaining that view, he was only echoing a founding father of modern anthropology, E. B. Tylor, who regarded death as the enigma which drove conscious human beings into becoming religious or animistic (that is, into seeing animation in all living things, and in regarding an *anima*, or soul, as able to be emancipated by death). Malinowski continued:

Death is the gateway to the other world in more than the literal sense. According to most theories of early religion, a great deal, if not all, of religious inspiration has been derived from it – and in this, orthodox views are on the whole correct ... Death and its denial – Immortality – have always formed, as they form today, the most poignant theme of man's forebodings.

The quest for the origin of religion has long since ceased for those who have given the matter any thought: no evidence has survived – nor could it – from which we might infer how belief began. But the account of religion *continuing* to attract believers because of its exploitation of their fear of death – and continuing, therefore, to exercise power, control and manipulation over oppressed and helpless humans – remains pervasive. As with Lucky, in *Waiting for Godot*, theology is then regarded as erupting from deprivation in a gibberish of frantic images and desperate design: Lucky, who has been driven and defeated through life by unending command and constraint – 'Stop-back-stop-turn-think' – suddenly bursts out (while the others pile on top of him):

Given the existence as uttered forth in the public works of Puncher and Wattmann of a personal God quaquaquaqua with white beard quaquaquaqua outside time without extension Who from the heights of divine apathia divine athambia divine aphasia loves us dearly with some exceptions for reasons unknown but time will tell and suffers like the divine Miranda with those who for reasons unknown but time will tell are plunged in torment plunged in fire whose fire and flames if that continues and who can doubt it will fire the firmament that is to say blast hell to heaven, so blue still and calm so calm with a calm which even though intermittent is better than nothing. (p. 42)

But what if time does *not* tell us anything except the story of its own process – a process which draws a line and makes an end of you or of me? In his recent Notebook, *To Be a Pilgrim*, Cardinal Basil Hume confessed: 'I fail to understand how anybody can go through life and think there is nothing after death. That is a totally inhuman thought' (p. 227). His failure in understanding is bizarre, when one considers how many people have held, and still do hold, exactly that belief and have not for that reason become inhuman. Bertrand Russell stated forthrightly: 'I believe that when I die I shall rot, and nothing of my ego will survive.' Russell no doubt was as much a sinner as any cardinal, and damaged some people during his life. But he could not be regarded as failing in humanity for that thought. His entire autobiography is held in a bracket of humanistic passion:

Three passions, simple but overwhelmingly strong, have governed my life: the longing for love, the search for knowledge, and unbearable pity for the suffering of mankind ... I have lived in the pursuit of a vision, both personal and social. Personal: to care for what is noble, for what is beautiful, for what is gentle: to allow moments of insight to give wisdom at more mundane times. Social: to see in imagination the society that is to be created, where individuals grow freely, and where hate and greed and envy die because there is nothing to nourish them. These things I believe, and the world, for all its horrors, has left me unshaken. (*Autobiography*, pp. 9, 728)

Far from being inhuman, the 'thought' to which the cardinal refers has driven the humanist vision, both ancient and modern, to insist on the natural nature of death – and, if necessary, to resist the pretensions of religious imagination which divert our energies into immature affections and unattainable goals:

> Our Father, who art in heaven,
> Stay there,
> And we will stay here on earth
> Which is at times so lovely
> With its mysteries of New York
> With its mysteries of Paris
> Which absolutely outweigh the mystery of the Trinity

Prévert's 'Pater Noster': it corresponds to the response of Peter Weiss' de Sade to Marat, when Marat remarks that 'the animating force of Nature is destruction, And that our only instrument for measuring life is death'. De Sade responds:

> Correct, Marat.
> But man has given a false importance to death
> Any animal plant or man who dies
> adds to Nature's compost heap
> becomes the manure without which
> nothing could grow nothing could be created
> Death is simply part of the process
> Every death even the cruellest death
> drowns in the total indifference of Nature
> Nature herself would watch unmoved
> if we destroyed the entire human race. (*Marat/Sade*, p. 32)

It is a thought already anticipated – and turned against the human construction of God, as it was by de Sade himself – by

Richard Hodgson, in his 'Meditations of a Hindu Prince and
Sceptic':

> You say that I must have a meaning! So has dung, and
> > its meaning is flowers;
> What if our lives are but nurture for souls that are higher than ours?
> When the fish swims out of the water, when the bird soars out
> > of the blue,
> Man's thought shall transcend man's knowledge, and your God be
> > no reflex of you!

MARX AND FREUD

The word 'reflex' takes us, very clearly, into the territory mapped
and described by Marx and Freud. For both of them, though in
different ways, the power of religion lies in its creation of illusory,
though persuasive, pictures of what lies ahead for human beings
beyond death. In fact, both Marx and Freud were capable of far
greater subtlety than the crude, compensatory understanding of
religion often attributed to them. But even so, there is no mis-
taking the thrust of the argument in both, that religions hold sway
over human affections precisely because they offer an escape from
the afflictions of this world, or a compensation for them. Even
if we go back as far as the fragments of Marx's earliest work, this
note is unmistakable. While he was still a student, he began a
novel, *Scorpion and Felix*, which (like many students who attempt
the same) he never finished. But in what he did complete, the
ambiguity of perspective is already apparent which was later to
culminate in his argument that the construction of heaven is a
reflection of the real world. In what van Leeuwen calls 'an ironic
comment on the New Testament parable of the Last Judgment
(Matthew 25)' (*Critique of Heaven*, p. 47), Marx asked how God
decides which is right and which is left. Of course, if God's
countenance sported a nose, it would be evident what is right and
what is left. But they are completely relative concepts. In contrast,
Marx argued,

we are all in the position of Faust: we don't know which side is right
and which is left: our life is a circus, we run in a circle, we look about
us in all directions, until we bite the dust at last and are killed by the

gladiator, life itself. We desperately need a new Saviour, because – agonizing thought that keeps me awake, ruins my health, slays me! – we cannot distinguish the left from the right side, we cannot tell the location of either.

So, Marx argued, if the criteria of judgement cannot be located in heaven, that is simply because they are a reflection in the imagination of the only real judgements of which we can be certain, those on earth. Where Feuerbach had glimpsed the way in which God is constructed as a projection of the ideals that humans hold of themselves at their best, Marx realised that that projection is never individual but always social. It arises in what we would now call 'the social construction of knowledge'; and *as* projection, it reflects, expresses and perpetuates existing social and economic relationships. Thus Marx was well aware that religion does important things even for the poorest and most oppressed ('Religious distress is at the same time the expression of real distress and the protest against real distress; it is the sigh of the oppressed creature, the heart of a heartless world, just as it is the spirit of a spiritless situation: it is the opiate of the people'); but it does even more for those who exploit them and, by removing profit for themselves, alienate the producers of wealth from the consequences of their labour. Religion must, therefore, be contested and eliminated, because the way in which it creates an illusory and fantastic world in heaven subverts those who are exploited and alienated from reversing the whole situation – if necessary, as it *is* necessary, according to Marx and his successors, by revolution: 'The abolition of religion as the illusory happiness of the people is required for their real happiness. The demand to give up the illusions about its condition is a demand to give up a condition which needs illusions. The criticism of religion is therefore in embryo the criticism of the vale of woe, the halo of which is religion' (p. 41).

The whole of that familiar passage is the clearest expression of Marx's understanding of the relation between religion, suffering and death. When he wrote of the criticism of religion stripping away the illusion with which people have attempted to alleviate their distress, not in reality, but in the imagination, then the connection with Freud is obvious. Not that Freud had particular sympathy with Marx; but Freud also believed that when he was reflecting on the continuing function of religion in human life, he was reflecting on the future of an illusion. The book of that particular title is one of Freud's later works (published in 1927). But if we retreat into his earlier life, as we did in the case of Marx, we find the root of his opinions on religion and on the connection between religion and death. In the second year of the First World War, Freud read a paper to the Bene Berith, the Jewish society to which he belonged in Vienna. It was called, 'Our Attitude Towards Death'. Together with another essay on 'The Disillusionment of the War', it was published under the title, *Thoughts for the Times on War and Death*. In the second section, on death, Freud first summarised his argument in *Totem and Taboo* (with its completely unverifiable and wholly improbable speculations about the primal horde and primal guilt) and he also anticipated a main argument in his later work, that man, confronting the reality of death, could not admit its finality, and therefore constructed imaginary ways in which its reality could be admitted and its finality denied. What Freud specifically added was the component of human guilt in the construction:

Philosophers have declared that the intellectual enigma presented to primaeval man by the picture of death forced him to reflection, and thus became the starting-point of all speculation. I believe that here the philosophers are thinking too philosophically, and giving too little consideration to the motives that were primarily operative. I should like therefore to limit and correct their assertion. In my view, primaeval man must have triumphed beside the body of his slain enemy, without being led to rack his brains about the enigma of life and death. What released the spirit of enquiry in man was not the intellectual enigma, and not every death, but the conflict of feeling at the death of loved yet alien and hated persons. Of this conflict of feeling psychology was the first offspring. Man could no longer keep death at a distance, for he had tasted it in his pain about the dead; but he was nevertheless unwilling to acknowledge it, for he could not conceive of himself as dead. So he devised a compromise: he conceded the fact of his own death as well, but denied it the significance of annihilation ... His persisting memory of the dead became the basis for assuming other forms of existence and gave him the conception of a life continuing after apparent death. (pp. 292–4)

Those reflections were evoked by the First World War. Freud's views remained much the same until January, 1920, when his daughter died. In May 1920 *Beyond the Pleasure Principle* was published, in which appeared, for the first time, his proposal of the 'death instinct'. Freud strenuously denied that the two events were connected. Perhaps he feared that the scientific independence of his discovery might be eroded if it were thought to be the product of chance occurrence and human emotion. He even asked his friend, Eitingon, to take part in an almost formal attestation that he (Eitingon) had read the manuscript before the beginning of January. Whatever the influence of his personal history may have been (and Max Schur has given a profound and detailed account of Freud's own fear of death), Freud was driven to introduce the death-instinct because he found that his post-war patients, who had suffered both physical and psychical trauma, kept reliving the psychical but not the physical trauma in their dreams. Yet the pleasure principle should be bringing them to a psychic equilibrium; therefore, he came to believe that beyond the pleaure principle there is an equally strong – or stronger – instinct to return to equilibrium in the opposite direction: to return the organism to its inorganic constituents. Hence, as he put it, 'the whole life of instinct serves the one end of bringing about death'; and again:

If we are to take it as a truth that knows no exception that everything dies for *internal* reasons – becomes inorganic once again – then we shall be compelled to say that 'the aim of all life is death'. (p. 70)

But there was another, reinforcing reason, which led Freud to postulate the death instinct. It came to him while watching his 18-month-old grandson playing a game – or rather, indulging in a repetitive action which many other parents will also have observed: he kept throwing or pushing everything he could grasp into a corner or underneath a bed. While he did so, he gave vent (as Freud described it) to a loud, long-drawn-out 'o-o-o-o', accompanied by an expression of interest and satisfaction. Freud and the child's mother believed that the sound was an attempt at the German word *fort* – 'gone'. Freud therefore concluded that the action was a game and that the only use the child made of any of his toys was to play 'gone' with them. A further game (of throwing a cotton reel out of his cot and retrieving it on a string), confirmed Freud in his view: the reel represented the going and coming of the mother. But since the emphasis was placed on the disappearance, the child was clearly reactivating a painful, not a pleasurable, event. Freud then applied this to psychoanalysis, and in particular to the fact that neurotic patients cease to make progress when they begin to 'recycle' the same material – the same symptomatic situations. They literally get stuck; and Freud therefore concluded that repetition is a basic constituent of our psychic life, and that the repetition will assert itself even to the detriment of the pleasure principle. So 'beyond the pleasure principle' there is a more basic instinct to revert to the prior condition of death, since life itself is preceded by non-life. The goal of life is therefore death: that is what life necessarily seeks. Transferred into the terms which Freud adopted from Greek, Thanatos (death) struggles with Eros (the drive to life): Thanatos strives to return all organic life to its inorganic condition, but Eros continues to assemble and integrate the constituent parts into their organic unity. In *The Ego and the Id*, published three years after *Beyond the Pleasure Principle*, Freud reiterated his conviction that both Thanatos and Eros are conservative, seeking stability, but in opposition to each other.

But why would life *seek* death? For the sake of peace. Eros is the restless, disruptive disturber of the peace; the instinct for death is the resolution of conflict – that text from the Prayer Book version of Psalm cxxvii.2, 'He giveth His beloved sleep', which appealed to many Victorians, to judge from memorials, and which, in Henrietta Huxley's version, was inscribed on the gravestone of T. H. Huxley (who had himself introduced the word and the concept of 'agnostic'):

> Be not afraid, ye waiting hearts that weep,
> For God still 'giveth his beloved sleep',
> And if an endless sleep He wills, so best.

On this basis, it is obvious why Freud could only think of religion as illusion: the ways in which religions resolve the conflict between Thanatos and Eros contradict the fact that Thanatos is, in the end, victorious; however, the religious attempt to contradict the fact does not rest on or point to further matters of *fact*. Since we know that life ends in oblivion, the religious claim can only be 'a hope beyond a shadow of a dream', with no more substance than that. Religions characteristically live, like children, 'as if' their dream worlds will one day be realised, 'as if' the end of the rainbow can be reached and the crock of gold secured. So Freud wrote, in *The Future of an Illusion*:

I am reminded of one of my children who was distinguished at an early age by a peculiarly marked matter-of-factness. Whenever the children were being told a fairy-story and were listening to it with rapt attention, he would come up and ask: 'Is that a true story?' When he was told it was not, he would turn away with a look of disdain. We may expect that people will soon behave in the same way towards the fairy tales of religion, in spite of the advocacy of 'As if'. (p. 14f.)

The words 'as if' have a very precise context in Freud's argument. The words 'as if' belonged, in his time, to a technical philosophical position, the *als ob* of Vaihinger, but Freud took Vaihinger's 'as if' as a basic example of the defect and error of religious belief in general. But in fact what happened, at least in part, was that he extrapolated a specialised issue in the philosophy of knowledge into a general definition of the illusory nature of religious belief: religion is clearly false, but it serves practical purposes. Above all, it enables humans to deny as final and absolute the two known realities of our condition: first, that life is a struggle between Thanatos and Eros; and second, that the struggle ends always in our complete defeat (and disappearance) in death. It is true that we are, for a short while (for about three score years and ten), *as if* living, but it is not for ever. It is only

> till the night of death
> ... severeth our memory from itself,
> and us from all.

It is equally true that humans together have endeavoured to find ways to hold back the frontiers of disease and death; and as Freud himself put it, 'the principal task of civilization, its actual *raison d'être*, is to defend us against nature' (*Future of an Illusion*, p. 11). But as he grimly continued, 'no one is under the illusion that nature has already been vanquished; and few dare hope that she will ever be entirely subjected to man'. In any case, there remains finally 'the painful riddle of death, against which no medicine has yet been found, nor probably will be. With these forces nature rises up against us, majestic, cruel and inexorable; she brings to our mind once more our weakness and helplessness' (p. 12).

In this state of weakness, what can an individual do? 'How does he defend himself against the superior powers of nature, of Fate, which threaten him as they threaten all the rest?' In his early infantile days, Freud suggested, he tries to come to terms with the impersonal forces ranged against him by 'humanising' them – in other words, by giving them personality: he

makes the forces of nature not simply into persons with whom he can associate as he would with his equals – that would not do justice to the overpowering impression which those forces make on him – but he gives them the character of a father. He turns them into gods. (p. 13)

So religion is to be understood as a construction made by those who cannot face the fact that the forces of nature *are* impersonal and hostile, and in the end overwhelming. In desperation they seek some consolation, or some way of rescuing something from the wreck, a way of marking their lives with a more permanent significance and value. But to achieve it would require the creation of a less hostile or more benevolent universe, something which can only be done in imagination, never in reality, because the reality is otherwise. It follows that the more effectively a religion provides consolation, the more certainly it has removed itself into the kind of fantasy and illusion which Flecker described:

> We who with songs beguile your pilgrimage
> And swear that beauty lives though lilies die,
> ... tales, marvellous tales
> Of ships and stars and isles where good men rest.

Freud suggested that the origins of religion are to be found in this area of fundamental need, constructing a store and system of fantastic and illusory 'realities', which is built up from the material of memories of the helplessness of our own childhood and the childhood of the human race. That, to Freud, is the gist of the religious illusion:

> Over each of us there watches a benevolent Providence which is only seemingly stern and which will not suffer us to become a plaything of the over-mighty and pitiless forces of nature. Death itself is not extinction, is not a return to inorganic lifelessness, but the beginning of a new kind of existence which lies on the path of development to something higher. (pp. 14f.)

The religious person is the person who lives 'as if' the comforting projection is true, 'as if' the world of complete fantasy and illusion has some actual substance; but in fact, according to Freud, every advance of scientific knowledge shows how insubstantial the world of make-belief is.

Freud certainly recognised the existence of other motives for belief, but the motive of seeking comfort and protection seemed to him to be dominant. Religion without consolation is no longer religion; a God who no longer rewards his faithful servants is no longer, *in effect*, God. However, what he called 'education to reality' (p. 45) will eventually expose the dubious motive for belief. The ensuing death of God will entail the death of religion, and Heaven can then be left, as Heine put it, to the angels and the sparrows. The fact that religions may happen to advance propositions which turn out, coincidentally, to be true, or even wise, is irrelevant to the erosion of religion by the discernment of its misplaced purposes. Even if some religious doctrines turn out to have a truth-value, it will be irrelevant, because they still rest in the context of the illusory wish-fulfilments of our distant ancestors. And how could they achieve worthwhile results without the benefits of nineteenth-century science and twentieth-century Freud? It would, Freud argued, be very remarkable indeed if 'our wretched, ignorant and downtrodden ancestors had succeeded in solving all these difficult riddles of the universe'. Furthermore, Freud made the claim that we know approximately at what period, and by what kind of people, religious doctrines were created.

Freud's writings, therefore, make it clear that he regarded our ancestors as dumb crumbs – an opinion which in any case he had already formed of many of his contemporaries, to judge from *The Future of an Illusion*, where he drew sharp contrasts between 'the great mass of the uneducated and oppressed' and 'educated people and the brain-workers' (p. 39). Yet at the same time it was essential for Freud to maintain that *plus ça change, plus c'est la même chose* – in other words, that there are universals, or at least recurring constants, in human behaviour, which arise as a consequence of the fact that we are all conceived and born in, broadly speaking, the same way: without that universal truth, the psychic discoveries (which in Freud's belief have the character of scientific laws) could not be inferred for individuals in the past; and with that truth taken to be universal, actual evidence about the origins of religion becomes unnecessary, as I have pointed out in *The Sense of God* (pp. 121ff.). Freud is thus the supreme exponent of conclusions based on the premise of 'what must have been the case' – not unlike the lawyer who declared at the beginning of a trial, 'Your Honour, here is the conclusion on which I intend to base my evidence.'

Together, then, Marx and Freud are dominating examples of the widespread conviction that death is the origin of religion. Because they were both working in the context of the nineteenth-century ambition to find scientifically universal laws which govern human behaviour (see my *The Sense of God*, ch. 1), their confidence is understandable. It does not mean, however, that they succeeded.

THE ARCHAEOLOGY AND ANTHROPOLOGY OF DEATH

How, then, can we proceed any further? To what extent is it true that religions began in the refusal of death? Or to put the question more directly, what did our remotest ancestors believe? Generally speaking, we cannot know. As the zoologist, J. Z. Young, put it, 'rituals and dances, like fears of devils or aspirations towards gods, leave few or no remains'. He is entirely correct in his conclusion that there is no body of facts that yet enables us to understand the origins of aesthetic creation or of religious beliefs and practices. We can no doubt speculate that both sorts of activity were somehow of assistance to Palaeolithic man in the business of getting a living. But, as he continues, 'This does not mean that carving, or painting, or offering prayers for the dead were crudely of "practical" value, for instance, by improving hunting technique' (p. 519). Activities so early and so pervasive are not going to be accounted for by naive reductionism, particularly in the absence of interpretation which comes from the period of the earliest artefacts. Therefore, Young concludes, 'The solution to the problem of the origins of religion would be of great value, but no one has yet found a way of using the earliest known burials and ornaments to solve them' (p. 524). In the absence of any oral or written evidence (through which some attempt was made to articulate the beliefs accompanying death and burial rites), opposite inferences can be drawn from the same archaeological data. Consequently, Kurtz and Boardman (to take but one example) concluded of Greek burials:

Archaeology can add little to our understanding of what the Greeks *thought* about death ... It can tell us a very great deal about what they *did* about death ... The limitation of all this evidence is that, while it tells us *what* the Greeks did, our understanding of *why* they did it has to depend on what we learn from other sources or our imagination. (*Greek Burial Customs*, p. 17)

Not surprisingly, therefore, while Chapman, Kinnes and Randsborg recognised recently (1981) that 'the archaeology of death is not a new subject', they also drew attention to how very little work had been done in the preceding decade, beyond the sociological approach of J. A. Brown. Their own chapter, 'Approaches to the Archaeology of Death' (in *The Archaeology of Death*) is, with its bibliography and its brief historical survey, an excellent point of departure in understanding the problems that face archaeologists. Their own solution is to bring theory to data: 'In this volume the central argument is that archaeologists need a body of theory in order to relate the mortuary data at their disposal to patterns of human behaviour within past human societies' (p. 2).

But that could easily reproduce, in more sophisticated form, the ways in which both Marx and Freud applied their own 'body of theory' to the data. Are there any controls over such application, where clearly beauty is all too often in the eye of the beholder? The most immediate (and it is a court to which Chapman, Kinnes and Randsborg appeal) is anthropology. Not that all anthropologists in the past have been reluctant to impose theory on data: Malinowski's attempt to modify Freud's theories, although it led to the acrimony of Ernest Jones' response (see my account in *The Sense of God*, p. 122), was not actually repudiating the generality of *some* psychoanalytic observations and their applicability to anthropological data. As for those anthropologists who failed to find the Oedipus complex among the most remote inhabitants of the furthest settlement, Geza Roheim simply accused them of suppressing or distorting the evidence because of their own failure to recognise and resolve their own Oedipal complexes.

In fact the achievement of anthropology has been to signal and describe, not uniformity, but extreme diversity in the ways in which individuals and communities deal with the fact of death. In a recent synthesis (dedicated nicely 'to our ancestors'), Huntington and Metcalf began their book (*Celebrations of Death*) in this way:

What could be more universal than death? Yet what an incredible variety of responses it evokes. Corpses are burned or buried, with or without animal or human sacrifice; they are preserved by smoking, embalming, or pickling; they are eaten – raw, cooked, or rotten; they are ritually exposed as carrion or simply abandoned; or they are dismembered and treated in a variety of these ways. Funerals are the occasion for avoiding people or holding parties, for fighting or having sexual orgies, for weeping or laughing, in a thousand different combinations. The diversity of cultural reaction is a measure of the universal impact of death. But it is not a random reaction; always it is meaningful and expressive. (p. 1)

And always, they could have added, it tends to be stable in any particular society: death customs and beliefs in particular societies do of course change, but such change usually evokes considerable conservative resistance. This stability in the midst of diversity is very well explored by Huntington and Metcalf, who based their work on two classic studies which have left both terms and concepts as a legacy in subsequent (academic) reflection on death. The first is van Gennep's *Rites of Passage*, which dealt only in part with death, but which discerned a recurrent pattern in all rites of passage. The pattern is one of one distinction, two categories, and three stages – thus:

death	marriage
alive/dead	single/married
alive > dying > dead	single > engaged > married.

Van Gennep also introduced the idea of 'liminality', later to be developed by Victor Turner in *The Forest of Symbols*: the mid-term of the three stages is (in the case of alive > dying > dead) the hardest for the living to handle, for obvious reasons (the 'item' in actual process is not in either firm category), so that the transitional phase frequently becomes independent and autonomous in the ritual process.

The 'autonomy of the liminal' was believed by Turner to be applicable to much more than death rituals – to what, in fact, he described as 'an ill-assorted bunch of social phenomena' (p. 125), by which he meant 'such seemingly diverse phenomena as neophytes in the liminal phase of ritual, subjugated autochthones, small nations, court jesters, holy mendicants, good Samaritans, millenarian movements, ''dharma bums'', matrilaterality in patrilineal systems, patrilaterality in matrilineal systems, and monastic systems'. But the 'autonomy of the liminal' is of particular importance in death rituals. Van Gennep had already drawn attention to the relative *un*importance of the rites of separation from the dead body, in comparison with the rites of transition which 'have a duration and complexity sometimes so great that they must be granted a sort of autonomy' (*Rites of Passage*, p. 146). Robert Hertz had also noticed the ritual recognition of the liminal stage, and he had concentrated on the widespread phenomenon of societies which do not regard death as instantaneous, and who therefore enact a second burial with elaborate rites. The second burial removed, not only the now-decayed corpse, but also the soul of the dead person, which in the transition stage has been living 'neither here nor there', on the margins of human habitation, capable of malevolent spite in its discomfort, unless its hostility and envy are diverted by particular rites or actions. Thus, in Hertz's view, death is not regarded as the immediate and total destruction of an individual's life. Death customs are related to the continuing process of society by assisting the dead to move over the *limen*, into the stable condition of being an ancestor.

The purpose of Huntington and Metcalf was to extend and modify the basic insight of Hertz's essay. In particular they drew attention to the frequency with which death-denying or death-opposing activities are incorporated in funeral rituals – particularly sexual and/or fertility behaviours. Of the Bara, for example, they wrote: 'During the time following death, extreme vitality is generated through the various excesses of the funeral celebration in an effort to counterbalance the extreme order of death. But this unstable situation cannot persist and the funeral activities become directed toward effecting a return to normality' (*Celebrations of Death*, p. 115).

A subsequent symposium (see Bloch and Parry, *Death and the Regeneration of Life*) made an attempt to apply those two themes (of the social importance of burial rites and of the sexual/fertility exuberance) to a much wider range of societies. The papers in that symposium make clear the extreme diversity of beliefs and practices, along spectra the opposite ends of which clearly contradict each other (or would do so if brought into conjunction). In other words, these papers call into question even the possibility of finding single, simple connections between death and the origins (or, indeed, the continuing power) of religions. The range of different customs extends from hunter-gatherer societies in Africa (which are very different from pastoral or agricultural groups, even in close proximity) where the dead body is relatively unimportant, to the Tantric Aghori cult in India where the dead are literally embraced as a way of transcending duality – and as a way of affirming detachment even from the most abhorrent circumstances or practices (Parry's description of the Aghori cult is referred to further in the chapter on Hindu understandings of death).

More recently, a third anthropological symposium was held on *Mortality and Immortality* which drew on both anthropology and archaeology, and it came to a comparable conclusion: that the fact of diversity is so paramount that generalised conclusions (which can be applied to societies where particular data are lacking) are extremely hazardous. The editor of the symposium, S.C. Humphreys, specifically reiterated the warning of Peter Ucko that 'there is variation in the treatment of the dead within all cultures as well as between cultures', and that 'it is in the highest degree unlikely that any two societies will resemble each other sufficiently for an archaeologist or historian to be able to make direct inferences from ethnographic data to fill gaps in our knowledge of past societies' (p.4).

It becomes clear, therefore, that the material collected by anthropologists cannot be claimed to support the view that the human consciousness of death led to the invention of religion, as a compensation for the fear which that consciousness evokes. Yet that view continues to be put forward as an assumption which can be taken for granted (see, for example, the passage from Cupitt, quoted on p. 218). David Premack considered recently whether, if the problems of communicating concepts to chimpanzees could be overcome, he would communicate to them a conception of their own death:

What if like man the ape dreads death and will deal with this knowledge as bizarrely as we have? ... The desired objective would be not only to communicate the knowledge of death, but more important, to find a way of making sure the apes' response would not be that of dread, which, in the human case, has lead to the invention of ritual, myth and religion. Until I can suggest concrete steps in teaching the concept of death without fear, I have no intention of imparting the knowledge of mortality to the ape. ('Language and Intelligence in Ape and Man')

The error in that paragraph does not lie in the claim that religion is a human invention. Of course it is. But so is everything else, from A(stronomy) to Z(oology), which humans put into concepts and language. The word '*invenio*' means 'I come into'. So the issue, as much for the sciences as for religion and theology, is the nature of the ground in reality which humans 'come into' and explore through their many different inventions, bearing in mind (as I have pointed out at length in *Licensed Insanities*) that all human accounts of everything (beyond the extremely trivial) are approximate, corrigible, provisional and frequently wrong; and yet that in the case of such long and well-winnowed accounts as those of the natural sciences or of religions (addressed though they are to different subject matters and purposes), great reliabilities are achieved. The error of the secular and reductionist accounts, which (like Premack) make the dread of death the cause of religion, is, first, their assumption that the religious accounts have achieved no reliabilities at all, even allowing for the fact that the language and descriptions of what is encountered in the religious domain are approximate and corrigible. The second error lies in the assumption that the concepts and explanations of our own culture are somehow exempt from the process of corrigibility, and that they provide an Archimedean point on which to stand and judge (impartially and correctly) the worth of other and earlier accounts of experience.

There are, of course, other errors involved (including, most obviously, the genetic fallacy). But the first two alone are enough to vitiate some of the most prevalent secular accounts of the causative relation between death and religion: since they know, *a priori*, what can and cannot be the case, they go to the evidence and find what they seek. Since they know that nothing survives death, it follows that beliefs to the contrary must be accounted for in other ways. The result is that these secular accounts of the early relation between religions and death completely misrepresent what the surviving evidence portrays, once we arrive at written reflections on the meaning and significance of death (and without that control, interpretations are, as we have seen, entirely speculative). Equally, their attempt to account for pervasive beliefs lapses into the ridiculous. To give but one example: Rosenblatt, Walsh and Jackson analysed ghost beliefs (in *Grief and Mourning in Cross-Cultural Perspective*) on the basis of 78 ethnographies included in the Human Relations Area Files. Material on ghost beliefs was recorded for 66 societies out of the 78, and of those 66, strong ghost beliefs were found in 65. Only the Masai seemed to be an exception, and even in that case the information was less reliable than for all other cultures except one (p. 51). The authors accordingly concluded:

The fact that ghost beliefs are present in all but one of the societies that raters could agree upon is startling. In the United States, ghosts are a topic for jokes, fanciful films, and fiction. To admit to the belief that one has seen a ghost is to invite being labelled as ignorant, superstitious, irrational or hallucinating. It is sobering to find American culture so much in the minority on this issue. What the cross-cultural literature seems to indicate is that belief in ghosts is natural; it is consistent with human nature. (p. 53)

What, then, constrains so many human beings into a belief that ghosts 'exist' in such forms that they can be discerned by the living? The constraints must arise in the environment which is 'natural' to a twentieth-century anthropologist, who knows *a priori* that there cannot be realities correctly referred to as 'ghosts', and that such near-universal references must be mistakenly reified accounts of more ordinary phenomena. Such at least is the underlying assumption of these three authors. What, then, do they identify as the constraints which control so many people into ghost beliefs? There are four sets of constraints (pp. 53 – 5): first, there are 'environmental cues', whereby sights, sounds or smells associated with the deceased trigger the sense of continuing presence; second, there are dreams; third, there is self-perception theory which argues 'that people make guesses about perceptions, emotions, and other internal states by drawing inferences from what they find themselves doing' (thus, to quote the authors, 'Consider a man lying in the bed he shared with his now-deceased spouse, thinking about her and finding himself sexually aroused. Self-perception theory would lead us to expect some people in such situations to tend to infer that they have perceived some kind of manifestation of the deceased'). Finally, there is the explanation that some individuals *need* to interact with ghosts of deceased people, in order to transact 'unfinished emotional, relational, or decision-making business with the deceased'.

But that account is extraordinarily 'thin' compared with the richness and complexity of actual ghost beliefs. Consider this account (by Goulart) of the Nakhi, a people of the far west of China:

The Nakhi, like many other people still unaffected by the materialistic Western civilization, lived in close and intimate contact with the world of spirits. They believed that the immensity of space was inhabited by big and small deities, spirits of the dead and a host of nature's spirits both good and bad. The relationship between mankind and these many spirits was not considered hypothetical or conjectural but factual and authentic. Unlike the taboo imposed by religion in the West on communication with spirits, no such restrictions existed in Likiang, and the communications themselves were looked upon as the normal and eminently practical means of solving certain intricate problems of life when other methods had failed. If there was an apparition, materialization or direct voice, people did not shrink from it but investigated the matter with sympathy and interest. In a word, a visitor from the unseen was treated as a person, with proper courtesy.

It was firmly believed that the dead survived. They did not live somewhere in the blue sky beyond the clouds but existed somewhere near, just on the other side of the veil. The veil could be lifted or, at least, a hole could be made in it for a short talk with the dear departed. It was not considered necessary or desirable to bother them too much for two reasons. One was that they had already accustomed themselves to their new existence and that it was a bad thing to remind them too much of earthly affairs and thereby induce them to become earthbound. The second reason was that if it could ever be demonstrated that the life beyond is as happy and felicitous as it is pictured in Nakhi scriptures, there would be the temptation to end it all and to migrate to a happier plane of existence in a hurry. As it was, the suicides in Likiang were too frequent and easy, and such revelations might cause a stampede, bringing the whole Nakhi race to a premature end. (*Forgotten Kingdom*, pp. 169f.)

It follows that interaction with the dead was realistic, not metaphorical, and certainly not evoked by the smell of cookies in the kitchen or memories of happy times in bed, though environmental cues of plausibility undoubtedly reinforced expectation. So the transactions with the dead were prosaic and literal, as Goulart went on to describe:

The dead, therefore, could only be approached in time of a severe crisis in the family, when for example, someone was dangerously ill, with all hope in drugs abandoned. Then a professional medium, called *sanyi*, was summoned and his visit was always arranged in the dead of night, when the neighbours were asleep. He chanted the incantations from the scriptures, accompanying himself on a small drum. He danced a little. Then he fell into a trance. There was no direct voice. The man gasped out what he saw. It might, for instance, be a tall old man in a purple jacket, slightly lame, leaning on a black stick. 'Oh, that is Grandfather!' cried the family, prostrating themselves. Then the sickness of the patient was described. 'The old man is smiling', reported the *sanyi*. 'He says the boy will recover in seven days if he takes this medicine.' There followed a slow dictation of what to take and when to take it. The family prostrated themselves again as the old man was reported to be going away. On the other hand, the old man might have said that the case was hopeless and that the boy would be with him in three days.

People always said that such prescriptions or prophecies were infallible: either the patient recovered with the aid of the prescribed medicine or he was dead on the day and hour announced by the departed ancestor. Moreover, murderers could be brought to justice through interviews with their dead victims, and certain family affairs cleared up. Conversations with the dead in dreams were a frequent occurrence in Likiang and were given much credence.

THE PHENOMENOLOGY OF DEATH

It is obvious, even from that brief and anecdotal account, that much more was constraining the Nakhi into ghost beliefs than the four sets of constraints proposed in *Grief and Mourning*. But the deficiency of that one account does not, of course, establish the *opposite*, that because many people report interacting with ghosts, therefore there are such realities to be interacted with. Still less does it mean that there must be some automatic truth in the widespread interest (common in every generation, including our own) in contacting the dead. So far as such things can be investigated, T. H. Huxley's comment is entirely justified, that it is scarcely worth paying out money to hear a medium communicate empty trivia, which have come, supposedly, from the dead:

The only good that I can see in the demonstration of the truth of 'spiritualism' is to furnish an additional argument against suicide. Better live a crossing-sweeper here than die and be made to talk twaddle by a 'medium', hired at a guinea a séance!

Even such well-known mediums as Doris Stokes were devastatingly exposed in the recent investigation by Ian Wilson:

For the television journalists [who had accompanied him with a view to making a programme] it was now transparently obvious that this Palladium show – and by implication all other of Doris Stokes' public performances – was nothing more than a set-up, with the audience, inevitably ignorant of the behind-the-scene arrangements, hapless dupes. (pp. 77f.)

Here, yet again, death (like religion) turns out to be big business. But despite all that, the task remains of trying to understand what underlies the widespread data which have evoked survival beliefs, and what has brought them into being; and that requires, first, an attempt to describe, as dispassionately and extensively as we can, what the reports of such claimed experiences actually are.

This is what is known as the first level of phenomenology – and it is by no means as easy to execute as it is to describe. Certainly, in the case of the phenomenology of death, the beliefs and practices are *so* diverse (as we have seen already, even with only the briefest reference to anthropology) that the description of the phenomena is still a long way beyond us. Virtually everything that *can* be imagined about death *has* been imagined. This means that *any* theory (to refer back to Chapman, Kinnes and Randsborg) can most certainly be illustrated and exemplified somewhere in the world's religions. On the other hand, it makes it equally certain that no single theory will be able to eliminate all others as being itself a sufficient and complete account. Thus explanations of the phenomena of death-related beliefs and practices in terms of, for example, alienation, compensation, projection, social order, individual dread, guilt, transference (to pick up the most important of those we have already encountered) are not in competition with each other; they are complementary. All complex eventualities (and human behaviours are certainly that) are constrained or controlled into their outcomes (into their being what they are as they make some claim on our attention) by *many* constraints, not by single, simple constraints. (The technical notion of 'constraint' in relation to cause is discussed in my *Licensed Insanities*, pp. 101 – 6, 137 – 9.) Such single constraints (as, in physics, the force of attraction between masses which we refer to as gravity) may well be identifiable *among* the constraints; but even in the case of what appears to be a relatively simple event, like the fall of an apple, gravity is not the *only* constraint which collapses the range of possibility into the eventuality that the apple falls.

It follows that the phenomenology of death requires us to be attentive to data and to be generous in our sensitivity to the extremely complex sets of constraints which control human beings into their death-related beliefs and practices. In particular, it is not possible to rule out, on *a priori* grounds, that among the constraints are those which are derived from an interactive reality which has come to be characterised (with great diversity, from the human point of view) as God.

This is the second level of phenomenology, which asks: given the phenomena built up and mapped by these extensive intersubjective networks of report, what are we entitled to infer as a sufficient ground to make them appear in consciousness? In the case of God, this is a great deal more important than a mere debating point, for this reason: when, in the earliest history of religions, we do have some access to the beliefs accompanying mortuary practice (through written or orally transmitted evidence), we encounter a paradox: at the root of all major, continuing religions, earliest speculations about death did *not* produce a belief that there is a desirable life with God beyond this life, after death. Yet the power and character of this-worldly, this-life experience of God, or of the Divine, were simply unmistakable, at least for some, perhaps many, of those who participated in it, even without any serious belief in life after death.

This means that the widespread account of the origin of religion, to the effect that it lies in the human fear of death and the construction of compensatory but illusory paradises, is certainly wrong, so far as we can judge from the evidence that survives. There is a subtle truth in Weininger's guess, that while it is often 'a cause for astonishment that men with quite ordinary, even vulgar, natures experience no fear of death, it is quite explicable: it is not the fear of death which creates the desire for immortality, but the desire for immortality which causes fear of death'. As de Fontenelle observed, 'Then came some of the *Iroquois* going to eat a Prisoner for their breakfast, who seems as little concern'd as his Devourers.'

It does not, of course, follow that compensatory accounts are wrong in all respects: what they say can certainly be exemplified in the later history of religions. But that is simply to say, yet again, that human behaviours are controlled into their outcomes by *multiple* constraints, not by abstracted theories. The basic fact is clear: when we get access to reflections on the nature of death and of a possible existence beyond death, then it is extensively the case that the earliest understanding of death and its aftermath (with one important category of exception) was the opposite of what Marx and Freud supposed. Extensively, death was regarded as something to be postponed for as long as possible, since there is nothing after death to which one might look forward as a place of compensation or bliss. For our ancestors, there was definitely no future in dying. At the most, a thin, insubstantial shadow of a person might continue (and there were reasons for that belief, as we shall see), which was a kind of memory-trace of a person, without any power or form through which to enjoy a continuing life. In Greece, Mesopotamia, India, China and perhaps most familiarly in Israel, the earliest beliefs in life after death were beliefs in the persistence of perhaps some trace of the dead, but of no substantial continuity; though occasionally some heroic individuals (with heroism differently defined in different cultures) are exempted from death and are taken, often literally, to some other outcome. Thus while in Jewish Scripture there is no belief, until the very end of the Biblical period, in a continuity of life with God after death, the heroic figures of Enoch and Elijah are literally taken (*ahad*) into the sky and exempted from the grave (see further p. 54).

It follows that in the earliest religious imagination to which we have access, it is life which is natural, and death which is un-natural, in the sense that it breaks into and disrupts what would otherwise be the natural and continuing circumstance of life. Lévy-Bruhl made exactly that point when he was attempting to portray what he called *Primitive Mentality*. He observed that Australian Aborigines do not regard death as natural, but as an interference caused by the magical power of enemies. He concluded: 'This attitude of mind is not peculiar to Australian tribes only. It is to be found occurring almost uniformly among un-civilised people who are widely removed from each other' (p. 40).

The belief that death is unnatural persists into the present. For example, in 1972 the BBC ran a series of short television program-mes, called 'Times Remembered', in which people reminisced about their earlier lives. In one of these, a boy, Michael Foster, who had been born in Ghana and who had subsequently come to live in England, was asked whether 'the pagans', as the interviewer called them, performed their firedance in relation to death, even if the person had died an old and natural death. He replied, 'No one dies naturally.'

In a different culture altogether, Simone de Beauvoir wrote almost exactly the same: 'There is no such thing as a natural death: nothing that ever happens to a man is ever natural, since his presence calls the world into question. All men must die: but for every man his death is an accident, and, even if he knows it and consents to it, an unjustifiable violation' (*A Very Easy Death*, p. 106).

This estimate of the significance of death is reinforced by the way in which so many myths, in so many different cultures, relate the origin of death to trivial accidents or to seemingly unimportant choices, such as stealing an apple in the Garden of Eden; or, among the Navajo, because Coyote threw a stone instead of a stick into a puddle; or, among the Melanesians, because five brothers had a family quarrel; or, among the Gilbert Islanders, because some people, given an either/or choice, happened to choose the wrong tree; or because they listened to the buzzing of a fly; or because they did not learn the lesson of a buried banana.

What they and so many other comparable stories make clear is that life *might* have continued undisturbed, but that relatively simple accidents or choices have introduced the disruption of death. Consider that last example, as Bendann recorded it, from Fiji:

When the first man, the father of the human race, was being buried, a god passed by the grave and inquired what it meant, for he had never seen a grave before. Upon receiving the information from those about the place of interment that they had just buried their father, he said: 'Do not bury him, dig up the body again.' 'No' they replied, 'we cannot do that. He has been dead for four days and smells.' 'Not so,' entreated the god, 'dig him up and I promise that he will live again.' But they refused to carry out the divine injunction. Then the god declared, 'By disobeying me, you have sealed your own fate. Had you dug up your ancestor, you would have found him alive, and you yourselves when you passed from this world should have been buried as bananas are for four days, after which you shall have been dug up, not rotten, but ripe.'

And whenever they hear this sad tale the Fijians say: 'Oh, that those children had dug up that body!' (*Death Customs*)

It seems absurd, perhaps, that so much catastrophe could be derived from so slight an offence and so unlucky a choice: never has so much been owed by so many to so little. But the theme is repeated again and again in countless myths of the origin of suffering and death, and it is far removed from quests for compensation, or for a substantial survival in some better land. To take but one example: there is no compensation or substance in the account of the suitors in Hades, in Book XXIV of *The Odyssey*: 'The souls of the suitors are like bats which, in the depth of a dark and gloomy cave, flit about, squeaking.' That is all that *can* survive, a memory-trace as thin as the squeak of a bat. Dietrich commented on early Greek beliefs that the gods, including Zeus, never significantly alter the code of man's life or the moment of his death. In Homer,

the knowledge of imminent death is always in the foreground in an epic of war and of adventure, but a hero's actions are untrammeled by a sense of fatalism, nor is his mind obsessed with constant fear of his end, though once dead he might well say that he 'would rather be a serf than king of all these dead men that have done with life'.

Dietrich goes on to make this point, specifically, that the people of Homer's time (and of his epic) sought fulfilment of their desires in this world, and that 'they rejected the belief of other people in a reward or penalty awaiting them in the next, the *au-delà*' (*Death, Fate and the Gods*, pp. 336f.).

But although Dietrich contrasts Greek belief with 'the belief of other people', in fact (with the one category of exception) the Greeks were in large company: there is equally no evasion or compensation in the Epic of Gilgamesh; there is no evasion or compensation in Israel, where the whole of Tanach (Jewish Scripture) except at the very end, is written without a belief that there will be a continuity of life with God after death; there is no evasion or compensation in the *anatta* of early Buddhism, although there will be continuity of consequence; with the exception of the immortality cult, there is no evasion or compensation in the earliest Chinese understanding of the fate of the dead. In the

famous response to Tzu-lu, when he asked about the importance
of serving spiritual beings, Confucius said, 'If we are not yet able
to serve man, how can we serve spiritual beings?' Tzu-lu then
said, 'Then let me ask about death.' Confucius said: 'If we do not
yet know about life, how can we know about death?' (*Analects*,
xi.II).

But some of his later followers were not even so agnostic as that.
Wang Ch'ung, an almost exact contemporary of Jesus, devoted
one of his critical essays to death and concluded that death is like
the extinction of fire:

When a fire is extinguished, its light does not shine any more, and when
a man dies, his intellect does not perceive any more. The nature of both
is the same. If people nevertheless pretend that the dead have
knowledge, they are mistaken. What is the difference between a sick
man about to die and a light about to go out? (*Lun Hung*, I, p. 196)

The analysis of Wang Ch'ung is equally austere in its refusal
of a continuing spirit:

People say that the dead become ghosts, are conscious, and can hurt
men. Let us examine this by comparing men with other beings:
    The dead do not become ghosts, have no consciousness and cannot
injure others. How do we know this? We know it from other beings.
Man is a being, and other creatures are likewise beings. When a creature
dies, it does not become a ghost; for what reason then must man alone
become a ghost, when he expires? Man lives by the vital fluid. When
he dies, this vital fluid is exhausted. It resides in the arteries. At death
the pulse stops, and the vital fluid ceases to work; then the body decays,
and turns into earth and clay. By what could it become a ghost? Anterior
to man's death, his mental faculties and vital spirit are all in order. When
he falls sick, he becomes giddy, and his vital spirit is affected. Death
is the climax of sickness. If even during a sickness, which is only a small
beginning of death, a man feels confused and giddy, how will it be, when
the climax is reached? When the vital spirit is seriously affected, it loses
its consciousness, and it is scattered altogether.

It is true that the *absolute* annihilationists in the classical
world or in India or in China may have been a small minority.
But they are a reminder that the human mind has been as capable
of raising sceptical questions in the past as in the present. However, the fact that total annihilationists were in a minority

raises the question why those distant ancestors of ours believed
that *something* survives, that a dead person has not wholly disappeared, and that at least some trace of him or her remains. The
answer is, because some trace of the dead undoubtedly remains.
The dead continue above all in memory and in children; *how* they
continue is another matter. But since our ancestors were as capable
as we are of observing that children often resemble parents or
grandparents, they could conclude, even without a knowledge of
genetics, that something continues from one generation to
another. And undoubtedly, the dead continue (for a time) to
inhabit human memory, especially in dreams. The plain and
rational fact is that the dead do not 'cease upon the midnight with
no pain': in some sense the dead are with us still. What the earliest
religious explorations seek to know is the state or the status of the
dead which allows them this continuing effect, without advancing
beyond the evidence of experience; and in their rituals, they did
much to reinforce memory and to effect the transition of ancestors
(of the fourth or fifth preceding generation) to the status of the
unremembered.

The nature of these rituals and beliefs will become more obvious
in the chapters dealing with the early religious traditions, east and
west. There it will become clear how little the earliest religious
explorations of the significance of death had to do with compensation or with a refusal to be realistic about the fact of death. But
to all that there remains the category of exception (p. 30) of which
Egypt is the most familiar example. As early as the 6th Dynasty,
around 2300 BCE, an inscription on the tomb of Herkhuf makes
it clear that one's condition after death depends on one's
behaviour in life:

I gave bread to the hungry, clothing to the naked, I ferried him who
had no boat ... Never did I say anything evil to a powerful one against
any people; I desired that it might be well with me in the Great God's
presence.

It was at around this time that the Egyptians were perfecting
mummification. Probably, in origin, they stumbled on this in as
accidental a way as other peoples (for example in Peru or in
Scandinavia) had discovered that in some circumstances – dried

in the burning air or frozen in the tundra – bodies do not necessarily decay and disintegrate. This gives rise to the inferential argument that this discovery lies at the root of speculations about more substantial survival than that of the body alone. It makes sense of the more elaborate burials that one finds in Egypt, or, at the opposite extreme of climate, in the frozen tombs of Siberia, and particularly of the High Altai. Those tombs were created by a deliberate enhancement of the process of freezing – an even more permanent deep-freeze than that of the Californians. In *Frozen Tombs*, the construction of the tombs is described (p. 23), and the artefacts from them are illustrated. Barkova then describes what else can be inferred:

The finds from the Altai enable us to reconstruct the customs and rites of the magnificent funeral of a chieftain. The funeral took place in the cold season of early spring or autumn. The bodies were embalmed, the muscle tissues removed through incisions in the skin and the cavities left filled with grass before the incisions were sewn up with sinews. The skulls were trepanned to remove the brains. After the funeral there was a feast and a ritual cleansing by fumigation with the smoke of hemp seeds. Small tents were built of thin rods covered by a rug, and bronze censers filled with heated stones were placed inside. The mourners then clambered into the tent, threw hemp seeds onto the heated stones and inhaled the narcotic smoke. These funeral practices in the Altai correspond to descriptions of similar rites among the Scythians of the Black Sea region in the fifth century BC. Herodotus' accounts of the custom of scalping enemies and the tattooing of the bravest and most renowned warriors are also confirmed. Other beliefs and superstitions are illustrated by finds of amulet-pouches containing roots of plants and herbs, locks of hair and nail-pairings. (p. 24)

However, if we wish to push further and discover what *beliefs* accompanied these rituals, we are held back by the familiar problem (pp. 18f.) that nothing has survived. Virtually nothing can be known, because the Southern Siberian tribes possessed neither writing nor coinage, and were remote from the ancient literate civilisations whose historians knew of them only as legendary tribes. Herodotus visited the lands north of the Black Sea in the fifth century BCE, and described the Scythians. But as Zavitukhuna puts it, 'the further east from Scythia the more mysterious were the inhabitants' (p. 11).

At least in the case of Egypt we do have access, at various different points, to the developing beliefs about a possible life beyond death. In the pre-Dynastic period (some time before 3100 BCE), bodies were not mummified but were desiccated in the sand. Basic artefacts were frequently buried with the dead, but the meaning even of that action is not unequivocal: artefacts, like pots or plates, can be interred with bodies, either because it was believed that the dead still have sufficient existence to have need of them, or because the living simply wish to dissociate themselves from death and the dead as formally and completely as possible.

In the earliest period, therefore, it is still uncertain what the beliefs of Egyptians may have been. But there is no doubt that they eventually developed strong and substantial beliefs in a worthwhile continuity of life beyond death. In the so-called *Egyptian Book of the Dead*, the means are provided for the dead to negotiate any kind of impediment; and in such myths as those of Isis and Osiris, the renewal of life is given symbolic expression. More obviously, the mortuary remains, often on a spectacular scale, reinforce the strength of those beliefs.

All that, in Egypt, is in strong contrast to the beliefs in Mesopotamia, where embalming and mummification were not discovered, nor were they imported from Egypt as a technique. Yet we know that there was considerable interaction between Egypt and Mesopotamia, and in other respects (for example, sacral kingship) they developed comparable, albeit different, beliefs and practices. In relation to death, they remained uncompromisingly distinct, even with visible consequences, as Giedion observed in his work on the architectures of both civilisations. In the case of Egypt, a belief in eternal continuity in the hereafter required co-operation on the part of the living. The departed needed a more permanent dwelling place on earth than the living, so that even into the Late Period, sun-dried bricks were considered adequate for the houses and palaces of the living, but the dead required the less destructible material of stone. Thus Giedion argued that the rise of stone architecture can, in the first instance, be attributed to the Egyptian conception of the nature of death. The consequences are still visibly with us. However, in Mesopotamia there was a deeply realistic, not to say pessimistic, approach to life after death: nothing but a vague shadow could continue, and for them it would be pointless to erect permanent dwelling places. So Mesopotamian graves were simply covered with earth. Even the so-called kings' graves in the Royal Cemetery of Ur (which date from the First Dynasty of Ur, c. 2500 BCE), are not made memorable by architecture. What Giedion called 'the most sensational of them' belonged to Queen Shudad, who was buried there with eighty sacrificed members of her household.

The golden vases and inlaid harps show a cultural standard which bears comparison with the elaborate furnishings, inscribed with hieroglyphs, found in the tomb of Queen Hetep-heres, the mother of Cheops. But architecturally, Mesopotamian tombs were without significance. Yet this was the period when the great pyramids of Cheops, Chephren and Mycerinus were storming the heavens. (*The Eternal Present*, pp. 11f.)

In Mesopotamia, therefore, we are back with the far more common estimation of death in early times, as something beyond which nothing much can be hoped for. It is not even certain that the slaughtered slaves reveal a belief that the dead Queen will require their services beyond the grave. It is equally possible that they illustrate the determination to sever all contact with the dead by the most dramatic form of dissociation. Certainly the Mesopotamian texts exhibit no belief that there is anything to be looked forward to beyond the grave. Nor is there any trace whatsoever that slaves will receive compensation for their miseries on earth or for their equally miserable deaths.

The earliest history of religions, both east and west, to which we have access makes it clear that religion did not originate in an offer of worthwhile life after death. It is equally clear that such widely influential people as J. G. Frazer (of *The Golden Bough*) were profoundly wrong when they tried to locate the origin of religion in the superstitious ignorance of primitive people who had not had the benefit, as he had, of spending a leisurely life in Trinity College, Cambridge. The religious exploration of death is a great deal more profound and interesting than that, since it is, basically, an assertion of value in human life and relationships which does not deny, and is not denied by, the absolute fact and reality of death. In place of the widespread and current view of religious origins (that religions derive their original and basic power over human lives from their 'sales pitch' on life after death) we have to recognise that the earliest religious explorations of death were focused much more on the disruption and disorder of death, and on how to maintain order in the face of chaos and malevolence and the deliberate willing of evil. The Norse myth of Ragnarokr joins hands with the Kali Yuga, and many other myths, in dramatising the real issue for the religious assertions of value: how can that value (however identified) be sustained in the face of the deliberate adversary and in the heart of darkness, of which the darkness of death and of the tomb are simply an epitome – what Rilke called, 'the deep epitome of things'?

'The heart of darkness': *that* is the territory which religions characteristically explore – not as a kind of intellectual curiosity, but because the very ground on which we stand trembles beneath our feet. The phrase 'the heart of darkness' is the title of Conrad's novel, superficially a story of class and race exploitation and its nemesis, but more deeply a study of human complexity and its capacity for disaster within the boundaries of the historically and geographically constrained. For what was it that Marlow saw playing through the face of Kurtz as he lay dying, as the moon struggled to reveal itself through a layer of ragged cloud? 'Sombre pride'? 'Ruthless power'? 'Craven terror'? Yes: but all three summarised as 'an intense and hopeless despair' (p. 297). And as Kurtz died, 'he cried out twice, a cry that was not more than a breath: "The horror! The horror!"' The next spoken words in the book are the words which T. S. Eliot set at the head of 'The Hollow Men', the words of the 'insolent' 'manager's boy', 'Mistah Kurtz – he dead.' Always the shadow falls:

> Between the conception
> And the Creation
> Between the emotion
> And the response
> Falls the shadow

We are the hollow men. The dried and shrunken heads, stuck on poles by Kurtz's house, were the first glimpse Marlow had into the heart of darkness, where the wilderness had whispered to Kurtz 'things about himself which he did not know, things of which he had no conception till he took counsel with this great solitude – and the whisper had proved irresistibly fascinating. It echoed loudly within him because he was hollow at the core' (p. 283). We are the hollow men:

> Those who have crossed
> With direct eyes, to death's other Kingdom
> Remember us – if at all – not as lost
> Violent souls, but only
> As hollow men.

And at the end, on his death bed, the voice of Kurtz was strong to the very last, hiding in the folds of eloquence the barren darkness of his heart:

'Oh, he struggled! he struggled! The wastes of his weary brain were haunted by shadowy images now ... The shade of the original Kurtz frequented the bedside of the hollow sham, whose fate it was to be buried presently in the mould of the primaeval earth' (p. 296).

> Between the idea
> And the reality
> Between the notion
> And the act
> Falls the shadow.

All this belongs very clearly to the religious exploration of death. It has nothing to do with compensation or projection. It has everything to do with the assertion and the affirmation of value, up against the boundary of death. Indeed, the more clearly a religion does *not* elaborate an imagination of a compensatory paradise or hell after death, the more sharply the question of values is raised: *why* affirm a particular value, if we do indeed go to oblivion (or, at the most, if we become a memory-trace, as thin as the squeak of a bat)? If we do indeed go to oblivion, then what is the point of resisting the occurrence within ourselves of what a German woman, during the last war, called *seelische Hornhaut*: the callousing – or, even more literally, the corneal blinding – of the emotional and moral self? The phrase comes from the diary of Ursula von Kardoff, later published as *Berliner Aufzeichnungen*. At a time when she first became aware of what was actually happening to the Jewish people, she noted that her brother Jurgen grew visibly pale when he saw in the street an old Jewish woman and a young girl, both clearly distressed. 'Jurgen,' she wrote, 'has as little as Father of that emotional callousing with which so many people try to get by' (p. 7). And on 3 March 1943 she wrote:

Frau Liebermann is dead [Frau Liebermann was the wife of a Jewish painter, Max Liebermann, and was a friend of the Kardoff family]. They came to fetch her with a stretcher to deport her to Poland – this 85 year old woman. She took poison at that moment, and she died a day later in the Jewish hospital without regaining consciousness. What ugly manifestation of evil shows itself here, and why does it show itself particularly among our people? By what transformation has a group of people who are basically good-natured and friendly been turned into such devils? (pp. 36f.)

It is on to *that* ground that the earliest religious explorations of death characteristically moved. They asked, in effect, how the assertion of moral, social and individual value can be maintained, even when (or particularly when) there is no belief that there will be a 'judgement of the dead', or a compensation or a punishment after death. In that respect, it is important also to remember from that same period in Germany the final episode of von Trott's life. Adam von Trott was one of those involved in the July plot of 1944. Before the war, he had been an apologist for the necessity of the Nazi regime, as representing the only possible means to Germany's revival. But he changed because of his experience of Nazi rule. He joined the plot, and he received the news of its failure in his flat in Berlin. As he waited for the inevitable arrest and execution, he was visited by a friend, Melchers, who knew about the plot, but was not himself arrested, and who therefore survived to record those last moments before von Trott's arrest. Melchers himself flew into a rage at the thought of how the conspiracy had been bungled, but in contrast:

Trott suddenly grew very gentle. 'Are you angry?' he said. 'Remember these people must pay for this thing with their lives!' There was a depressed silence between us ... I asked if he had any hope for the future. 'No,' he answered, 'there is no hope left now, or for the future. This is the end. The disaster must take its course – till there shall be left no stone upon another. Hitler will carry on this madman's war till everything is destroyed.' 'And yet', he added, 'it is good all the same that there were people ready to break this reign of terror. It remains an historical fact, and more than that, a symptom.' (Sykes, *Troubled Loyalty*, p. 438)

Here there is no appeal to some compensation for himself. There is no future for himself, here or anywhere: not one stone shall be left upon another. Yet still he makes his choice and stands his ground, as an affirmation of fundamental value as fact, and as a mark of that fact, transcending the interest of his own survival, to whatever subsequent generations there may be. Christopher Sykes, who wrote the life of von Trott, commented on this:

The story of Adam von Trott's life is not that of a saint of anti-Nazism; it is something more human. To see it in hagiographic terms is to miss its significance, as though one were to see *Hamlet* solely as an edifying play on the subject of stainless filial duty. His story is of a man who met temptation and resisted it, sometimes with difficulty and sometimes without perfect success; of a man whose perception could be clouded, and who sought for moral truth within the stumbles of our human weakness. All the more wonderful is his ultimate moral triumph. (p. 455)

All this is much more fundamental to the religious exploration of death than the pervasive accounts of religion as illusion realise. It is an exploration of how value can be maintained at the limit of life without seeking illusory compensation. Beyond the ultimately trivialising generalisations of Marx and Freud (exemplified though those generalisations often are) there lies more serious ground to be explored: the human capacity to gain the whole world and lose its own soul; the recognition that life yields to life, part to part, and that the attainment of the whole, whether it be the forms of life on a coral reef or in a modern city, seems to demand a sacrifice that few of the components of the scene are anxious to volunteer on their own account, but which some nevertheless do volunteer, thereby making of their death a sacrifice for the benefit of others.

And it is sacrifice which is by far the earliest category through which religions explore the nature and significance of death. It is the theme of life yielding not simply *to* life (giving way to other life), but life yielding *for* life, to enable its possibility. Sacrifice is a far earlier and more widespread theme through which religions have explored the nature of disorder and death, than is the pursuit of compensation or of a desirable life after death. It is a theme which, as Blake among many others realised, embraces death instead of acquiescing in evil:

> 'Do I sleep amidst danger to my Friends? O my Cities and Counties,
> Do you sleep? rouze up, rouze up! Eternal death is abroad!'
> So Albion spoke, and threw himself into the Furnaces of affliction.
> (*Complete Writings*, p. 743)

It is the religious exploration of death which brings us, still, to a more sensitive – and resistant – awareness of evil. So it follows that to reflect on death may be morbid in the literal sense of the underlying Latin word, but not in the pathological sense of a disturbed or distorted preoccupation. What we think about death and its occurrence (for example, is it so natural that it is insignificant? Are people expendable? Is death an evil or a good? Or both?) flows back into our moral and aesthetic and political judgements within life. Not surprisingly, the human exploration of death occurs much more in such enterprises as liturgy, ritual, music, art, architecture, monuments, poetry, than it does in books about death such as this. Words are so much the currency of our consciousness that we sometimes rely on them where they cannot bear the weight. People who talk at grief, instead of holding hands with grief, are a menace. Words come later, but only after tears.

But what a book can do – or what at least this book attempts to do – is to show something of what has happened in the religious explorations of death, not as a comprehensive history of death, but as an indication of what lies at the root of some of the main religious traditions, and gives to each of them its characteristic style. We will look at the themes of sacrifice and friendship, in both western and eastern religious traditions, in order to argue, finally, that in both these themes there are points of vital contact with secular understandings of death 'beyond Marx and Freud'. Recovering the value of death, and recovering value in death, is important to us all, not least in the medical professions and in the hospice movement. What will be argued here is that there is now an important congruence of the religious and the secular and that these can now reinforce each other in a human attitude to death.

II

Religions and the origin of death

CHAPTER 2

Judaism

Judaism is constituted by the command, *Shema Israel*:

Hear, O Israel: the Lord our God, the Lord is One. You shall love the Lord your God with all your heart and with all your soul and with all your strength. These words which I command you this day are to be kept in your heart. You shall repeat them to your sons, and speak of them indoors and out of doors, when you lie down and when you rise. Bind them as a sign on the hand and wear them as a phylactery on the forehead; write them up on the doorposts of your houses and on your gates. (Deut. vi. 4 – 9)

But that command requires a context; and the context in which it first arose was the long process of time (increasingly perceived as history) through which a kinship group, the *bene Jacob* (the sons of Jacob), came to recognise the consequence and the demand of God upon them. Through that process they came to recognise the nature of what other nations took to be god or gods (*El* or *elohim*) as being Yhwh (the Lord) transliterated conventionally as Yahweh. That process, through which an originally nomadic kinship group became the children of Israel, and through which the many possible gods of the ancient near East were dissolved in the recognition that there is only One from whom all things and all events are derived, I have tried to describe briefly in *The Religious Imagination and the Sense of God*, in the first section on Judaism. The central point, in relation to the command, *Shema*, is that the people of Israel understood themselves to be a people constituted by common and coherent descent (hence the importance of genealogies throughout the Jewish Bible, Tanach), but also constituted far more importantly by the creative act and promise of God. That special intention in relation to the people of Israel was eventually believed to go back to the first act of creation itself. The opening chapters of Genesis describe a creation in which harmony prevails. But from the original condition in which 'God saw all he had made, and indeed it was very good', Genesis describes the progressive disintegration which follows from the first acts of disobedience, which in themselves introduce death (Gen. iii): the alienation of man from woman, and of both from God; of one life form (the serpent) from others; of man from his labour and from his environment; of Cain from Abel; of one mode of labour from another; of one generation from another; culminating in God's despair, when 'he saw that the wickedness of man was great on the earth, and that the thoughts in his heart fashioned nothing but wickedness all day long. Yahweh regretted having made man on the earth, and his heart grieved' (Gen. vi.6). Since death is in the disposition and control of God, he decides to make absolute the punishment of death: ' "I will rid the earth's face of man, my own creation", Yahweh said "and of animals also, reptiles too, and the birds of heaven; for I regret having made them" '(Gen. vi.7).

'But,' the narrative goes on, 'Noah had found favour with Yahweh' (verse 8). And Genesis then goes on (with the rest of Scripture) to become the story of God's work of repair and of restoration, through the covenants beginning with Noah, including the transmission of Torah through Moses, on to David and his descendants, and embracing all his people under Ezra and Nehemiah, when 'the Book of the Law of Moses which Yahweh had prescribed for Israel' (Neh. viii.1) was read before the whole people; and when it was finished, 'all the people raised their hands and answered, "Amen! Amen!" ' (Neh. viii.6). In that context of repair and renewal, made formal by the specific promises and commands of covenanted agreements, the detailed laws become a means of saying 'Yes' to God: they become a language through which people can make explicit their affirmative response.

So what constitutes Israel is the gratuitous, creative act of God, which became focused on a particular family and people, the *bene Jacob*, the sons of Jacob. Yet what also constitutes Israel is their response, their willingness to hear and to fill out the substance of their life with the guidance, the instruction, and the command which God has entrusted to them for the construction of their life, and which is contained in Torah. It is in the realisation of these conditions that the covenant-bonding between God and his people is established.

Why, then, *Israel*? Why the focus on one particular people? It is ultimately for the repair of the whole human condition. What Israel displays, in hearing and in implementing what they hear, is a proleptic representation (a representation in miniature and in advance) of what will ultimately be the entire human case, when 'the earth shall be full of the knowledge of the glory of Yahweh as the waters fill the sea' (Hab. ii.14). When Israel hears and obeys and fills out her life with that obedience, she is representing in the midst of time what God intended at the beginning, in the paradisal conditions of unbroken harmony which Genesis describes and which God still intends to realise through the faithfulness of this one particular people.

The word 'Torah' is sometimes translated as 'Law' but it means something more like 'guidance' or 'instruction'. It is the term applied to the whole of the Pentateuch (the first five books of the Bible) – and it can also be used as a term for the whole of Scripture. So Torah is guidance, which includes the stories of creation and of the patriarchs, and which also includes specific 'decrees, laws and customs' which Israel must keep.

Why must Israel keep them? Simply because God has laid this demand on them. To attempt to find a rational explanation for particular commands (for example, that the prohibition on eating pork was originally a recognition that pork goes bad rapidly in hot climates) is completely irrelevant. As a Jewish woman told me, when I asked her in *Worlds of Faith* why she kept the commands:

Just because God commanded it. It's not like people suggest sometimes, because of hygienic reasons: there isn't any such reason, we don't believe in such reasons. We do it because God commanded it. It's a positive commandment. (p.143)

A much earlier text, from the Rabbinic period, makes a comparable point, that to respect a prohibition against something one has no wish to do anyway, has no point compared with respecting a prohibition on something one does wish to do. This is not to say that all Jews have felt like this. Even the great Maimonides believed that the original reasons were hygienic: 'I maintain,' he argued, in *The Guide for the Perplexed* (iii.48), 'that the food forbidden by the Law is unwholesome. There is nothing among the forbidden foods whose injurious character is doubted except pork and fat, but even in those cases the doubt is unjustified.' But much more common has been the opinion of Isaac Abarbanel:

God forbid that I should believe that the reason for forbidden food is medicinal: for were it so, the Book of God's Law would be in the same class as any of the minor brief medical books ... Furthermore, our own eyes see that people who eat pork and insects and such ... are well and alive and healthy at this very day ... Moreover, there are more dangerous animals ... which are not mentioned at all in the list of prohibited ones. And there are many poisonous herbs known to physicians which the Torah does not mention at all. All of which points to the conclusion that the Law of God did not come to heal bodies and seek their material welfare, but to seek the health of the soul and cure its illness.

Torah, then, for Israel is the language of love. It is a way of saying 'Yes' to God and to the dream of a restoration of Paradise, here on earth. But in all this there is no promise that the reality of death will be cancelled or suspended if the people are obedient – if, in other words, they reverse the disobedience of Adam and Eve. They remain, therefore, *bene* Adam – sons of Adam, those who live in a succession of generations: consequently, the phrase 'son of man' (*ben Adam*) in Scripture, although it is a poetic parallel to other words for 'man', occurs almost always in contexts which stress the frailty and mortality of human beings:

Yahweh, what is man, that you are mindful of him.
Or a son of man that you take notice of him?
Man's life is a breath of wind,
His days are as a shadow that passes away.   (Ps. cxliv.4)

Put not your trust in princes
Nor in a son of man, in whom there is no help.
He gives up his breath and goes back to the earth from which
    he came,
And on that day all his purposes perish.   (Ps. cxlvi.3f.)

Could any man ever think himself innocent, when confronted
    by God?
Born of a woman, how could he ever be clean?
The very moon lacks brightness,
And the stars are unclean as he sees them
What, then, of man, maggot that he is,
A son of man, a worm?   (Job xxv.4–6)

The condition of being *bene Adam*, subject to the penalty of death
('Dust thou art and unto dust shalt thou return', Gen. iii.19), and
of therefore living in a succession of generations, is not cancelled.
Such promises as there are have to do with the future of the people
on earth, not with individual survival after death, as Deuteronomy
makes clear:

In times to come, when your son asks you, 'What is the meaning of the
decrees and laws and customs which Yahweh our God has laid down
for you?', you shall tell your son, 'Once we were Pharoah's slaves in
Egypt, and Yahweh brought us out of Egypt by his mighty hand … He
brought us out from there to lead us into the land he swore to our fathers
he would give us. And Yahweh commanded us to observe all these laws
and to fear Yahweh our God, so as to be happy for ever and to live, as
he has granted us to do until now. For us right living will mean this:
to keep and observe all these commandments before Yahweh our God
as he has directed us.' (Deut. vi.20–5)

It is because God has shown himself so unequivocally in their
past, from the creation onward, that they can trust him now, in
the present (in contrast to trusting mere mortals) – no matter
if, as with the Babylonians, those 'mere mortals' overwhelmed
Israel in battle. Therefore God can proclaim:

I, I am your consoler:
How then can you be afraid
of mortal men, of a son of man,
whose fate is the fate of grass?
You have forgotten Yahweh who made you,
who spread out the heavens and laid bare the earth's
    foundations.   (Is. li.12f)

From all this it can be seen that the Jewish understanding of
death in the Biblical period belongs inextricably to the context in
which Israel's *self*-understanding was formed. There would have

been no Israel, in their estimate, apart from the providence and power of God who called his people out of Egypt to live in the covenant-bond of faithfulness with himself and with each other. But the consequent trust in God is *not* for the sake of reward after death. It is clear that the enduring reality of God can guarantee the restoration of the people he has chosen – 'I am he who says of Jerusalem, "Let her be inhabited", of the towns of Judah, "let them be rebuilt", and I will raise their ruins once more' (Is. xliv. 26). But, despite this basic trust, there is no offer of a comparable restoration of individuals beyond death. There can be continuity only in the nation and in one's own children, a point which underlies the Levirate law of Deut. xxv.5 (which requires of a widow, if she is still childless, that she marry her late husband's brother, and that she name the first son after the dead brother). But there is nothing offered by way of promise or compensation to the individual, that he or she will enjoy a happy life with God after death. Exactly the reverse. What is promised is Sheol, a domain beneath the earth (see Num. xvi.31–5). The nature of Sheol is described in Job's challenge to God:

> Why did you bring me out of the womb?
> I should have perished then, unseen by any eye,
> A being that had never been,
> To be carried from womb to grave.
> The days of my life are few enough:
>   turn your eyes away, leave me a little joy,
> before I go to the place of no return,
>   the land of murk and deep shadow,
> where dimness and disorder hold sway,
>   and light itself is like the dead of night. (Job x.18–22)

Again and again the plea of the Psalms is, not for an entrance into some paradise, but that the entrance into Sheol may be postponed for as long as possible:

> Yahweh, hear my prayer,
> listen to my cry for help,
> do not stay deaf to my crying.
> I am your guest, but only for a time,
> a nomad like all my ancestors.
> Look away, let me draw breath,
> before I go away and am no more.   (Ps. cxxxix.12f.)

Sheol is not to be equated with later ideas of hell, as a place of torment. But it is definitely to be avoided as long as possible – it is exactly as Sophocles in *Ajax* said of Hades, *ton apotropon Haidan*, Hades to be turned away from. In the same way, also, as the Greeks, the Jews of this early period hoped that one's own insignificant life might be overlooked and forgotten about, thus postponing the moment of departure into a condition so dismal and abandoned. The Greek Bias (c.570 BC) (whose opinion Diogenes recorded, that it is a disease of the soul to be enamoured of things impossible of attainment) was once on a sea voyage with some godless men, but when they ran into a storm, even they began to call on the gods for help. 'Peace!' said he, 'lest they hear and become aware that you are on the ship.'

But the Jews, in general, did continue to call on God, even though it could not possibly lead them into a life with God beyond death. Indeed, the particularly bitter misery of Sheol is that it severs all connection with God:

> Come back, Yahweh, rescue my soul,
> save me, if you love me;
> for in death there is no remembrance of you:
> who can sing your praises in Sheol?   (Ps. vi.4f)

The only return that can be offered to God is to continue to praise him for as long as he extends the span of life on this earth. All this is caught poignantly in the Song of Hezekiah – the song attributed to Hezekiah, when he recovered from what had seemed a mortal sickness: it is full of prayer and praise, but not of immortality (Is. xxxviii.10 – 20; cf. Ps. cii, cxvi).

But Sheol is not oblivion. There, in wretched separation from life and God, a thin shadow, as vague as memory, continues. Thus when Saul needed the advice of Samuel who had died, he went (contrary to his own recent law) to the 'witch of Endor' who summoned the shadow of Samuel from Sheol. Samuel is recognisable, not from his appearance, but from the prophetic mantle which the figure wears. Saul asks the woman what she can see:

The woman answered Saul, 'I see an *elohim* [a usual word for God or gods, but here a figure apart from this life] rising up from the earth.'

'What is he like?' Saul asked. She answered, 'It is an old man coming up; he is wrapped in a cloak.' Then Saul knew it was Samuel and he bowed down his face to the ground and did homage. (1 Sam. xxviii.17)

So the dead are perhaps recognisable: when the King of Babylon, the mighty tyrant who has 'angrily thrashed the peoples with blow after blow' at last is flung down into Sheol, he is recognised, but is still derided by the other shades as having become 'weak as we are':

> So you too have been brought to nothing, like ourselves.
> You, too, have become like us.
> Your magnificence has been flung down to Sheol
> with the music of your harps;
> underneath you a bed of maggots,
> and over you a blanket of worms.   (Is. xiv.10f.)

But nothing significant survives. After all, what *could* survive? The basic Biblical anthropology is one of dust animated by the breath breathed in by God: 'Yahweh God fashioned Adam of dust from the soil [*adamah*]. Then he breathed into his nostrils a breath of life, and thus man became a living being' (Gen. ii.7). At death, the body returns to dust, and the breath, the *ruah*, returns to the air, or returns to God. There is nothing that *can* survive – not unless that basic, and very realistic, anthropology is extended, either by giving to the 'animating breath' a more enduring status (an independent self or soul), or by God deliberately continuing or renewing his original creative act (by reconstituting the original person, body and breath).

Both of those developments occurred in Judaism, though scarcely within the Biblical period. Where the anthropology is concerned, there are three words which express the vitality which is bestowed by God, *nephesh*, *neshamah* and *ruah*; but although they are often translated as 'soul' or 'spirit', they do not, in the Biblical period, have any overtones of an enduring, immortal reality, which, like the Platonic soul, can escape from this body into a better existence. Thus when Elijah prays to Yahweh to return the widow of Zarephath's son to life, he is praying that God will return his animating breath to him:

He stretched himself on the child three times and cried out to Yahweh, 'Yahweh my God, may the soul [*nephesh*] of this child, I beg you, come into him again!' Yahweh heard the prayer of Elijah and the *nephesh* of the child returned to him again and he revived. (1 Kgs. xvii.20f.)

But of course, that language (of a distinct gift from God which gives life to a particular individual) is open to the interpretation that there is a continuing identity between the individual and the soul, so that what is taken back by God at death is not lost or destroyed. That interpretation certainly developed in later Judaism, as one can see now in the morning prayer of the Authorised Daily Prayer Book (p. 5):

O my God, the soul [*neshamah*] which you gave me is pure: you created it, you formed it, you breathed it into me, you preserve it within me; and you will take it from me. But you will restore it to me in the hearafter. Therefore, so long as the soul is within me, I will give thanks to you, O Lord my God and God of my fathers, sovereign of all works, Lord of all souls: blessed are you, O Lord, you who restore the souls to the bodies of the dead.

In this much later understanding, the soul clearly pre-exists the body, since it comes from God and is bestowed on a particular body; and in some forms of Judaism, particularly in Kabbalah, it came to be believed that souls can go from one body to another, in what is known as *gilgul*, a kind of transmigration. According to some opinions, all souls have to undergo transmigration, and are undergoing continual judgement; but more generally, it was not believed that *all* souls are reborn, but only those deserving punishment. As Scholem (*Kabbalah*, pp. 351ff.) summarises the point, the majority saw *gilgul* connected especially with offences against procreation and with sexual transgressions. It is, therefore, a very severe punishment, but it is nevertheless an act of mercy on the part of God, because it means that even those who deserve to be entirely 'cut off' have a chance to be restored. Conversely, the extremely righteous may be reborn, not for their own sake, but for the benefit of others and the good of the universe. A different kind of transmigration in Judaism is that of the *ibbur* and the *dibbuk*. The *ibbur* (literally, 'impregnation') is the entry of another soul into a person, to reinforce a particular action or characteristic (thus, according to the Zohar, Judah's soul was present in Boaz when he begat Obed). The *dibbuk* is an evil *ibbur*, often the soul of a sinner, which possesses another life – as in the example of the unclean spirits of the New Testament. The belief in *gilgul* remains alive in Judaism, as can be seen from the responses in *Worlds of Faith* (pp.182, 262).

But none of that is yet explicit in the Biblical period. During all that time, when Israel and its faith were being formed, there is an austerely realistic acceptance that nothing lies beyond death – nothing at least to compare with that quality of relationship with God which enabled later writers to describe it, in the case of Abraham, as 'friendship' (2 Chron. xx.7; Is. xli.8). Consequently, the most that can be hoped for, or prayed for, is that the breaking of that relationship with God will be postponed for as long as possible. Rather than illustrate so basic a theme, it is far more instructive to sit down and read the Psalter, to see how fundamental it is.

So the exploration of death in the Biblical period is not one of seeking for each individual an immortal compensation with God. It is an exploration of how the facts of living and of death can be taken on their own terms, and of how, within those conditions, the order and stability of the process of life and of succeeding generations can be maintained in conjunction with God. It is true that both Enoch (Gen. v.24) and Elijah (II Kgs. ii.1–11) were exempted from death and were taken to a life with God; but everyone else, including (as we have seen) the mightiest tyrants, comes to the same final condition.

Not surprisingly, therefore, the exploration of death and of the maintenance of order and succession in the face of death, takes place in the Biblical period far more in relation to the concept of 'blood' than it does in speculations about the status of *nephesh* or *ruah*. It is the blood which is the summary of life, just as the shedding of blood is the epitome of death. Therefore at the very root of God's work of repair in the covenant with Noah, the prohibition on the shedding of blood, and even on eating meat with the blood still in it, is fundamental:

'I give you everything,' says God, 'with this exception: you must not eat flesh with life, that is to say blood, in it ...' He who sheds man's blood shall have his blood shed by man, for in the image of God man was made. (Gen. ix.4–6)

The eating of meat, on this view, was a later concession (cf. Gen. i.29, where meat is not mentioned). Deut. xii.20 seems to suggest the same, and in any case emphasises that the life (the blood) must be separated from what is dead (the meat). The same passage in Deuteronomy goes on to stress the importance of blood in sacrifice, as that which belongs to God (the giver of life) and is rightly returned to him: 'The blood of your sacrifices shall be poured out on the altar of the Lord your God, but the flesh you may eat' (verse 27).

This identification in the blood of the vitality which belongs to God leads directly into the laws of *shehitah*, of ritual slaughtering in a way which sheds the blood directly and immediately, without which no meat can be *kosher*. As Dresner and Siegel summarise the point:

There is no clearer visible symbol of life than blood. To spill blood is to bring death. To inject blood is often to save life. The removal of blood which Kashrut teaches is one of the most powerful means of making us constantly aware of the concession and compromise which the whole act of eating meat, in reality, is. Again, it teaches us reverence for life. (*Jewish Dietary Laws*, p. 29)

It is a comparable intuition which makes many Hindus refuse the compromise and eat only vegetarian food (see p. 164). In Judaism, that basic intuition (that blood is the focus of the transition between life and death) extends in many different directions. For the Jews, since life comes from God and is in his disposition, nothing less than the shedding of blood will effect reconciliation and atonement, when things have gone wrong or when sins have been committed which deserve that same penalty of death as did the disobedience of Adam. In Lev. xvii.10 – 12, the prohibition on blood is extended even to Gentiles, and the point is made that 'the life of the flesh is in the blood': 'This blood I myself have given you to perform the rite of atonement for your lives at the altar; for it is blood that atones for a life'.

Supremely, it is the shedding of blood and the carrying of it through the veil to the mercy-seat which effects the cleansing of Israel from its transgression on the Day of Atonement (Lev. xvi). This exploration of death through the shedding of blood (especially in sacrifice) as a necessary condition for the continuity of life on this earth is far more fundamental and pervasive in Scripture than speculations about a life with God after death – which scarcely existed, as we have already seen. So deep is this intuition about the shedding of blood and the attitudes it carries with it, that in the attempt, as recorded in the Book of Acts, to find some minimal conditions which will enable Jewish and Gentile Christians to live in community with each other, this is included: '"I rule, then", proclaimed James, "that instead of making things more difficult for pagans who turn to God, we send them a letter telling them merely to abstain from anything polluted by idols, from fornication, from the meat of strangled animals and from blood"' (Acts xv.19f.; cf. Rom. xiv). Five centuries later, when refugees from many different persecutions were attempting in Arabia to re-establish a basic 'religion of Abraham', to which all monotheists could belong, their 'minimal' conditions remained much the same. Zayd b. Amr was one of four men who broke with Meccan polytheism, shortly before the time of Muhammad's birth. According to ibn Ishaq, he abandoned the religion of his people, but did not accept either Judaism or Christianity. Instead, 'he abstained from idols, animals that had died, blood, and things offered to idols' (*Life of Muhammad*, p. 99).

It is thus through sacrifice that the reality of death and its necessity were recognised, in the Biblical period. Not only for that, of course, but for many other purposes as well: sacrifice in Scripture is an extremely complex phenomenon, and there is certainly no single 'meaning of sacrifice' in the texts or in the practices which they describe. It would be wrong, therefore, to suggest that atonement is the only theme in the exploration of death through sacrifice, just as it would be wrong to suppose that there is only one, uniform understanding of how sacrificial death effects its purpose. Daly makes it clear that no significance is attached to the death of the animal, since its death, in itself, effects nothing. This means that at least those theories of sacrificial atonement which emphasise the suffering and death of the victim or the destruction of the material being offered are wrong. It follows that in the Biblical understanding, there is very little trace of substitutionary ideas associated with sacrifice – that the death of the victim is substituted for the (deserved) death of the offender. In contrast, Daly argues,

the process of atonement had a twofold function: the *positive* function of making persons or objects 'acceptable' to Yahweh, of preserving them in this condition, of making them eligible to participate in Israel's religious life and sacrificial cult; and the *negative*, apotropaic, function of interrupting or averting the course of evil set in motion by sin or transgression, whether knowing or unknowing (Lev. 10.6, Num. 1.53, 17.11, 18.5). (*The Origins of the Christian Doctrine of Sacrifice*, p. 27)

Thus an important point in sacrifice is that the domains of life and death, both of which belong to God, should be kept clearly separate and unconfused (as Calum Carmichael has explicitly argued) and that sacrifice involving death should play its deliberately costly part in maintaining both the community and the individual in the domain of life. Life is given up that life may continue. Thus Israel turned away from human sacrifice, though the *aqedah* (the binding) of Isaac 'writes into' the very root of the tradition a recognition that even human life belongs to God. Through formal and deliberate sacrifice, life is willingly returned to God from whom it came, in order that other life may continue in order and profusion:

The angel of Yahweh called Abraham a second time from heaven. 'I swear by my own self – it is Yahweh who speaks – because you have done this, because you have not refused me your son, your only son, I will shower blessings on you, I will make your descendants as many as the stars of heaven and the grains of sand on the seashore. Your descendants shall gain possession of the gates of their enemies. All the nations of the earth shall bless themselves by your descendants, as a reward for your obedience.' (Gen. xxiii.15 – 19)

It is by a comparable obedience that the faithful can hope, not for a life with God after death, but for the postponement of death to a full term – to the 'three score years and ten' of Ps. xc.10. Yet there, precisely, is the seed of the peculiarly Jewish problem of suffering as I have tried to summarise it, both in *Problems of Suffering in Religions of the World* and in ch. i.5 of *The Religious Imagination and the Sense of God*, 'The Death of God in the Greek and Jewish Worlds.' If there is no desirable life with God after death, and if we all, just and unjust alike, go to the same dismal state in Sheol, why are the just so often unrewarded in this life? There are, after all, no rewards *after* this life: so why does God apparently abandon in this life those who try to keep faith with him in the boundary of his covenant conditions? It is a commonplace observation that

> The rain it raineth every day
> Upon the just and unjust fellas,
> But mainly on the just because
> The unjust steal the justs' umbrellas.

What, then, is the point of being just, if there is no ultimate reward? The problem became dramatic in the Maccabean revolt, where it was precisely the just who were most likely to be slaughtered by their enemies, the Seleucids: if the just are defined as those who endeavour to keep the commands of God, they are precisely the ones who refuse alien commands which conflict with Torah, and who therefore refuse to fight on the Sabbath, as 1 Macc. ii.29 – 38 records. The result was that 'the attack [against them] was pressed home on the Sabbath itself, and they were slaughtered, with their wives and children and cattle, to the number of one thousand people' (1 Macc. ii.38).

It is in this period and just before it (2nd century BCE), that beliefs or affirmations began to take shape that, as the Book of Wisdom puts it with great nobility, 'the souls of the righteous are in the hand of God, there shall no torment touch them. In the eyes of the foolish they seem to have died, ... but they are in peace' (iii.1ff).

The problem of the martyrs (of those who are not rescued from death even though – obviously – they are keeping the Law) provided a sharp focus for these growing beliefs in a life restored by God beyond death. But it is not the single or simple cause of them. The first beginnings of those beliefs can be seen earlier than the revolt, and they arose from a recognition of what God *is*, as the creator and guardian of Israel, unmistakable in their experience both past and present: why not, therefore, in the future?

The promise for the future is already explicit in the choice of Israel and in the many covenant agreements which are recorded throughout the Biblical period and beyond: 'I have set before you life and death, the blessing and the curse: therefore choose life, that you may live, you and your seed' (Deut. xxx.19f.; cf. Baruh iv.1ff).

The promise became even more detailed and visionary when, after David's introduction of kingship, the hopes centred on *haMashiach*, the anointed one (or in English transliteration, 'the messiah'), were transferred from existing descendants of David to a future figure – a transition which took place in and beyond the Exile (6th century BCE), and which I have described briefly in *The Religious Imagination and the Sense of God* ch. i.5. Hopes focused on the Messiah (or Messiahs) are extremely diverse, right through the Rabbinic period (to c. 7th century CE), but in general beliefs in the Messianic Age look to a time of peace and prosperity when the rule of God will be both effective and recognised. This is a restoration of Israel which is as much a consequence of the initiative and the action of God as was the first choice of Israel – and as, indeed, was the moment of creation itself. Why, then, should it not be possible for God to include in that promised act of restoration a re-creation of his faithful friends – a return of life (of breath and blood) to the scattered remains of those who kept faith with him before?

The answer seemed increasingly to be that it was *not* impossible. Indeed, in a sense, to doubt its possibility would be to doubt the power of God to do as he wills. In this way, hopes began to develop in the later Biblical period – for example, in the so-called Isaianic apocalypse (Is. xxiv–xxvii – see esp. xxvi.7–19), and most obviously in the vision of Ezekiel xxxvii of the dry bones being literally reassembled:

Then Yahweh said, 'Son of man, these bones are the whole House of Israel. They keep saying, "Our bones are dried up, our hope has gone; we are as good as dead." So prophesy. Say to them, "The Lord Yahweh says this: I am now going to open your graves ... I mean to raise you from your graves, my people. And I shall put my spirit (*ruah*) in you, and you will live, and I shall resettle you on your own soil; and you will know that I, Yahweh, have said and done this – it is the Lord Yahweh who speaks."' (Ezek. xxxvii.11–14)

By the time of the Maccabean revolt, the possibility of God restoring his faithful to life was established, though not necessarily widely believed. The book of Ecclesiasticus, written not long before the Maccabean crisis, stays well within the boundary of the more general Biblical expectation: it reiterates the view that retribution takes place in this life (iii.26, ix.12(17), xi.26 – 8, xii.1 – 7) and that conversely the just are rewarded here and now (ii.10f.), particularly by being kept from Sheol (li.6(8)ff.). Certainly there are no punishments in Sheol: 'Fear not death: whether it be ten or a hundred or a thousand years, there are no chastisements for life in Sheol' (xli.3(5)). In general, the only immortality that *can* be hoped for is the retrospective kind, conferred by the living on the dead when they obey the exhortation of Ecclesiasticus (much beloved of school Speech Days), 'Let us now praise famous men, And our fathers that begat us' (xliv.1).

Yet even in Ecclesiasticus there are limited hopes, based on the exegetical opportunities in the tradition, Enoch and Elijah (xliv.16, xlviii.5, 9), and Ezekiel xxxvii. They are expressed in the prayer – in conjunction with 'may they be remembered' – 'may their bones flourish again out of their place' (xlvi.12, xlix.10). It was therefore not without precedent for Daniel, written in the midst of the Maccabean crisis, to hold out hope for the faithful that they will be vindicated beyond death, although Daniel expresses this in a novel form, in apocalyptic imagery:

> I gazed into the visions of the night.
> And I saw, coming on the clouds of heaven,
> one like a son of man [*bar enash* in Aramaic = *ben Adam*].
> He came to the one of great age
> and was led into his presence.
> On him was conferred sovereignty,
> glory and kingship,
> and men of all peoples, nations and languages became his servants.
> His sovereignty is an eternal sovereignty
> which shall never pass away,
> nor will his empire ever be destroyed.   (Dan. vii.13f.)

In the interpretation of the vision, it is 'the saints of the Most High' (cf. Num. xvi.3, Is. iv.3, Ps. xxxiv.9) who are identified with those granted sovereignty for ever; the beasts, including the Seleucid king, Antiochus Epiphanes, are overthrown.

But if Daniel is allusive in encouraging the faithful to believe that they can be vindicated beyond death, the books written as commentary on the Maccabean revolt, especially II and IV Maccabees, are not. Both those books tell stories of martyrs – and, indeed, they tell the same story. But they handle the issue of what exactly may be able to survive death, or may be restored beyond death, very differently indeed. II Maccabees undoubtedly sees resurrection of the body as the reward for the righteous, particularly for the martyrs, and it constructs its ideas out of material lying in the tradition which was (much later) designated as Scripture. For example, it retains a Biblical view of Sheol to which both the righteous and the wicked go at their death without distinction, but the implication that Sheol itself is in the control (and creation) of God is developed. Thus Eleazar refuses to partake of the pig's flesh which is being forced upon him, with the words, 'Even if for the present I shall escape the punishment of man, yet I will never escape the hand of the Almighty, either living or dead' (vi.26). And Eleazar accepts death, not because he believes or expresses any hope that it will lead to a reward for him, but because he cannot betray his *present* experience of God: 'Just before he died under the blows, he groaned aloud and said, "The Lord whose knowledge is holy sees clearly that, though I might have escaped death, whatever agonies of body I now endure under this bludgeoning, in my soul I am glad to suffer, because of the awe which he inspires in me"' (vi.29f.).

But when II Maccabees tells the story of the seven brothers who are killed in succession in front of their mother (who is then herself killed at the end) Sheol has become a kind of transit camp for the righteous and obviously, in particular, for those faithful Jews who refuse to break the commands of Torah. So the fourth brother 'when he neared his end, cried, "Ours is the better choice, to meet death at men's hands, yet relying on God's promise that we shall be raised up by him; whereas for you there can be no resurrection, no new life"' (vii.13f.).

The same general hope is expressed by the second brother:

After stripping the skin from his head, hair and all, they asked him, 'Will you eat, before your body is tortured limb by limb?' But he retorted in the language of his ancestors, 'Never!' So he too was put to the torture in his turn. With his last breath he exclaimed, 'Inhuman fiend, you may discharge us from this present life, but the King of the world will raise us up, since it is for his laws that we die, to live again for ever.' (vii.7 – 9)

II Maccabees is clear that this continuing renewal of life requires the resurrection of the body, as the third brother explains: 'It was heaven that gave me these limbs; for the sake of his laws I disdain them; from him I hope to receive them again' (vi.11). This belief is extremely literal, as one can see in the death of Razis. He had been denounced to Nicanor, and when the troops surrounded him, he attempted to fall on his own sword, but, as the narrative puts it,

in the heat of conflict he missed his thrust, and while the troops swarmed in through the doorways, he ran up with alacrity onto the wall and bravely threw himself down among the troops. But as they instantly drew back some distance, he fell into the middle of the empty space. Still breathing, and blazing with anger, he struggled to his feet, blood spurting in all directions, and despite his terrible wounds ran right through the crowd; then, taking his stand on a steep rock, although he had now lost every drop of blood, he tore out his entrails and taking them in both hands flung them among the troops, calling on the Master of his life and spirit to give them back to him one day. Such was the manner of his passing. (xiv.43 – 6)

The Biblical roots of this are extremely clear. Where II Maccabees goes much further is in its affirmation that the living can assist the dead by prayer and sacrifice, in chapter xii.38 – 45. It is this passage alone (in a book which no Jew and not all Christians regard as Scripture) which underlies, as basic justification, the later Christian beliefs in purgatory and masses for the dead. After a victory in battle, Judas gathered the bodies for burial in the sepulchres of their fathers, and he made a collection 'to offer a sacrifice for sin (on behalf of the fallen), doing thereby well and honourably, in that he took thought for a resurrection. For if he were not expecting that those who had fallen would rise again, it were superfluous and idle to pray for the dead ... Therefore he made the propitiation for the sin'. But even in that passage there is a recognition that not all Jews held that belief. The author added a parenthesis, 'And if he did it looking for an honourable memorial of gratitude laid up for those who die [or literally 'fall asleep'] in godliness, holy and godly was his thought'. That is the Sadducaic and Biblical position, just as it expresses an anthropology (an account of what constitutes the human being) which is fundamentally Biblical. Body, blood and breath constitute the self, the individual and immortality lies in being remembered by others.

But once the language of *nephesh* and *ruach* (life and breath) were being written in Greek (and an increasing number of Jews were beginning at least to write in Greek, that *lingua franca* of the Mediterranean world), the possibility of Greek philosophical reflection became obvious, because a Greek reader would see such familiar words as *psuche* and *pneuma*. That would not immediately suggest to him a single or simple concept of the soul and its immortality, because such issues were much debated in Greek philosophy. But it would at least allow the engagement of Jewish hopes with Greek speculation. In particular, it would encourage the speculation that the soul or spirit might be a self-sufficient reality, which might be detached from the body and continue in its own right, even if it would require to be reconnected with this body, or *a* body, for its full expression; and that is well on the way to some kind of Platonic dualism.

What Plato himself believed is much disputed, but certainly some form of dualism of that kind was attributed to him, as one can see from the epitaph which Diogenes Laertius wrote for him: 'Phoebus gave to the mortals Asclepius and Plato, the one to save their souls, the other to save their bodies.' And, indeed, the actual inscription on Plato's tomb makes the same point: 'Earth in her bosom here hides Plato's body, but his soul has its immortal station with the blest.' Some Jews made deliberate attempts to meet the Greek quest for wisdom and for God, by showing how the Jewish faith and tradition are the truth for which the Greeks were seeking. By the time of Jesus and Paul (and later) so many of the best minds were being persuaded of the truth of Judaism, that several Roman authors protest angrily against their folly. IV Maccabees is explicitly a part of this endeavour to show how Judaism meets the needs expressed in the Greek quest. At the outset, the book states its basic theme: 'The question which we have to determine is whether the reason is complete master of the passions' – a question which many Greek philosophers also addressed. The answer of IV Maccabees is that reason alone is not enough: what is required is reason controlled and inspired by piety – what the book calls *eusebes logismos* – and the book argues that that piety is only attainable within the Jewish religion. It follows that the faithful Jew should never be frightened of death, because death leads to life: indeed, it leads to life for others, because the death of the faithful (as martyrs) is sacrificial.

But what IV Maccabees emphasises, as the way in which the faithful can indeed continue to live in the company of God, is the immortality of the soul, not the reconstruction of the body. The Patriarchs receive the souls of the faithful at death (v. 37, xviii.23), and those souls are then rewarded in the presence of God (ix.8, xv.2, xvii.5).

The Jewish writer who makes an even more explicit and deliberate attempt to interpret Judaism in terms which make real connection with the Greek imagination is, of course, Philo. However much Philo may later have been disowned by Judaism, at the time when he was alive he was by no means alone in remaining (as he emphatically believed) faithful to Torah, while interpreting Torah in terms established in Greek philosophy. In terms of anthropology, therefore, he had no difficulty in seeing an equivalence in experience between the Jewish notion of two *yezer*-s (inclinations) pulling the individual between good and evil, and a dualistic struggle of the soul to emancipate itself from its entanglement in evil desires and inclinations. As Goodenough put it, he accepted the Platonic notion 'that man's problem lies primarily in the struggle between matter and the immaterial. This struggle is represented within each individual in the conflict which his body, along with perhaps its organising bodily mind, wages against the divine soul, spirit, or higher mind within it'.

In the context of that anthropology, what did he have to say about death? Fundamentally, he emphasised an uncompromising realism about the fact of death as the inescapable prospect for all people. Thus on the prayer in Deut. xxxiii.6, 'let Reuben live and not die', he commented: 'Is Moses here praying that he should never know death and corruption, a thing impossible for a man? Surely not.' He also, on occasion, seems to have been expressing a belief in a literal heaven or hell, at least conceived as places of reward and punishment. So in *De Cher.* 2 he wrote:

One who is weighed down in helpless subjection to this severe and incurable illness [of sin] must bear undying horrors to all eternities; he is thrust out to the place of the impious, there to endure misery unmitigated and unrelieved.

But far more frequently, Philo emphasised that terms like 'heaven' and 'hell' have only what he calls 'a mythological value', and in a famous passage (*Questions on Exodus* 2.40) he wrote of the soul being deified or divinised by its ascent after death to God:

A holy soul is divinised by ascending not to the air or to the aether or to heaven which is higher than all, but beyond all heavens; for beyond the cosmos there is no place but God [*non locus sed Deus*].

That last phrase summarises the real centre of Philo's interest. Rather than map out a literal heaven and hell, as the other major imaginative exercise in Judaism at that time, Apocalyptic, was doing, Philo was content simply to talk of undying life and eternal death:

In my judgement, preferable to life with impious men would be death with pious men; for awaiting those who die in this way there will be undying life, but awaiting those who live in that way there will be eternal death. (*de Posteritate*, 39)

The question then necessarily arises: What is it that experiences this undying life? It is not possible to extract a single, consistent answer from Philo's surviving works, but some themes recur frequently. Thus he argued more than once that the soul of man is material, and that it is made of a fifth substance, *aether*, the fifth substance being different from the four elements of a body. For that reason, he called the soul an *apospasm*, a fragment. This gave him a natural sequence, of death disintegrating the elements, and of the soul returning 'as to its father'. This is particularly clear in a crucial passage in *Quis Rerum* 282:

Just as nouns and verbs and all parts of speech which are composed of the 'elements' in the grammatical sense are finally resolved into the same, so too each of us is composed of the four mundane elements, borrowing small fragments from the substance of each, and this debt he repays when the appointed time-cycles are completed, rendering the dry in him to earth, the wet to water, the cold to air, and the warm to fire. These all belong to the body, but the soul whose nature is intellectual and celestial will depart to find a father in *aether*, the purest of the substances ... Out of this the men of old thought the stars in the whole of heaven had been made, and deduced as a natural consequence that the human soul also was a fragment thereof.

But the driving force for Philo in all this was not the intellectual speculation and its satisfaction, but the sense, which he clearly had in himself, of the connection between the human and the divine. Thus, much as Eleazar had appealed to the experience of God in this life as the foundation for hope, so Philo did the same, though with entirely different words and concepts. So he claimed in *De Gig.* 13 and 14 that those 'who soar upwards and return to the place whence they came' are 'those who have given themselves to genuine philosophy, who from first to last study to die to life in the body, that a higher existence, immortal and incorporeal [*asomatos kai aphthartos*], in the presence of him who is himself immortal and uncreated, may be their portion'.

The important point here is that these very different pictures (of how a continuity of experience of God beyond death might be possible) *are* extremely different; which makes it apparent that the experience in this life comes first, and that the picturing activities are secondary. It is clear that they are parasitic on the reality of what has been experienced in this life. This becomes even more obvious when one adds the graphically literal imaginations and pictures of Apocalyptic, which (in addition to being maps of the future) are also frequently what Austin Farrer called 'Cook's tours of heaven'. Yet despite the temptations of a Freudian wish-fulfilment, picturing activities do not go uncontested. The very speculation itself (that there will be a life with God beyond death) *was* contested, not least on the grounds that it cannot be justified from the Biblical tradition. That opposition is most obvious in the case of the Sadducees. Their opposition is well known not least because they appear in the Gospels posing highly sceptical questions to Jesus, particularly about the status of the unfortunate widow who, according to the Levirate law

(p. 50), was compelled to marry seven brothers (so if there *is* to be this resurrection, whose wife will she then be?); and because Paul was able to divide the Council on the question of resurrection, 'for the Sadducees say that there is no resurrection, neither angel nor spirit' (Acts xxiii.8). As Josephus says very firmly of the Sadducees: 'As for the persistence of the soul after death, penalties in the underworld, and rewards, they will have none of them' (*War* 2.165); and in *Ant.* 18.16 he repeats: 'The Sadducees hold that the soul perishes along with the body.'

What the Sadducees themselves believed is impossible to reconstruct, since virtually nothing from their own writing or opinion has survived. But what is certainly clear is that they would not advance beyond the Biblical evidence; and, even more to the point, that they refused to search for terms on which to live their life other than those which are clearly given to us. In other words, they affirmed the goodness of the created order as it now is, including death. It would be a kind of blasphemy to reject the present life by supposing that there is a better one to come. That is certainly what seems to underlie the grudging comment on the Sadducees by their opponents, in *Aboth DeRabbi Nathan*: 'The Sadducees used silver vessels and gold vessels all their lives, but it was not because of arrogance [or 'ostentation']; but the Sadducees said, "It is a tradition among the Pharisees to afflict themselves in this world; but in the world to come they will have nothing."' What that brief comment shows is that the Sadducees were not simply negative in their attitude to life after death. They received life from God as his creation and were prepared to live it on the terms given to them by God. If they had any further hope it could only be in the context of God's creative act, as the book of Ezekiel would allow them to believe.

But this hesitation about explicit belief in life with God after death was certainly not confined to the Sadducees. Inscriptions on tombstones frequently reflect the beliefs of those who bury their dead, and in this period (before and immediately after the emergence of Christianity), very few tombstones bear any sign of a vigorous belief that the dead person has gone or will go to a life with God beyond death. The most usual inscription is some variation on *shalom* (which in itself is a reminder that it was no doubt an expensive business to have long inscriptions carved on a tombstone); otherwise, the word 'rest' occurs frequently, sometimes in combination with *shalom*, as on a tombstone from Naples: 'Peace to your place of rest'. But there are some which express a much clearer hope, occasionally in quite elaborate form, as in this example from the Monteverdi Catacomb in Rome:

> Here lies Regina, buried in so beautiful a tomb,
> which her husband, prompted by his love, erected ...
> She will live again, she will return to the light,
> for she can hope to rise into that eternity
> which is promised with utter surety to those who are worthy and
>   pious,
> She deserves to have a throne in that blessed country.
> This your piety will guarantee for you, your chaste life,
> your love of the people, your observance of the Law.
> This is the reward of your marriage, for whose honour you were
>   solicitous,
> you have great hopes for the future from those things which you
>   have done,
> and in them your sorrowing husband seeks his consolation.

Less elaborate are those inscriptions which express a belief in the *olam haBa*, the age or the life to come, as in two Greek inscriptions from a site near Haifa: one says that anyone who disturbs the grave will have no share in the life to come, and the other says that the man and his wife have a share in the life to come. It is even more rare for a tombstone to endorse the Greek picture of an independent soul, though one moving example has been recovered from Egypt:

This is the grave of Arsinoe, wayfarer. Stand by and weep for her ... I had a small span of years, but great grace flowered in the beauty of my spirit. This grave hides in its bosom my chaste body, but my soul has fled to the holy ones. Lament for Arsinoe. (*Corpus Inscriptionum Iudaicarum*, 1510)

But in general, to judge from the tombstones, popular opinion was as cautious as were the Sadducees. Occasionally it seems to be even more pessimistic:

Black death stays without end in the everlasting dwelling places
And the thin ghost possesses an eternal home.
Life goes back to the sky while the body is held by the earth.
All things thus seek out what is rightful for them, and their own
    places.
Thus does the nature of things require, as does also the order of
    time,
That what things exist today perish, and what things will be in
    the future will pass away.
Now, my wife, if any faculties are left the dead, receive
The offices due to holy shades ...
O jealous fate, why hast thou plunged her cruelly into the tragedy
    of things
And not even the new love of her husband has turned thee?

She enjoyed this light seventeen years, ten months, twenty days,
of which she lived one hundred days with her husband.
She was ill forty-five days, and has gone to rest in peace.

There is no sign here of spiritual terrorisation or of attempts to
manipulate and control people through the imposition of heaven
or hell. The belief that there may be a continuity of life with God
arises from the unmistakable consequence of God in this life, an
experience which creates a faith and an allegiance which will not
hesitate to die rather than deny it. Josephus, the Jewish historian
in and of this period, summarised that faith:

For those who live in accordance with our Laws, the prize is not silver
or gold, no crown of wild olive ... no. Each individual , relying on the
witness of his own conscience and the lawgiver's prophesy, confirmed
by the sure testimony of God, is firmly persuaded that to those who
observe the laws, and (if they must needs die for them) willingly meet
death, God has granted a renewed existence and in the revolution of
the ages the gift of a better life.

That hope undoubtedly did take hold and become widespread.
In the Rabbinic period, its detail was filled out. But the speculative
imagination swung back very firmly to the Biblical materials –
in other words, the Greek speculation was largely abandoned.
That, of course, is not surprising, because the Rabbis were
concerned with the reconstruction and continuity of Judaism
beyond the failure of the two revolts against Rome and the

emergence and spread of Christianity. Under such threats of dissolution, the Rabbis delineated anew the boundary of Israel, with scrupulous attention to Torah and its interpretation. Indeed, those interpretations eventually acquired a comparable status, becoming known as Torah Shebeal Peh, Torah transmitted by word of mouth. The Rabbis perceived their task to be the implementing of the basic advice in Pirqe Aboth: 'Be careful in judgement, establish many disciples, and make a fence [*syag*] for Torah.' The Rabbinic enterprise, therefore, in relation to life beyond death, was to elaborate and fill in the basic Biblical opportunity from materials within Scripture itself, in order to elaborate and make more detailed those elementary beliefs. They opted very firmly for resurrection, since that belongs to the Biblical tradition, and Greek speculation certainly does not.

There were then many disputes about what could be inferred from the Bible. Some held the view that only those who were buried in the promised land could be raised to life. Others accepted the premise, but believed that the faithful dead, buried elsewhere, could be transported to the soil of the promised land. So, for example, commenting on the passage in Ps. cvi.9, 'I will walk before the Lord in the land of the living', the Palestinian Talmud records a comment that this refers to the land whose dead will be revived first in the days of Messiah (i.e. Israel). But that would mean that the Babylonian Rabbis – amongst many others – would not be equally rewarded; therefore, 'the Holy One, Blessed be He, will tunnel through the earth before them, and their bodies will roll down the tunnels like bottles, and when they arrive under the soil of Israel, their souls will be reunited to them' (J. Ket.35b).

Belief in the resurrection becomes from this point on one of the basic principles of Judaism. Maimonides, the great unifier and codifier of the rabbinic interpretations of Torah, went so far as to say that anyone who does not believe in the resurrection of the dead is not an adherent of Judaism. He himself made one further attempt to show that belief in the resurrection is coherent with philosophy, as philosophy had then developed under the great impetus of the Muslim rediscovery of Greek philosophy. Yet that was precisely one of the points isolated by the opponents of Maimonides, in the so-called Maimonidean controversy, as demonstrating that he was himself unfaithful to Judaism, by subordinating revelation to reason. For his opponents, the belief in the resurrection was not to be doubted, since that is what Scripture allows and requires Jews to believe.

For all that, Jews have frequently remained cautious and reticent in their own personal beliefs and affirmations. This is particularly clear in the contributions made by many different Jews to *Worlds of Faith*, especially on pp. 263f. Many different hopes – and doubts – are expressed. But the strong and fundamental Biblical themes constantly recur, above all the assertion that the main continuities worth talking about, and living for, are those in the people and in one's own children. It is still very much as R. Jochanan ben Nappacha (c. 190 – 279) put it when he finished reading the book of Job:

The end of man is to die, and the end of a beast is to be slaughtered, and all are doomed to die. Happy is he who was brought up in the Torah and whose labour was in the Torah and who has given pleasure to his Creator and who grew up with a good name and departed the world with a good name; and of him Solomon said: 'A good name is better than precious oil, and the day of death than the day of one's birth.' (Eccles. viii.1)

From this it follows that the Jewish understanding of death is an affirmation of affinity. That is why it is a very basic duty to be with the *goses*, the dying person, and to be present at the *yetziat neshamah*, the departure of the soul; and also to recite at the parting moment at least the last part of the *Shema* (p. 45). It is equally a duty, noticed at least as long ago as the time of Josephus (*Contra Apionem* II.205), to accompany the body to the grave. Even study of Torah should be suspended (B. Ket. 17a) in order to fulfil this duty, even if only by walking with it for four paces.

It follows that the customs of mourning and remembrance of the dead are at least as important as those of the funeral (which are described in Rabinowicz, *A Guide to Life*). *Shivah* (lit. 'seven') is the period of seven days immediately after the funeral. Rabinowicz says of it: 'The *Shivah* is a unique institution. For seven days, the mourners, irrespective of status or disposition, are united in their common sorrow. Daily routine and work cease. Death, with its awesome majesty, casts its shadow on the mourners' (p. 55).

But the real shadow that is being cast is that of the person who has died, and the shadow is a long one. The *Yahrzeit* (lit. 'year's time') is the anniversary of the death, when memorial is made through the mourner's *kaddish*. The word *kaddish* is derived from the Hebrew word meaning 'holiness' and 'praise', and it is another fundamental obligation. Few things summarise better, not only the Jewish emphasis on affinity and community, even in the face of loss or of holocaust, but also the emphasis on the truth of God *for its own sake*, not for the sake of a transaction whereby we calculate the gain for ourselves:

Mourner: Magnified and sanctified be his great name, in the world which he has created according to his will. May he establish his Kingdom during your life and during your days, and during the life of all the house of Israel, even speedily and at a near time; and to this say, Amen. *Congregation and mourner*: Let his great name be blessed forever, and to all eternity. *Mourner*: Blessed, praised and glorified, exalted, extolled and honoured, magnified and lauded be the name of the Holy One, blessed be he, even though he is high above all the blessings and hymns, praises and consolations which are uttered in the world; and to this say, Amen.

May there be abundant peace from heaven, and life for us and for all Israel; and to this say, Amen.

He who makes peace in his high places, may he make peace for us and for all Israel; and to this say, Amen.

Judaism is thus a religion of radical self-offering. As there is, for a Jew, a blessing for virtually every occasion, so every occasion is an opportunity for recognising God, and for affirming the community which, through time, has existed only because of him. Including the Holocaust? That has cut very deep – how could it not? Yet Rabbi Israel Spira, the Rabbi of Bluzhov, had this to say:

Every day, every child, after studying the daily lessons prescribed by our sages, should learn about the Holocaust, for it says in our holy Torah: 'Then it shall come to pass, when many evils and troubles are come upon them, that this song shall testify before them as a witness' (Deut. xxxi.21). The suffering and the testimonies, when told by Holocaust survivors, are a song, a hymn of praise, a testimony to the eternity of the Jewish people and the greatness of their spirit.

He also told this story of his time, in the Janowska camp, to Baruch Singer, which summarises so much of the Jewish attitude to death – and to life.

It was a dark, cold night in the Janowska road camp. Suddenly a stentorian shout pierced the air: 'You are all to evacuate the barracks immediately and report to the vacant lot. Anyone remaining inside will be shot on the spot!' Pandemonium broke out in the barracks. People pushed their way to the doors while screaming the names of friends and relatives. In a panic-stricken stampede, the prisoners ran in the direction of the big open field. Exhausted, trying to catch their breath, they reached the field. In the middle were two huge pits. Suddenly, with their last drop of energy, the inmates realised where they were rushing, on that cursed dark night in Janowska. Once more the cold, healthy voice roared in the night: 'Each one of you dogs who values his miserable life and wants to cling to it must jump over one of the pits and land on the other side. Those who miss will get what they rightfully deserve – ra-ta-ta-ta-ta.' Imitating the sound of a machine gun, the voice trailed off into the night followed by a wild, coarse laughter. It was clear to the inmates that they would all end up in the pits. Even in the best of times it would have been impossible to jump over them, all the more so on the cold dark night in Janowska. The prisoners standing at the edge of the pits were skeletons, feverish from disease and starvation, exhausted from slave labour and sleepless nights. Though the challenge that had been given them was a matter of life and death, they knew that for the S.S. and the Ukrainian guards it was merely another devilish game.

Among the thousands of Jews on that field in Janowska was the Rabbi of Bluzhov, Rabbi Israel Spira. He was standing with a friend, a freethinker from a large Polish town whom the rabbi had met in the camp. A deep friendship had developed between the two.

'Spira, all of our efforts to jump over the pits are in vain. We only entertain the Germans and their collaborators, the Askaris. Let's sit down in the pits and wait for the bullets to end our wretched existence,' said the friend to the rabbi.

'My friend,' said the rabbi, as they were walking in the direction of the pits, 'man must obey the will of God. If it was decreed from heaven that pits be dug and we be commanded to jump, pits will be dug and jump we must. And if, God forbid, we fail and fall into the pits, we will reach the World of Truth a second later, after our attempt. So, my friend, we must jump.'

The rabbi and his friend were nearing the edge of the pits; the pits were rapidly filling up with bodies.

The rabbi glanced down at his feet, the swollen feet of a fifty-three-year-old Jew ridden with starvation and disease. He looked at his young friend, a skeleton with burning eyes.

As they reached the pit, the rabbi closed his eyes and commanded in a powerful whisper, 'We are jumping!' When they opened their eyes, they found themselves standing on the other side of the pit.

'Spira, we are here, we are here, we are alive!' the friend repeated over and over again, while warm tears streamed from his eyes. 'Spira, for your sake, I am alive; indeed, there must be a God in heaven. Tell me, Rebbe, how did you do it?'

'I was holding on to my ancestral merit. I was holding on to the coattails of my father, and my grandfather and my great-grandfather, of blessed memory,' said the rabbi and his eyes searched the black skies above. 'Tell me, my friend, how did *you* reach the other side of the pit?'

'I was holding on to you,' replied the rabbi's friend. (Eliach, *Hasidic Tales of the Holocaust*, pp. 3f.)

CHAPTER 3

Christianity

The Christian understanding of death is dominated by the belief of the first friends and associates of Jesus that he had died on a cross and yet had been raised by God to a life beyond death. Christianity is thus a celebration of the Easter exclamation marks:

> Christ the Lord is risen again!
> Christ hath broken every chain!
> Hark, the angels shout for joy,
> Singing evermore on high,
> > Alleluya!

It seems rather obvious to say so. But it was not obvious before the event. Jesus was not even acknowledged as 'Christ' during his lifetime, except, at most, in a tentative way which he seems (as we shall see) to have regarded as misleading. What the Gospels make clear is that Jesus was recognised, not as a special religious creation (like an angel), but as a disturbing, challenging man, whose unequivocal humanity was obvious, and whose words were accompanied by actions of a powerful and God-claiming kind.

Thus the Christian understanding of death begins in a Jewish context, with a teacher who: took up very independent positions on many of the major religious and political issues of his day; anticipated his own death in a specific way; asserted, nevertheless, that it is in and through death that that 'truth of God' which is so fundamental to Judaism will be unequivocally manifest; and was believed by his followers to have been dramatically right, but in ways that took them, at least initially, by surprise.

It follows that the Christian understanding of death cannot be summarised in an exclamation mark. It has to be set in that

original context, in which Christianity emerged as an interpretation of what Judaism should be – of how, in other words, the
covenant promises and commands should be implemented in that
day and at that time; for at the time when Jesus was alive, there
were many competing interpretations of how Jews (defined by
birth or conversion) should live as the true children of the
covenant: Sadducees, Pharisees, Zealots, Essenes, Dead Sea
sectarians, Hellenisers, even Samaritans, saw themselves as the
faithful children and interpreters of the covenant. What the Israeli
novelist, Amos Oz, has said of Jews in contemporary Israel was
as true then as it is now, that 'Judaism' is an abstraction. What
we find in practice is a coalition of traditions and, even more, a
coalition of dreams – dreams based on Biblical promises, and
not least, in those days, dreams of a coming messiah (or messiahs;
there was not even agreement about the nature of the messianic
hope).

Christianity represents a belief that the dream has been realised
in life, and that the messiah (or in Greek, the Christos or Christ)
has arrived:

> Wake up, you who sleep, and arise from the dead,
> And Christ shall give you light!   (Eph. v.14)

But who has been identified as Christ? And why? Obviously, with
hindsight, it was the man Jesus, for whom the term 'Christ' has
become virtually a part of his name. But it was not so obvious
at the time, nor has it remained so: it is a continuing Jewish
objection to the interpretation of Jesus as Christ that very few of
the so-called 'messianic signs' (the signs located in the Biblical
promises of what will be the case when the messiah comes) have
in fact been realised.

So it is not obvious or inevitable that Jesus should have been
regarded as Christ. According to Acts xi.26, it was not until long
after the death of Jesus that 'the disciples were for the first time
called Christ-ians'. And that reflects the record of a general hesitation in the Gospels to call Jesus 'Christ'. In fact what one finds,
particularly in the first three Gospels, is a very wide range of
different attempts to interpret who Jesus is and how he does
and says what he does: 'On the way, Jesus asked his disciples,

''Who do men say that I am?'' And they told him, ''John the Baptist; and others say Elijah; and others one of the prophets.'' And he asked them, ''But who do you say that I am?'' Peter answered him, ''You are the Christ.'''

Surely right? But the *immediate* response of Jesus (according to Mark viii.30 and Luke ix.20) was to stop this interpretation of himself: 'He charged and commanded them to tell this to no one, saying, ''The son of man must suffer many things, and be rejected by the elders and chief priests and scribes, and be killed, and on the third day be raised''' (Luke ix.21f.).

The point here is very simple but completely fundamental for the Christian understanding of death. The man Jesus has made manifest what the Gospels call in Greek a *dunamis*. The word 'dunamis' underlies such English words as 'dynamic' and 'dynamo'. So the Gospels claim that Jesus set forward into the world, through his own life and body, a consequence and an effect: both in words and in actions, lives are changed; there was an *effect*, which made a dramatic difference; and it was an effect, a *dunamis*, which Jesus did not claim to be his own. To the contrary, he claimed and knew in his own experience that it came from God whom, in his teaching, he was characterising as Abba, as father, as one involved in the lives of his children. Thus some of those effects, like the healing of illness in conjunction with the forgiveness of sins (which were believed to be the cause of illness), were thought at that time to be the property of God alone. Yet Jesus spoke the word of forgiveness and healed the disease. So not surprisingly people began to ask, from what resource, or with what authority, does this man do these things?

The issue is put as briefly and sharply as it can be, in Mark vi.2f.:

On the sabbath he began to teach in the synagogue; and many who heard him were astonished, saying, 'Where did this man get all this? What is the wisdom given to him? What mighty works are wrought by his hands! Is not this the carpenter, the son of Mary and brother of James and Joses and Judas and Simon, and are not his sisters here with us?'

The first question is even more brief in the Greek, consisting of only three words, *pothen touto tauta* – whence to this man these things? From those three words derives the necessity for Christology – that is to say, for attempts to give an adequate (or a not entirely inadequate) account of the relation of the un-equivocally human Jesus ('and are not his sisters here with us?') to the reality and being of God whom Jesus believed was the source and resource of all that he was doing and saying. His claim, in life and in word, is that the domain of God's effect, the kingdom of God, is already here, in himself and in those who recognise it in faith (the episode above continues by recording how the *absence* of that faith frustrates the consequence of God). It is also his claim that that domain is about to be extended much more widely: 'Truly, I say to you, there are some standing here who will not taste death before they see the kingdom of God come with power' (Mark ix.1).

It is the connection with death which makes it clear why the interpretation of Jesus as Christ was met immediately by his command not to spread that interpretation around. That same command to silence can be found elsewhere in the Gospels, when those who had actually felt or experienced in their own case the *dunamis* of God transmitted through Jesus, attributed an equally high status to Jesus in relation to God: 'He had healed many, so that all who had diseases pressed upon him to touch him. And whenever the unclean spirits beheld him, they fell down before him and cried out, "You are the Son of God." And he strictly ordered them not to make him known' (Mark iii.10–12).

The point is clear: no one denied that something unusual was going on. Even the enemies of Jesus, at the time and in subsequent history, did not question the fact that his words and actions were full of independence and power. The issue for them was to know from what resource he acted in these ways, because he was speaking and acting well within the boundary of Israel (literally in the synagogue and metaphorically within the tradition); but he was doing so with challenging independence: 'You have heard that it was said to you of old ... but I say to you ...' (Matt. v.21, 27, 31, 33, 38, 43). The issue *had* to be: on what *basis* does he speak and act in this way? Or in their language, 'By what authority [*exousia*] are you doing these things, or who gave you authority to do them?' (Mark xi.28, Matt. xxi.23, Luke xx.2) – a question in response to which Jesus was as uncommunicative as he had instructed others to be. Why? The answer seems clear: there were *many* ways in which Jews believed that an individual might be in a 'special relationship' with God and might therefore be able to advance an independent opinion or action. He might be a prophet, or an angel, or specially endowed with Wisdom, or Elijah returned to usher in the messianic kingdom, or even one of the two different kinds of messiah – one of the two anointed figures ('messiah' = 'anointed'), the high priest or the descendant of David. There were many figures through whom a special effect, or *dunamis*, of God might be made manifest.

But however much some of those descriptions seemed appropriate for what was happening in the case of Jesus, Jesus resisted them all. In the Gospels, many of those categories were 'floated towards' Jesus as possible interpretations, and while Jesus did not apparently repudiate at least some of them, he did not embrace them either. Instead, he referred to himself most frequently by a phrase which is not a title, nor even a category of special relationship with God, except in so far as it emphasises the relationship in which *all* people are included, the relationship of creature to Creator, subject to the universal fact of death.

That phrase is 'the son of man'. The meaning of that phrase is completely uncertain. The *possible* meanings I have reviewed and summarised elsewhere (*The Religious Imagination*, pp. 139ff.). Yet what at least is clear is that for any Jew who was hearing Scripture read in synagogue (or Temple) or who recited the Psalms as prayer and praise, there are two Biblical associations of the phrase which reinforce each other: one is the poetic parallel for 'man', where the phrase 'a son of man' is used most frequently in contexts associated with death (p. 48); and the second is the use of the phrase in Daniel (p. 60) to refer to a coming figure who (in that context) represents those who have kept faith with God (despite death and martyrdom) and who have been vindicated by God beyond death.

In that phrase in Greek, the definite article (*the* son of man, the one you all know about) requires a sufficiently well-known reference: this could certainly include Daniel, since (in the evidence that has survived) there is only the one other usage which appears sufficiently frequently, or over a wide enough area, to be recognised. Putting it the other way round, to a Biblically literate person, the phrase 'the son of man' would immediately trigger the Danielic image, particularly since Daniel was important in reinforcing Jewish faith in times of persecution or testing (cf. the allusions to Daniel in the so-called 'Markan apocalypse', xiii.26).

But the same argument points with equal inevitability to the other (more frequent) association in Scripture, to man as 'less than God' and subject to the penalty of death (p. 49). In Hebrew (though not in Aramaic or Greek, which many Jews spoke as their everyday language) the point is even stronger, since the phrase is *ben adam*, literally 'son of Adam', the name Adam being one of several Hebrew words for 'man'; for it was Adam who was first subject to the penalty of death.

The two Biblical phrases in conjunction suggest that when the phrase is attributed to Jesus in the Gospels, or was originally used by him, it meant, in paraphrase: it is as one who is subject to the penalty of death (like any other human) that he speaks and acts as he does (*not* as a *super*-human figure, such as an angel or messiah); and yet also it is as one who believes that he will be vindicated by God beyond death. It is, in other words, a radical assertion that God can be as much of effect *now*, *en dunamei* (in power or consequence), as he has ever been in the past, for those who look for that effect in the faith that it can and will be so. The action of God is not confined to supernatural figures or events. It can be known and realised here, within the human boundaries of life and death.

Jesus, then, resisted the more extravagant titles, in order to insist that he spoke and acted as he did as one who is subject to death, but who believes that he will be vindicated by God, without whom not even a sparrow falls.

The phrase 'the son of man' is not only the obvious way to insist on those two points together: it is the only way, in the Jewish resources available to him at that time, through which to make that point. So the problem that Jesus posed to his contemporaries is obvious: he restored the *dunamis* of God (the difference that God can make) in and through his own person, not just in action (healing the sick) but even more in word. He spoke and acted with an independence which he claimed came directly from God whom, in his authority and accessibility, he characterised as Abba, father; and that evoked, inevitably, the repeated question: By what delegated authority on earth do you speak and act in this way?

In that context it immediately becomes clear, not only why Jesus felt compelled to go to Jerusalem, but also why the likely outcome, in his own death, was involved in that transition from Galilee to Jerusalem. All four Gospels emphasise both points. The Synoptic Gospels use strong Greek words of necessity for the journey (for example, *dei*, 'it is necessary') and they all record strong predictions of the passion and death of Jesus (Mark viii.31ff.; Mt. xvi.21ff.; Luke ix.22). These are often explained as constructions composed, after the event, by those who believed that Jesus must have been in control of his own destiny, at least in obedience to God. So he seems indeed to have been, but in a way which makes his awareness (that his own death is predictable, if he goes to Jerusalem) a matter of historical fact, not a matter of post-resurrection construction. The reason is obvious: Jesus had claimed in word and in action that the *dunamis* of God is as real and as much available now as it ever has been to those who have faith that it can be so. This led him to realise that that possibility is not confined to the people of Israel (to those in the boundary condition of the covenant). He came to realise that the consequence of God is just as real and possible for those outside that boundary, Samaritans, gentiles, Roman soldiers; in other words, for those who have the faith that it can be so. Faith becomes the new boundary condition of a covenant friendship with God.

But then the issue is unavoidable: is God, so to speak, available 'to all sorts and conditions of men', simply on the basis of faith and trust? And if so, what then of Torah? What of those particular conditions of which the *shema* constantly reminds all Jews? (pp. 45–8). By what authority could he teach and act in such a way that it threatened to destroy the covenant boundary of Israel? The issue of his authority could only be avoided in one way: Jesus could have stayed in Galilee. We know of other aberrant teachers, who were emphatically repudiated, but who were not crucified. They simply stayed away from the centre and locus of Jewish authority. By insisting on the necessity to make the journey to Jerusalem, Jesus was *ipso facto* insisting on the truth of his understanding of the *immediacy* of God's effect and authority: it does not have to be mediated through high-priest or religious court. That becomes a different kind of challenge in Jerusalem, because it was in Jerusalem that there was located (for most Jews, though not for those who belonged to deliberately schismatic movements like the Dead Sea Sect) the final and absolute authority in deciding what truly constitutes covenant faith and practice.

The foundation for that goes back to Deuteronomy xvii.8 – 13:

When the issue in any lawsuit is beyond your competence, whether it be a case of blood against blood, plea against plea, or blow against blow, that is disputed in your courts, then go up without delay to the place which the Lord your God will choose. There you must go to the levitical priests or to the judge then in office; seek their guidance, and they will pronounce the sentence. You shall act on the pronouncement which they make from the place which the Lord will choose. See that you carry out all their instructions. Act on the instruction which they give you, or on the precedent that they cite; do not swerve from what they tell you, either to right or to left. Anyone who presumes to reject the decision either of the priest who ministers there to the Lord your God, or of the judge, shall die; thus you will rid Israel of wickedness. Then all the people will hear of it and be afraid, and will never again show such presumption.

This is the most deeply fundamental offence in Israel, because it is a kind of blasphemy: it is a negation of the work of repair which God initiated in his covenants, articulated in Torah and entrusted to his people. As I argued in more detail, in *The Religious Imagination*, there can hardly be a clearer statement of the boundary condition which is required to be observed if Israel is to continue. If the aberrant teacher, after careful preliminary examination, insists on his own opinion when he is brought before the highest and final authority on earth, then he must be executed. Some of the later rabbis maintained that even if he recanted on his way to execution, he must still be executed, as a warning against this most destructive of all offences in Israel.

On that basis, it is not surprising that the Gospels record a constant and recurrent interrogation of Jesus, as he moved to

Jerusalem, on major political and religious issues: remarriage after divorce, the *kelal* (summary) of Torah, tribute to Caesar, resurrection from death, the nature of the messiah. The independence of Jesus is obvious and the question of his authorisation is explicit (Mark xi.27 – 33). In the context of Deuteronomy xvii, and of all that that chapter represents in maintaining the people of God within the boundary of God's command and covenant, the issue and the confrontation were inevitable.

It is not that Jesus was wholly independent of everyone – the only one in step. On some issues his teaching was indistinguishable from that of other Jewish groups. Thus his teaching on life after death sides very much with the Pharisees against the Sadducees:

But as touching the dead, that they are raised, have you [the Sadducees] not read in the book of Moses ... how God spoke to him saying, I am the God of Abraham, and the God of Isaac, and the God of Jacob? He is not the God of the dead, but of the living. You do greatly err. (Mark xii.26)

In the parable of Dives and Lazarus (Luke xvi.19 – 31), it is the belief of the Pharisees themselves which is turned against Sadducees, to whom the issue would have been an idle speculation. Both themes (of Lazarus, maybe as an echo from Eleazar of the Maccabean revolt, p.61; and of the living continuity of Abraham, Isaac and Jacob) are profoundly elaborated in St John's Gospel, where they are involved in the person of one who claimed to be the Resurrection and the Life. That is indeed idiosyncratic in relation to Judaism. But the basic teaching of Jesus is not aberrant: it is one option in the fluid explorations at that time of the true meaning of the covenant.

But what was certainly aberrant, from any central Jewish point of view, was the way in which Jesus tied *all* his teaching, and his action, to God as the immediate source and direction of his life. The consequence of God is no longer mediated by Torah interpreted by priest or rabbi (at least as a *necessary* condition). It may be mediated simply by faith. To bring that assertion to Jerusalem was to know that the issue of its truth and legitimacy was inevitable: indeed, it was to create the issue.

In that context, it is not surprising that the last supper of Jesus with his disciples, and the time after it in Gethsemane, are recorded in such a way that they make the theme of his voluntary and unevaded death unequivocally clear. It is why the Christian understanding of death begins, not in the Crucifixion, but in the Eucharist. All five accounts of the institution in the New Testament interpret the actions and words of Jesus as a summary of the significance, and of the continuing significance, of the death of Jesus, and of the involvement of others (including subsequent generations) in that death. It is epitomised in 1 Corinthians xi.26, 'For as often as you eat this bread and drink the cup, you make public the Lord's death till he come'; and it is followed by the immediate statement of consequence in judgement, if the participation is made unworthily.

How far did Jesus intend this interpretation of his actions and words at the Last Supper? In the strict sense, of course, we can never know, because historical judgements of that kind are not possible. But the probability seems clear enough, that Jesus continued in and through the moment of crisis his affirmation that even those who are *bene adam* (children of Adam and subject to death) will not be abandoned by God in death, but will be vindicated by him if they trust that it can be so; and he included himself in that affirmation.

What Jesus also added was the enacted statement that everything which the disciples had begun to discern and experience of God in and through Jesus would continue, even if he was removed from them by death. This extraordinary claim he tried to bring home to them in the most powerful language available at that time. This was the enacted sign of a prophet, like that of Agabus in the book of Acts (xxi.11). The point of those signs was not simply to illustrate an argument, like a diagram on a blackboard. They were believed to enact the event, so that it has already happened. That is why, in the example of Agabus, the friends of Paul immediately began to weep: the sign was not *warning* Paul; it was producing the event. All that remained was for Paul to appropriate the event at some point in the future. There is no other Jewish context which would make it intelligible that someone should stand up and say of a piece of bread, 'This is my body' while he is still standing there in front of them.

Even in the ancient world, where no doubt many strange things were believed, that would be disconnectedly bizarre – except for the fact that the formal prophetic action was still recognised as creating the reality of a future event in the present. The difference between the action of Jesus and that of other prophetic actions is then obvious: whereas with all other prophetic actions there is only one future event which has to be realised and appropriated in life (there is just one imprisonment that Paul has to go into), in this case the sign is to be appropriated over and over again, exactly as Paul emphasised, by repeating twice over, *hosakis ean*, *hosakis ean*: 'as often as you do this, as often as you do this', you make manifest the Lord's death till he comes (1 Cor. xi.25f.).

Of course the historical reconstruction of what happened at the Last Supper remains uncertain. What is not uncertain is the way in which the Eucharist has been seen, throughout the whole history of the Church, as the epitome of human salvation, achieved in the death of Jesus, in which others have already become incorporated through baptism.

The ways in which the Eucharist has been understood to effect that connection with the saving death of Jesus have varied enormously in the history of the Church, from the explicit affirmation that the sacrifice of Jesus, made once for all, is nevertheless continually being offered, to the implicit affirmation that the saving power of Christ's death moves into others with effect through the constant remembrance of him. Hence at one extreme the Tridentine canon (1753) affirms:

If anyone says that the sacrifice of the Mass is merely an offering of praise and thanksgiving, or that it is a simple commemoration of the sacrifice accomplished on the cross, but not a propitiatory sacrifice, or that it benefits only those who communicate; and that it should not be offered for the living and the dead, for sins, punishment, satisfaction and other necessities, *anathema sit*.

And at another, the Lima text (see bibliography under World Council of Churches) states:

The eucharist is essentially the sacrament of the gift which God makes to us in Christ through the power of the Holy Spirit. Every Christian receives this gift of salvation through communion in the body and blood of Christ ... The eucharist is the great sacrifice of praise by which the Church speaks on behalf of the whole creation. For the world which God has reconciled is present at every eucharist: in the bread and wine, in the persons of the faithful, and in the prayers they offer for themselves and for all people. Christ unites the faithful with himself and includes their prayers within his own intercession so that the faithful are transfigured and their prayers accepted. This sacrifice of praise is possible only through Christ, with him and in him. The bread and wine, fruits of the earth and of human labour, are presented to the Father in faith and thanksgiving. The eucharist thus signifies what the world is to become: an offering and hymn of praise to the Creator, a universal communion in the body of Christ, a kingdom of justice, love and peace in the Holy Spirit.

The eucharist is the memorial of the crucified and risen Christ, i.e. the living and effective sign of his sacrifice, accomplished once and for all on the cross and still operative on behalf of all humankind. The biblical idea of memorial as applied to the eucharist refers to this present efficacy of God's work when it is celebrated by God's people in a liturgy. (pp. 10f.)

Interpretations differ. But all interpretations agree in connecting the Eucharist to the death of Christ, and in seeing the Eucharist as relating ourselves to that death which is the means of our salvation and in which we are already involved through baptism. To quote the *Response by the Church of England to the Agreed Statements by ARCIC*:

Believers must be incorporated into that death, and for each individual the incorporation into Christ's death is by baptism. The effect of this incorporation is renewed and made continually manifest by the eucharist: the eucharist links the passion and resurrection with what happens to us.

Here is the root and foundation of the Christian understanding of death: it does not evacuate the factual reality and pain of death by some compensatory promise of resurrection. It goes through Gethsemane and through the passion, where Jesus affirms as son of man (as one who is subject to death but who believes that God will vindicate him) that the route to vindication is not by supernatural intervention (not by angels), nor by armed resistance (not by a sword). How then is it to be? That was the question also for Jesus, as he moved from Gethsemane to the 'trial' and the cross.

The so-called trial of Jesus was not in truth a trial. It seems to have been the kind of investigation envisaged in Deuteronomy xvii to establish whether he might count as an aberrant teacher. That is why the accusation against Jesus had nothing to do initially with blasphemy, or any other such matter. In Matthew and Mark he is accused of threatening the Temple, and in John he is questioned about his teaching and about those whom he had taught. To those questions, Jesus remained silent. And it was his silence which condemned him (or at least put him in the Deuteronomic category of an obstinate and aberrant teacher), because it was in itself a refusal to accept the authority of the high priest as 'the judge who shall be in those days'. The high priest then demanded to know whether he was seriously claiming a direct authority from God, as one of the specially anointed figures, or messiahs. He clearly cannot be the *high-priestly* messiah, because it is the high-priest who is asking the question. 'Are you, then, the Christ, the Son of the Blessed?' Jesus replied that he is claiming direct authority of that kind, but not in the way the high priest supposed: it is as the son of man, who will (in a Danielic way) be vindicated by God. There was no need of further witnesses: the Deuteronomic point is proved. Yet even so, one last attempt was made to find if he was acting with the independence of the only other person recognised in Scripture as directly inspired, namely, the prophet – hence the otherwise strange episode where they cover his eyes and say, 'Prophesy'.

Once again, historical reconstruction is uncertain. What is at least clear (and it makes the issue inevitably one of death) is that Jesus was seen as a threat to the Temple – a threat which he had made deliberate by coming to Jerusalem so publicly.

It is exactly the same issue in the only other Christian trial recorded at length in the New Testament, the trial of Stephen in Acts. There, also, if Stephen had not got involved in a *synagogue* dispute (if he had been content to remain of the private opinion that Jesus is the Christ), then there would have been no problem. But the charge is unequivocal:

This man never ceases to speak blasphemous words against this Holy Place, and the law; for we have heard him say that this Jesus of Nazareth shall destroy this place, and shall change the customs which Moses delivered to us. (Acts vi.14)

The defence which Stephen offered, which looks at first sight like a recital of Biblical history, down to the time of Solomon, is in fact deliberately designed to make the point that God never wanted a Temple in the first place, and certainly does not locate authority there. It is an issue of death (at least according to Deuteronomy) to emphasise the direct inspiration of the Holy Spirit, as Stephen did; for that immediately rejects the authority of 'the judge who shall be in those days'.

So also it had been with Jesus: as the son of man, he was subject to death and yet he knew the effect and consequence of God in and through his own person, and he knew it to be immediate and direct. It is not surprising that Stephen is given the only use outside the Gospels of the phrase 'the son of man' as a description of Jesus (as opposed to a self-designation by Jesus of himself), in Acts vii.56. The connection here is extremely close. Stephen saw in Jesus the second reference in that phrase, the Danielic vision (as in Rev.i.13, xiv.14), through which the claim is made that even one súbject to death will be vindicated by God, as Jesus clearly had been. Yet Jesus said on the cross, 'My God, my God, why have you forsaken me?'

It is this cry of dereliction from the son of man that makes the belief of his family and friends that he rose from the dead all the more dramatic and demanding. The son of man had indeed proved to be *ben adam*, subject to death; and at the last moment it seemed that the vindication which he also claimed through that phrase had not happened. In the Jewish context of the time, with its realistic anthropology and Biblical uncertainty about life after death, the form of the resurrection *must* have been sufficiently substantial for it to have counted as vindication. Of all theories of what happened, the suggestions that it was mass-hallucination, or that the disciples could not bear to let his teaching go to oblivion, simply cannot be true. Beyond that basic certainty, the accounts of the resurrection present innumerable questions and problems – certainly beyond the scope of this book to summarise. The account by Murray Harris, *Raised Immortal*, offers a wise, albeit conservative, survey. In relation to the Christian understanding of death, what is clear is that the Christian way begins in the knowledge that Jesus, who was dead, is alive, and that, in the figurative language of the Ascension, he has not abandoned his humanity, but has taken it into the new authority which is now demonstrated to extend to the whole cosmos. Even in the New Testament itself, there is a clear sense that the resurrection goes against the grain of common sense and natural probability. And yet the restoration of Jesus to a living form beyond death is precisely what appeared to them, historically, to have happened; and in the context of Jewish anthropology, that living form had to be substantially and recognisably the one whom they had known before his death if any sense of resurrection was to be for them the truth.

But given that whatever happened *is* a matter of history, and ancient history at that, how can it have any importance for others, so many centuries after the event? The first friends of Jesus (or at least those whose writings now stand in the New Testament) had no doubt: they seized upon the realisation that the death and resurrection of Jesus are the vindication, not just of his own affirmation of God, but of all who claim that truth by faith as well. But it was the *death* of Jesus, much more than the resurrection, which they saw as liberating others also from death, because in some way it dealt with the fact of sin, whose deserved penalty (in the story of Adam) is death. Thus the Christian understanding of death is dominated by the recognition that our own death is already involved in his, and that the fact of our estrangement from God and from each other in sin is overcome and dealt with.

That involvement is not left as a matter of words alone, but is enacted in baptism and in the Eucharist. There the reconciliation between creature and creator, between humans and God, is made real. The atonement (at-onement) with God becomes true, not for a few, but for many. But how? How is the death of Jesus understood as effecting that atonement?

The New Testament does not give any single or systematic account (as Hengel, *The Atonement*, makes clear). Nor did the Church subsequently arrive at any dogmatic definition, as it did for the Trinitarian nature of God or for the person of Christ. Therefore, as C.J. Wright put it, it is 'to individual thinkers such as Paul, Origen, Anselm, Abelard, Grotius, to name but a few – and not to Councils – that we have to go for anything in the nature of a philosophy of the Cross' (p. 179).

John Burnaby put the matter more strongly:

There never was, and there never can be, a theory of the Atonement that is worth the paper it is written on. If we want to understand God's reconciliation of the world to Himself, there is nothing that we can do but to listen to those who have known it as a reality in themselves. If we ask them, How do you know that the one Christ died for all? – they can only answer, At any rate he died for me; and if we ask them how they know that, they will say with St Paul that they have known the power of his resurrection and the fellowship of his sufferings (Romans 8.31, 35, Philippians 4.13). Yet it is only too manifest that 'all' have not known that fellowship and that power: 'all' have not died with Christ and found their life renewed and strengthened by his. Once more we ask: What can it mean to speak of an atonement consummated on the Cross? Does not the world still wait to be reconciled? The only answer is that the finality of the Atonement is the finality of the Incarnation. (pp.101f.)

The doctrine of the Incarnation is an eventual and more formal articulation of what the Gospels display, that it was the *human* life of Jesus which nevertheless made manifest the *dunamis* of God. For that reason the Church ended up (inevitably, in terms of evidence) with the recognition that in Jesus the absolute reality of God was present, in and through his whole person, without diminishing or destroying the equal reality of his human nature, which remained subject to death. How that affirmation can still be maintained in terms of information process I have summarised in *The Religious Imagination*. Here it is enough to note that the atonement is supremely effected in the person of Jesus; and that theories of atonement explore how others can be brought into a living relation with him, in whom the atonement is a living fact. That is why the New Testament does not usually relate the believer to the death and resurrection of Jesus in any way which is evasive of life here and now, by offering a compensatory paradise. The obvious symmetry would seem to be: death of Jesus/resurrection of Jesus; death of believer in baptism/resurrection of believer to paradise. In fact what Paul wrote in Romans vi.4 was: 'We are buried with him by baptism into death, that like as Christ was raised up from the dead by the glory of the Father, even so we also should walk in newness of life.' Exactly the same is true of Titus ii.14 and 1 Peter i.18ff., where Jesus is described as ransoming us, not to eternal life, but to a blameless and purer way of life here and now.

This means that the New Testament understanding of death and atonement begins in a paradox: the death of Jesus was understood as the key, the cross-shaped key, which opens the door to forgiveness and a new way of life. Yet the teaching and practice of Jesus, long before his death, makes it clear that forgiveness and reconciliation are as simple as the change of heart (or, as the New Testament words for repentance prefer, 'change of direction') which makes it possible: 'I will arise and go to my father, and I will say ...' The story of the Prodigal Son repenting and being welcomed home is a continuing theme, not only of Jesus, but of John the Baptist and other prophets. Even while Jesus was alive in Galilee and Judaea, the reconciliation of sinners with God could take place, and it manifestly did so, with dramatic consequences, not just in healing, but in behaviour. What, then, does the death add to the life, in which the reconciliation with God was already effected for so many?

The New Testament answer is that it universalises the reconciliation. What applied to a few (those who met Jesus while alive) is now offered to all. After the Exile, the prophet of Isaiah lix had proclaimed:

Behold, the Lord's hand is not shortened that it cannot save, neither is his ear heavy that it cannot hear. But your iniquities have separated between you and your God, and your sins have hid his face from you, that he will not hear.

In Jesus, the reversal of that situation was believed to have happened. Consequently, everything that was believed to have been effected in and through the sacrificial system of the Jewish Temple (culminating in the Day of Atonement) for the people of Israel; and everything that had been effected for some individuals through Jesus' word of absolution, is now claimed, through the death of Jesus, to be true for all – even if its truth is not claimed by all.

It is the dichotomy in that last sentence (true for all, even if not accepted by all) which leads to objective and subjective understandings of atonement. The objective understanding takes

the cross to be the absolute statement, demonstration and achievement of a truth without qualification, that God was in Christ
reconciling the world to himself: there is nothing in the human
condition which remains as a kind of incurable cancer, multiplying
its cells of evil in some way that God cannot, or has not, dealt
with. Even the last enemy is not, so to speak, an incurable
illness. Death, to change the metaphor, is not the unmarked
and untilled corner of a field, where weeds and poison ivy
can flourish. The cross, in the New Testament understanding,
ploughs even that corner of the field and makes it, in its own
way, fruitful for harvest. Consequently, there is nothing, neither
life, nor death, nor angels, nor principalities, nor things present,
nor things to come, nor powers, nor height, nor depth, nor
any other creature, which can unravel that reconciliation; there
is nothing which is able, reverting to Paul, to separate us from
the love of God, which is in Christ Jesus our Lord. Not surprisingly, therefore, Paul described his work as a ministry of
reconciliation, and his gospel as a message of reconciliation
(2 Cor. v.18f., cf. Rom. v.8 – 11) but in those verses he emphasises
that God is the author of this reconciliation, and Christ is its
agent. Whatever has been achieved through the body of Jesus
dead on a cross had its origin in the purpose and initiative of
God: 'For God so loved the world that he gave his only-begotten
Son, to the end that all that believe in him should not perish,
but have everlasting life' (John iii.16).

So the objective understanding of reconciliation in the New
Testament emphasises that the initiative of God precedes the
particular history on earth of Jesus. Or, to put it more precisely,
Jesus is the initiative of God to make universal the truth which
particular individuals already knew for certain in their own case
– the truth that before I was blind, but now I see. The New
Testament is thus the living consequence of this truth, that there
is a new way of being human which is already a way of friendship and co-operation with God and with each other. It results
in (or should result in) an entirely different quality and style of
life, by the urging or urgency of his Spirit, that inbreathing which
is God, and which becomes manifest in joy, peace, longsuffering,
and all the other 'fruits of the Spirit'.

The death of Jesus, with which Christians are involved in the Eucharist, states that it is not just for the few assembled at that Last Supper that this blood is shed; it is for you and for many (for a vast multitude) for the forgiveness of sins. The Eucharist is thus the great reunion party: it is the re-established union with God.

The subjective understanding of the cross and of atonement simply recognises that the truth and the fact are indeed universal (it is for many), but that we can still refuse to participate in that reunion party: it is not for me. Thus salvation is a final and accomplished fact ('there is no other name under heaven by which we may be saved'), but salvation is not inevitable; we may refuse to acknowledge the name; and the possibility of being eternally unsafe, unsaved, is clear in the New Testament.

How, then, according to the New Testament, is salvation related to the death of Jesus? Sacrifice would seem an obvious category through which to answer that question. After all, the New Testament writers were exploring why the death on the cross achieves/demonstrates/proclaims/initiates the new fact of reconciliation which becomes *he kaine diatheke*, *novum testamentum*, the new covenant. The old covenant had required the solemn confirmation of blood when it was initiated; 'and according to the law, I may almost say, all things are cleansed with blood, and apart from shedding of blood there is no remission'. So the Epistle to the Hebrews argues (ix.22). But it is only in Hebrews that the theme of sacrifice in relation to the death of Jesus is worked out in much detail. Christ is described as one who

has appeared once, for all, at the end of the age to put away sin by the sacrifice of himself. And just as it is appointed for man to die once, and after that comes judgement, so Christ, having been offered once to bear the sins of many, will appear a second time, not to deal with sin, but to save those who are eagerly waiting for him. (ix.26f.)

The Epistle to the Hebrews is drawing a deliberate contrast between the old sacrificial system and the effect of Christ: the former is located in time and had to be repeated over and over again, but the latter is eternal and unique; the sprinkling of the blood of animals cannot compare with the consequence of the shedding of the blood of Christ (ix.12), not least because the priests of old were themselves frail 'and prevented by death from continuing in office' (vii.23), whereas Christ, by the defeat of death in his own person, demonstrates the corresponding negation of sin in that same person, and is thus 'able for all time to save those who draw near to God through him, since he always lives to make intercession for them. For it was fitting that we should have such a high priest, holy, blameless, unstained, separated from sinners, exalted above the heavens' (vii.25f.).

Thus, in the contrasts drawn in the Epistle to the Hebrews, Christ is both priest *and* victim, abolishing those sacrifices of old which simply foreshadow ineffectively what Christ has done effectively for all, and for all time. Drawing out the distinctions between the giving of Torah on Mount Sinai and the self-giving of Jesus, the Epistle claims that Jesus is the mediator of the new covenant, the sprinkling of whose blood speaks better things than that of Abel (xii.18 – 24).

The Epistle to the Hebrews is the most deliberate of the New Testament writings in working out the implications of the death of Christ (and particularly its consequence for us) in terms of sacrifice. Elsewhere Jesus is described as the Paschal Lamb which has been sacrificed for us (the passover lamb being sacrificed to mark the deliverance from Egypt) (1 Cor. v.7); as 'a fragrant offering and sacrifice to God' (Eph. v.2); as *hilasmos* for our sins (1 John ii.2, iv.10) – *hilasmos* meaning 'expiation', 'propitiation' or 'sin-offering'; and as *hilasterion* in Rom. iii.23ff.: 'There is no distinction: since all have sinned and fall short of the glory of God, they are justified by his grace as a gift, through the redemption which is in Christ Jesus, whom God put forward as *hilasterion* by his blood, to be received by faith.' The meaning of *hilasterion* is again diverse, being 'that which expiates' or 'propitiates', 'a gift to secure expiation', or 'the place of propitiation', especially 'the mercy-seat' associated with the Ark of the Covenant, as in Hebrews ix.5. In two other passages, Romans viii.3f., 2 Corinthians v.21, Jesus may be being described as a sin-offering, depending how the relevant phrases are translated. 'Him who knew no sin [like the scapegoat of the old sacrificial system, Lev. xvi] he made to be sin on our behalf, that we might become the righteousness of God in him.' In yet another image, Jesus claims of himself, in Mark x.45, that he has come to give himself as a ransom (*lutron*) for many. In the Jewish context, where there was a tense argument between Pharisees and Sadducees about whether a *lutron*, or ransom payment, is allowed in Torah for humans (or only for non-human property) it is certainly conceivable that Jesus made this interpretation of himself. It simply epitomises the costly consequence of affirming the reconciliation which his whole life is already effecting; and that is how Jesus is understood, who made of himself an *antilutron*, in 1 Tim. ii.6.

But *the* place where the Christian Church came to see the death of Christ most clearly as sacrificial was in the re-enactment in the Eucharist of his offering of himself, his body and his blood, to his disciples at the Last Supper. The extent to which that interpretation was developed – to the point where it seemed that the sacrifice 'once, and for all' was being repeated in a succession of further sacrifices at every celebration of the Mass – became one of the most bitter points of argument in the Reformation. This explains the strong emphasis, in the prayer of Consecration in the Anglican prayer-book of 1662, on the one oblation of himself offered once, and once only:

Almighty God, our heavenly Father, who of thy tender mercy didst give thine only Son Jesus Christ to suffer death upon the cross for our redemption; who made there (by his one oblation of himself once offered) a full, perfect, and sufficient sacrifice, oblation, and satisfaction, for the sins of the whole world; and did institute, and in his holy Gospel command us to continue, a perpetual memory of that his precious death until his coming again; Hear us, O merciful Father, we most humbly beseech thee; and grant that we receiving these thy creatures of bread and wine, according to thy Son our Saviour Jesus Christ's holy institution, in remembrance of his death and passion, may be partakers of his most blessed Body and Blood ...

In apparent contrast, the 3rd Canon of the (Roman Catholic) Council of Trent has already been quoted affirming 'the most holy sacrifice of the Mass' (p. 85). However, the Council also emphasised that the Mass is not a sacrifice *independent* of the cross through which the salvation of all has been effected. This enabled the Commission exploring Anglican and Roman Catholic relationships to issue an agreed Elucidation:

There is therefore one historical, unrepeatable sacrifice, offered once for all by Christ and accepted once for all by the Father. In the celebration of the memorial, Christ in the Holy Spirit unites his people with himself in a sacramental way so that the Church enters into the movement of his self-offering. In consequence, even though the Church is active in this celebration, this adds nothing to the efficacy of Christ's sacrifice upon the cross, because the action is itself the fruit of this sacrifice.

We are back once more with the basic New Testament theme of salvation through participation in the death and resurrection of Christ, but here made real – and realised – by the repeated enactment of his self-offering, his body and his blood given for a multitude for the remission of sins: 'As often … as often as you eat this bread and drink the cup, you proclaim the Lord's death until he comes.' By the time of Ignatius' letter to the Ephesians (first century AD) the Last Supper is being called *pharmakon athanasias*, the medicine of immortality.

It becomes clear that there are many allusions and themes underlying the New Testament interpretations of the death of Jesus and its relation to our own death and life. There is a swarm of images, none of which is worked out in detail, but all of which invade the Christian understanding of death – sometimes in ways which seem impressive but in fact are imprecise:

> Paschal Lamb, by God appointed,
> All our sins on thee were laid.

On this, Hodges commented:

The effect is impressive, and one does not stop to remember that the sins of Israel were never laid on the Paschal Lamb, and that the beast on which they were laid, the scapegoat, was not sacrificed. (*The Pattern of Atonement*, p. 47)

But despite the allusiveness of the images, some negatives at least are possible. Thus what is *not* found in the New Testament (except perhaps in the most marginal way) is any claim that Jesus is the propitiation for our sins. How could that be, since God initiated the work of our salvation in Christ, and that is hardly the model of an angry god needing to be propitiated? Nor do we find much support in the New Testament for the view that Jesus is a penal substitute for us on the cross, although that theme has been extremely important for some Christians in the subsequent history of the Church. There is certainly the preposition *anti* (in the saying about *lutron* being a ransom payment), picked up also in 1 Timothy ii.6 (but that was understood as an alternative, or as an equivalent, not as a substitution); there is the preposition *huper* in 2 Corinthians v.14, 15; and *peri* in Matthew xxvi.28; and there is the long section in 1 Peter ii.21 meditating on Isaiah 53. But, ironically, it is precisely to that passage that advocates of the theory of the atonement, which sees it as exemplary, appeal.

Exemplary theories of atonement follow 1 Peter ii.21 in affirming that 'Christ suffered for you, leaving you an example, that you should follow his steps.' The power of the cross is then understood as the appeal it makes to people to change their ways. That was the view particularly of Moberley's *Atonement and Personality*, which seemed in effect to be saying that our salvation (and, *ipso facto*, the forgiveness of our sins) does not happen until we repent – until we are won by love. That view is also associated with Abelard. As Hodges summarised the point,

The winning power of Christ, his power to break down indifference and ill-will and bring us to the point where we are willing to let him have his way with us, this is what impressed Abelard. In an age when all France was discussing the different forms of love, here Abelard saw divine Love. (*The Pattern of Atonement*, p.40)

Abelard's view was open to the objection that the cross was not the necessary act, or the necessary operation on a mortally sick patient: it was getting the consent of the patient to have the healing happen in him. In contrast, vicarious theories of atonement see our salvation as achieved by a victory over the forces of evil (Satan or the devil) who justly hold us in their grip. This is the Christus Victor theme, renewed by Gustav Aulén in this century.

But none of these ways of understanding how the cross effects our atonement, and hence our salvation, is sufficient on its own. Theories of atonement are somewhat like lymphocytes in the body: they are solutions going around looking for a problem, and taking the shape of the problem as it is identified. Theories of atonement know what the answer is:

> As the heaven is high above the earth,
> So great is God's mercy toward them that fear him;
> As far as the east is from the west,
> So far has he removed our transgressions from us.
>
> (Ps. ciii.12)

So the Psalmist: draw the two lines, mercy from heaven to earth, and our sins banished as far from us as east from west, and the two lines, the horizontal and the vertical, make the sign of a cross. That is what Christians, from the first, saw in the crucified figure: the meeting point of mercy and forgiveness, at the furthest limit of its cost: nothing will defeat the will of God to save us, except our freedom to refuse.

Theories of atonement are simply applications of the cure (the death and resurrection of Christ) to the problem of sin or mortality however it is identified. This is already apparent in Paul, whose whole letter to the Romans is an answer to the question: What was there about the human condition, that made Jesus necessary? Paul did not argue the case that Jesus *is* the effective action of God: accepting that he is, then to what crisis was Jesus, so to speak, addressed or sent?

Here we arrive at the second great theme of universalisation in the New Testament: as the death of Christ was believed to have universalised the reconciliation or atonement with God (p. 91), so Pauline anthropology universalises the corresponding human condition which is in need of repair or salvation: 'For *all* have sinned, and come short of the glory of God … The good that I would, I do not do, and the evil that I would not, that I do.' In the Genesis story, Adam epitomises the disorder which results in death (p. 46); Christian anthropology recognises that that disorder, or sin, is true of all humans, without exception. But the fault or estrangement which is universally evident, and which is summarised in the figure of Adam, is now balanced (and contradicted) by what Paul calls (for that reason) the *second* Adam. Paul understands Jesus as the last Adam reversing the penalty of death suffered by the first Adam and shared, since then, by all. The symmetry, moreover, is extended by the claim that *we* can participate in that reversal of the penalty of death by our association with (or involvement in) the Christ (especially in baptism and Eucharist) who died but who nevertheless is living still: the *dunamis* is still at work in the transformation of human life into love:

For as by man came death, by a man has come also the resurrection of the dead. For as in Adam all die, so also in Christ shall all be made alive. It is written: 'The first man Adam became a living being (*psyche*); the last Adam became a life-giving spirit (*pneuma*). But it is not the spiritual which is first but the physical, and then the spiritual. The first man was from the earth, man of dust; the second man is from heaven. As was the man of dust, so are those who are of the dust; and as is the man of heaven, so are those who are of heaven. Just as we have borne the image of the man of dust, we shall also bear the image of the man of heaven. I tell you this, brethren: flesh and blood cannot inherit the kingdom of God, nor does the perishable inherit the imperishable. (1 Corinthians xv.21f., 45–50)

The symmetry is impressive. But how could Paul have come to make so startling an extension of that fundamental story of Adam through which Jews had identified the origin of death as our now-natural condition? Only because he believed that one man (Jesus), who shared that natural circumstance of death with us, had in fact been seen by many of his followers (1 Cor. xv.1–7) *after* his death, in resurrected form; and has been seen, not only by them, but by Paul himself. The symmetry, therefore, can be taken further: as Jesus has entered into our condition of death, so we can enter into his condition of life resurrected beyond death (which means *living* in that condition already) – and can enter through the enacted sign of baptism (Romans vi.3–11).

As, then, death is universal, so also is the atonement, effected through the death of Christ:

For if, when we were enemies, we were reconciled to God by the death of his Son, much more, being reconciled, we shall be saved by his life. And not only so, but we also joy in God through our Lord Jesus Christ, by whom we have now received the atonement ... For as by one man's disobedience many were made sinners, so by the obedience of one shall many be made righteous. (Romans v.10f., 19)

The New Testament, therefore, portrays death as defeated. II Timothy i.10 even speaks of it as 'abolished', using a word (*katargesantos*) which in classical Greek means 'to render idle' or 'useless', 'to have missed an opportunity'. II Timothy proclaims as gospel (as good news) 'the appearance of our Saviour Jesus Christ, who abolished death and brought life and immortality [*athanasia*: cf. Ignatius, p. 96, and Philo, pp. 65f.] to light through the gospel'. So death is not only impotent: it has already begun to yield up its prey (see Luke vii.11f.; Matthew ix.18ff. and xxvii.52f.; John xi.1ff.), and it falls back before the followers of Jesus (i.e., those who, by participating in him, extend through the Spirit the same *dunamis* or effect of God: Matthew xi.3ff.; Acts ix.36ff., xx.7ff.). Anyone who hears his word, as John v.24 puts it, 'and believes him who sent me, has eternal life: he does not come into judgement, but has passed from death to life' – exactly as Jesus has passed through death to life, because, as Acts ii.24 puts it, 'it was not possible for him to be held by death'. Why? Because God is the agent of his own activity in Christ, and it is he who 'raised him up, having loosed the pangs of death'.

So the victory of Christ has implications for the whole *cosmos* (Colossians i.15–20); the cosmos is no longer what it was, because death, which was final in the process of the universe, is now, and is now known to be, after the resurrection, the base from which we are transacted into that kind of 'quantum leap', into a new disposition and alignment of a relationship, which we already anticipate here and now. It cannot be of our own making or achievement: it can only be the action of God working in those who allow that action to occur. At the opposite extreme, there can be refusal: there can be that 'sin against the Holy Ghost', which in context in Mark iii refers to those who see the *dunamis*, or effect of God, but who then ascribe it to other causes – in the paradigm case, to Beelzebub, the prince of devils: if one admits the effect, but refuses to recognise God as the agent of that effect, how can God 'take up residence' (as 1 John ii.14ff. puts it) in that life? Heaven has its corollary in hell in all religions, because if it is possible to be religiously right (in the Christian case, to be declared in the right and thus to be saved), it is logically – and perhaps actually – possible to be religiously wrong.

Christian history is then replete with debates: about the nature of eternal loss; or whether such loss can be eternal; or whether after death there is a long purgation of some human souls before they are ready to enter the final vision of God (on the rise and fall of purgatory, for which there is no unequivocal Biblical warrant, see le Goff, *The Birth of Purgatory*); or even on the nature of the human self and soul. The New Testament articulates a thorough-going Biblical anthropology, but does so in Greek. Terms like *psyche* and *pneuma* then allow the articulation of a more philosophical anthropology, influenced by Plato in terms of Christian spirituality, and by Aristotle in affirming that the characterised self, the subject of its own experience and the agent of its own activity, is not identical with the brain or the body. So far, no philosophical argument, and no amount of speculation about computers and artificial intelligence, has come close to dislodging that position, though many of course believe that it has (see further pp. 221–5). Whether such a characterised self, independent as it is in some important respects from the body, will survive the death of its body, is an entirely separate issue. The Christian affirmation is that it will, only because it lives already in the resurrection of Christ:

Then shall be brought to pass the saying that is written, Death is swallowed up in victory: O death, where is thy sting? O grave, where is thy victory? ... Thanks be to God, which giveth us the victory through our Lord Jesus Christ. (1 Corinthians xv.54f., 57)

CHAPTER 4

Islam

Islam began, historically, in the quest of a young man, Muhammad, to find the absolute truth of God in the midst of the many conflicting claims which he encountered about the nature of God. In Mecca (where he was born in the year c. 570 CE) and in the surrounding territories (which he came to know when he took part in trading caravans), there were many such claims: Christians (of different kinds), Jews, polytheists, animists. Surely, if they were claiming to be worshipping God, it must be God (however inadequately described) that they must be worshipping? How then could they be in dispute or conflict with each other?

Muhammad went off for periods of increasing isolation during which he struggled in prayer to find *alHaqq*, the underlying and fundamental truth of God. It was in a cave, on the hillside of Mount Hira, that there came to him the overwhelming sense of that reality, impressing itself on him and demanding of him that he speak words, not of his own construction, but impelled upon him from God: *iqra*, 'Proclaim, in the name of your Lord ...' (s.xcvi.1). Later, he identified the presence in the cave with the messenger, Jibril (Gabriel). But it did not alter the sense he had of words from *God* being spoken through him, in response to that initiating command, *iqra*, 'proclaim'.

From that same Arabic root comes the word Quran. The Quran is the collection of all the subsequent utterances of Muhammad which were observably unlike his ordinary words and conversation, and which were believed to come directly from God. Not many, initially, thought that they did so. Even Muhammad felt that he must surely have gone insane. But both he and others came to recognise the totally different nature of Quranic utterance when it pressed forward in his speech. He even looked visibly different when the words of Quran were being spoken through him. Muhammad and his first followers came to have no doubt that the words of Quran came directly from God, making clear *sirat ulMustaqim*, the straight path which leads to God.

There can be no possible doubt about the disturbing and compelling nature of Muhammad's experience, or of its powerful consequence. He was possessed by the conviction that God is; and that it is *only* God who can be what God is. If God is indeed God, Allah, (*the* God), then there can only be what God is, the One who is the source of all creation, the unproduced Producer of all that is. The life of Muhammad and the message of the Quran then becomes the working out and the application of that fundamental vision. All people (divided as they are from each other at present) should become a single *umma*, community; every action and every aspect of life should become an act of witness 'that there is no God but God'.

It follows that the words of previous prophets, of whom Moses and Jesus have high status in the Quran, must also have been identical in *content*, even though they were related and addressed to different circumstances. Nevertheless, if the scriptures of the Jews and the Christians now differ in content from each other, and if in addition Jews and Christians oppose or reject Muhammad (or for that matter, each other), it can only be because they have corrupted the revelation (the Quran) entrusted to them. Because God is One, what he reveals must also be one. The 'Mother of the Book', as the Quran says of itself, is with God in Heaven. Yet manifestly Jewish and Christian scriptures do *not* agree, either with each other, or with the Arabic Quran. In particular, they have confused the revelation (the word from God) which has been transmitted *through* each prophet, with stories *about* the prophets, which are known in Arabic as *ahadith*, or collectively in English as Hadith. Only in the case of Muhammad has Hadith (stories about what Muhammad and his companions did and said) been recorded and kept separate from Quran. Hadith is undoubtedly of real authority in Islam, because Muhammad was the first living commentary on what the Quran means. But it cannot supersede or contradict the Quran, which is *the* Word of God, in the strongest, literal and inerrant sense; and only in Islam (according to Muslim belief) has Quran been recorded and preserved without corruption.

It follows, from that brief introduction, that the Islamic understanding of death is determined by the Quran, and by the practical interpretation of Quran in Hadith. Both Quran and Hadith may be supplemented by custom and exegesis, but never in any way that erodes the final and absolute authority of Quran. What then does the Quran say about death? Death, like all else in the created order, belongs to the will of God, and cannot occur without his leave: 'It is not possible for a soul [*nafs*] to die except with the permission of God at a term set down on record' (iii.139). Since the Quran embraces (and, from the Islamic point of view, corrects) earlier revelations, it takes the origin of death back to the offence of Adam and Eve in succumbing to the seducing whisper of Shaitan/Iblis (Satan/the *diabolos* or devil): his tempting is expressed in the subtle Arabic word *waswasa*, 'he whispered'. As a result God said: 'In the earth you will live, and in it you will die, and from it you will be brought out' (vii.24).

The resurrection of dead bodies is thus already asserted, from the earliest moment, in a way that it is not in Genesis (although in later Judaism the passage concerning the serpent being trampled beneath the heel was interpreted messianically). The same is true in xx.123f., where the promise and the threats are generalised:

God said: 'Go forth from it [the Garden] altogether, both of you, with enmity to each other. But whenever there reaches you a guidance from me, then whoever follows my guidance will not go astray or fall into misery. But whoever turns away from my reminder/remembrance [*dhikr*], surely for him will be a life constrained, and we will raise him up on the day of resurrection, blind.

So Adam and Eve and their descendants are not to be destroyed and sent to permanent punishment immediately; they are given a respite, for the duration of this life, to return to the *dhikr*, the recollection, of God – just as Iblis is also given a respite until the day when the dead are brought back again from their graves; in the meantime Iblis seeks to pervert and corrupt human beings from their *islam*, their allegiance to God (xv.26 – 42; xxxviii.71 – 85). As Jabir recorded: 'I heard the messenger of Allah say: "The throne of Iblis is upon the ocean and he sends detachments in order to put people to trial, and the most important figure in his eyes is one who is most notorious in sowing the seed of dissension"' (Muslim, *Sahih*, 1167.6754). So far as humans are concerned, Iblis has no power over them unless they yield to his enticements:

Surely, where my servants are concerned, you have no jurisdiction over them except for those who put themselves in the wrong in following you. Surely, Jahannam is the promised place for them all: it has seven entrances; to each of them a class has been assigned. (xv.42 – 4)

The purpose of death, therefore, is to set a term or limit on this period of respite, in which individuals are free (within the boundary of what God's creative will determines and allows) to direct their lives along the *sirat ulMustaqim*, the straight path that returns them to God (i.5), *or* to join the *kafirun*, the kafirs who reject and repudiate God. This period of life becomes a period of probation or trial: 'We have not granted to any man [lit. 'flesh', *bashar*] before you unending life; so if *you* die, will *they* live unendingly? Every living person [*nafs*] shall taste of death, and we test you by evil and by good as a trial, and to us you will return' (xxi.35f.; cf. xxix.57f.).

So death is not itself a punishment: it simply brings to an end a particular stage in a much longer process culminating in the day of resurrection and the final judgement. The period in the grave is not discussed in detail in the Quran, but it is in Hadith. In Hadith, two angels, Munkar and Nakir, come to interrogate the dead. The dead are asked, 'Whom have you worshipped? and who is your prophet?' If they answer, Allah and Muhammad, they rest until the Day of Judgement. But those who have rejected God and Muhammad will immediately be punished by the angels, either physically, or by being shown the torment that awaits them after the Judgement. What this means to a Muslim now was expressed very strongly in *Worlds of Faith*:

Islam says, and the prophet of Islam has said, and the Quran has said, once a person dies and reaches into the grave, all of a sudden two angels appear and wake him up. His soul returns to the body. The very first question which is asked of the person, whether it's a man, woman or child, big or small, is: who is your God, what is your religion, who is your prophet? If the person has been good ... what I have been told is this (because nobody has been into the grave; but we believe that what the prophet has said is true – every single word is true; and what the Quran has said is that, because it is the Word of God, it's true): if the person has been good and has done the five prayers a day, once he opens his eyes in the grave, he would be looking at the sun as it is setting (because that's the time the two angels come), and he would think that somebody is just standing by. He wouldn't think that he is dead and he is in the grave. He'd say, 'Leave me alone.' You see, the time of the third prayer comes exactly when the sun is setting. So he would say, 'My prayer time is gone and I have overslept, so please let me pray.' And if he has said that by the help of God, I don't think that the angels would bother him any more – because he has answered every question. And if he hasn't done this, if he has been into the pubs and clubs and doing all the worldly things, and trying to snatch the things off anybody else, then the punishment would start from that very moment.

None of this is explicitly stated in the Quran, though it is certainly clear in Hadith (see, for example, the anthology of *ahadith*, *Mishkat alMasabih*, I, 340–2). The two angels may be the two recording angels who accompany each individual through life, 'one sitting on the right and one on the left – he does not utter a word without there being an observer ready' (l.17f.); and the punishment in the tomb may be implied in vi.93, viii.50, ix.101, xxxii.21, xlvii.27, lii.47. However, in Hadith, the punishment in the tomb is strongly emphasised: 'Seventy dragons are given power over a kafir in the grave, and they bite and gnaw him until the Hour comes. If one of those dragons breathed on the earth, it would not bring forth any green things' (at Tirmidhi, *Sunan Jami*, Qiyama 126).

Yet for all that elaboration of the punishments in the tomb, death *itself* is not a punishment – though its occurrence may be a test or trial. It is true that premature death can be brought by God as an immediate and additional punishment – as on the people of Sodom, when 'we rained down on them a shower, so see how there was an end for those who do what is forbidden' (vii.82; cf. xvi.28–31 and xvii.60, before the day of Resurrection). But in general it is not death itself which is the punishment:

punishment lies ahead of the grave and at the end of the process, after the Judgement. Death is simply the natural term to a period of probation: 'Blessed be he in whose hand is the kingdom, and he over all things has power, who created death and life, that he may test which of you is best in deed' (lxvii.1 – 4).

So the characteristic words through which Muslims describe death occur in ii.151/6, 'Surely we belong to God, and surely to him we are returning', in the context of the test which God sends in this life:

Certainly we will try you with something of fear, and hunger, and loss of goods and lives and fruits; but give good news to those who bear up patiently, who say, when afflicted with calamity, Surely we belong to God, and surely to him we are returning.

As a Muslim put it in *Worlds of Faith*:

The soul, what we call the soul, is the *ruh*, spirit from God, which will return to him. When someone dies we say: 'From God we are, to him shall we return.' And we do return, but the next life is a different stage. So we look at death like a door, an entrance. Once we go through that door there is no coming back. You go on to the next phase.

There is, therefore, no chance to come back and try again. The kafirs (according to xxxv.33) will burn undyingly in the Fire of Jahannam (Greek: Gehenna), and from it 'they will cry out, "Our Lord, bring us out! We will do good deeds, far removed from those we used to do." Did we not extend life to you so that he who would, would receive warning? And the warner came to you. So taste to the full! For those who have done dark things, there is no helper' (cf. xlii.42 – 7).

Already, therefore, the main components of Muslim anthropology become clear – though the exact meaning and reference of each of the words involved remained a matter of argument for many centuries after: a human being is a compound of *bashar*, *nafs* and *ruh*. *Bashar* (the equivalent of the Hebrew, *basar*, flesh) is the word used scornfully by Iblis, explaining why he will not prostrate himself (as God has commanded) before God's creation of man (*insan*) from clay moulded into form (xv.76) Iblis retorts: 'I am not one to prostrate myself to *bashar*.' But the *bashar*, the bodily form of man, has had God's *ruh* breathed into it (verse 29).

The *ruh* (the equivalent, etymologically, of the Hebrew *ruah*) is more than the breath of Genesis, because it is bestowed by God on the individual and continues to live apart from the body after death, until it is reunited with the body on the Day of Resurrection. Linking body and soul is the spiritual vitality which is referred to as *nafs* (Hebrew *nephesh*) and that too is in the control (and gift) of God. *Nafs* (and the plurals *anfus* and *nufus*) may be nothing more than reflexive pronouns – 'I will take him *linafsi*, to myself' (xii.54); and they may elsewhere mean simply 'a person', 'someone', 'everyone' (as probably in the sentence, 'every *nafs* shall taste of death', iii.185/2, xxi.35/6, xxix.57). But lvi.83/2 – 87/6 suggests that something leaves the body at death, although *nafs* is not specifically mentioned (and it was believed that Muslim soldiers, if strangling an enemy to death, would relax the grip very slightly to allow the soul to escape, before the final moment). It is this which is taken at night and returned in the morning (unless death intervenes) so that sleep and uprising become natural models of death and resurrection (vi, 6of., xxv.47/9): 'God removes the *nafs* at death and of those who do not die, in their sleep. Those on whom he has passed the decree of death, he keeps back; but the rest he sends back until the appointed time. Surely in that are signs for a people who reflect' (xxxix.43). But although a separation is implied, there is only one single and persistent subject at the beginning and the end: 'Your creation and your being sent for [at the resurrection] is only as a single *nafs*. Surely God is the one who hears, the one who sees' (xxxi.28). One can remain animate and still (literally) have lost one's soul: 'Those are the ones who have lost their souls [*anfus*] and what they have invented has led them astray' (xi.23). It is the *nafs* which is the agent of action as well as the subject of experience: 'It is we who created man [*insan*] and we know what his *nafs* whispers within him, for we are nearer to him than the jugular vein' (l.16).

In the great Islamic renaissance, when the Greek philosophers (particularly Plato and Aristotle) were rescued from possible oblivion, these terms were mapped on to an adopted philosophical scheme. *Ruh* came to be identified with the pure, underlying reality – spiritual substance, in philosophical terms. It is thus immortal, bestowed by God and temporarily inhabiting this body. Although it may be separated from the body at death, it will be reunited with the body on the Day of Resurrection, the *yaum ulQiyama*, and will thus appear before God on the Day of final and absolutely divine Judgement, the *yaum udDin*, of which God is *malik*, or sovereign. Until then (according to one Hadith) the soul may assume the form of a bird, and hangs from a tree in heaven (in other words, it is in a suspended state); or, more commonly, it is immediately raised into an interim body, to be questioned by the angels and receive its provisional fate, pending the final judgement (as on pp.105f.).

The Days of Resurrection and Judgement are frequently described in the Quran: liv.7 imagines the bodies swarming out of their graves like locusts, lxx.43 sees them rushing out like runners in a dash for the winning post, and xviii.99 envisages them surging together like conflicting waves. Then, as that verse says, the trumpet will sound (see also xx.102, xxiii.101, xxvii.87, xxxvi.51, xxxix.68, lxxviii.18), the heavens will be split open (xxv.26) and the mountains will be levelled (xviii.47) as completely as clouds drift away (xxvii.88) or as sand is sifted and poured away (lxxiii.14) or as a mirage dissolves (lxxviii,20). On that day the angels will be seen:

So, when one blast is sounded on the trumpet, and the earth and the mountains are moved and are crushed to dust all in one blow, then on that day the happening will happen, and the sky will be rent asunder, for on that day it will be without strength; and the angels will be at its sides, and eight will bear the throne of your Lord above them on that day. That day you will be brought to judgement: none of your deeds that you hide will be hidden. (lxix.15 – 18; cf. lxxviii.19)

Those who previously have mocked, saying they have never seen an angel, will see them now, to their sorrow (xxv.21f.):

No, but when the earth is ground down into dust upon dust and your Lord comes and the angels, rank upon rank, and he brings Jahannam forward on that day, on that day man [*insan*] will recollect, but how will the recollection help him then? (lxxxix.21)

On the Day of Judgement, books will be produced and opened in which every word and action has been recorded.

On the day of Resurrection we will bring out a written record: each man will see it spread open: 'Read your record: it is sufficient for your own *nafs* to make the account against you on this day.' (xvii.14f.)

The reaction of those who have done wrong is described in xviii.49:

The book will be put down, and you will see those who have done wrong terrified because of what is in it. And they will say, 'Ah, woe to us! what a book this is! It does not omit anything, small or great, without taking account of it.' And they will find what they have done laid out, and your Lord will not treat a single one of them wrongly. (cf. xxiii.64)

It follows, on the Day of Judgement, that everyone will be rewarded according to an exact and precise reckoning. This is one of the most insistent themes in the Quran. A summary statement occurs in ii.281 ('And fear a day when you will be returned to God; then every *nafs* will be paid what it has earned, and they shall not be wronged'), but it recurs frequently (see, for example, ii.286, iii.155, 182, vii.38ff., x.55, xi.18, xiv.51, xxii.10, xxiii.64, xxxvi.54, xl.16f.).

The deeds of each individual are weighed literally in the balance on that day:

The day of clamour! What is the day of clamour? And what will bring home to you what the day of clamour is? It is a day when men will be like moths scattered in a flurry, and the mountains will be like carded wool. Then he whose balance will be found heavy, will be in pleasure and delight; but he whose balance is light, his company will be that of the pit. And what will bring home to you what the pit is? It is a fire blazing fiercely. (ci; the balance, *alMizan*, is mentioned further in xlii.16, lv.7, lvii.25, where it is related to human justice).

So exact is the measure that 'you will not be wronged even by so little as a date-thread' (iv.79, 123):

On that day, men will come forth in groups, sifted, to see their deeds. Then whoever has done an ant's weight of good will see it, and whoever has done an ant's weight of evil will see it.

It would seem, from all this, that Islam is a religion of salvation by works. Yet in fact Abu Huraira recorded a saying of Muhammad, 'None among you will attain salvation purely because of his deeds.' Someone asked him 'Messenger of God, including you?' He answered, 'Yes: not even I; but that Allah wraps me in mercy.' So if Islam *is* a religion of salvation by works, it is by works enabled by God and done in co-operation with his mercy, grace and will (*qadir*). It is also important to remember of Islam, that the intention (*niyya*) with which anything is done is an essential part of an act's evaluation. At the very opening of his immensely revered collection of Hadith, alBukhari set this tradition:

Umar ibn alKhattab said: I heard the Messenger of God say: 'Actions are nothing except according to their *niyya*, and there will not be to anyone except according to what he intends. So whoever has made the *hijra* [made the move from his existing home and security] for the sake of God and his Messenger, his *hijra* is for God and his Messenger. But whoever has made the *hijra* for this world and its gain, or for a woman he hopes to marry, his *hijra* is for that for which he made it.'

But in addition to the importance of *niyya*, any crude estimate of 'works' is deeply modified by the ever-open possibility, *this* side of death, to return in repentance to God who is constantly described in the Quran as the merciful, the all-forgiving. Abu Huraira reported a story of Muhammad concerning a man who had never done anything for his family. Just before he died, he told his family to burn his body and scatter his ashes in two parts, one part in the sea, the other on the land, to make it impossible for God to find him and reassemble him for the punishment he knew he deserved. But God commanded the sea and the earth to gather the ashes together, and then he asked him, Why did you do this? The man replied, 'Out of fear of you, O Lord: you know it well'. And immediately God forgave him.

However, within the context of mercy (of which the guidance given in Quran is the supreme example), the fact remains that nothing is lost, either of good or evil (ii.104, xxi.94), and everyone is rewarded according to the exact balance. The only marginal exceptions are at the extremes of good and evil: xlvi.14ff. records the command to treat one's parents rightly, and also the prayer of thanksgiving and commitment in Islam to be said by those reaching the age of forty. Then it continues: 'Those are the ones from whom we will accept the most righteous of their deeds, and we will pass over their evil deeds; among the companions of the

Garden – a promise of truth which has been promised to them'
(cf. xvi.99 with a stress on both men *and* women). Conversely,
xvi.27 warns that those who have misled others will have to bear
their burdens, in that respect, as their own, on the Day of
Resurrection.

But in general each person has to come to the reckoning of his
or her account. This means that no one can be accountable for
the faults of others – even if they want to be (that is, even if they
want to take some of the debit of another on to their own account):
'To them what they have earned, and to you what you have
earned; and you will not be questioned concerning what they did'
(ii.128, 135, referring to 'people of old'); or, in an equally
characteristic sentence, 'Each *nafs* will be reckoned only according
to itself, and no bearer of burdens will bear the burden of another'
(vi.164; cf. xxxiv.42, xxxix.9, liii.39, lxxxii.19). The proverb which
Jeremiah and Ezekiel had refuted long ago (that our teeth are set
·on edge because our fathers ate sour grapes) still (as an attitude)
has to be refuted, 'lest you should say, ''Our fathers before us
may have worshipped false gods, but we are their descendants
after them. Will you then destroy us for what those men of error
did?'' ' (vii.172).

It follows that a father cannot help his child on that day, nor
can a child help his father (xxxi.33); nor even can the man who
has undertaken the formal role of protector help the one to whom
he owes this obligation:

Surely, the *yaum ulFasl* [p. 119] is an appointed time for all of them, the
day when there is no profit for any one under protection from his
protector – they shall not be helped. (xliv.40f., iv.109–12)

On that day, it will be too late for repentance or for pleas for
mercy. Repentance *before* death is possible, as we have already
seen, because God is (as the Quran frequently says) *arRahman
arRahim*, the merciful and the forgiving; but after death it is too
late:

God accepts the repentance of those who do evil in ignorance, then turn
soon after. To them God will turn, because God is knowing and wise.
Of no effect is the repentance of those who continue to do evil until death
visits one of them, and they say, 'Now I repent indeed' – nor of those

who die as kafirs: for them we have prepared a painful punishment. (iv.21f./17f.)

After death, a wall is built up behind the dead person so that he cannot get back to this world to relive his time of trial:

When death comes to one of them [those who have done evil], he says, 'My Lord, return me, in order that I may do good in the things I neglected'. By no means! It is but a word he speaks. Behind them is a barrier until the day they are sent for. (xxiii.101f.; cf. ii.162/7, xxxv.34/7, xlii.42/44)

Even more to the point, there cannot be any kind of transaction whereby the virtues of one can be set against the vices of others. There is no sense of redemption or ransom, least of all of the Christian understanding of how the death of Christ effects atonement. Indeed, at the opposite extreme, Muslims do not believe that Jesus died at all: on the contrary, as a faithful prophet God rewarded him by exempting him from death (like Enoch and Elijah in Jewish Scripture) and taking him straight to Paradise. The Jews *thought* they had crucified him, but God created the likeness of Jesus instead.

This rejection of the death of Jesus (and therefore of the saving consequences of his death) is based on iv.156/7, in the context of a list of accusations against *ahl ulKitab*, the People of the Book – including the accusation (literally translated)

that they said, 'Surely, we killed the messiah, Isa, son of Maryam, the apostle of God.' And they did not kill him, and they did not crucify him, but his [or 'its'] appearance was to them; and surely, those who dispute about him [or 'it'] are full of doubt concerning him/it. They have no knowledge about him/it, but only the following of guesswork. And they did not kill him, beyond all doubt.

As can be seen, the Arabic pronoun, *hu*, is ambiguous, because it can be masculine or neuter. If it is neuter, then the denial of Christian belief is not so strong, since the passage is then simply affirming that it appeared to the Jews that they had crucified and killed Jesus, but (because of the resurrection) they were wrong. But that is not how orthodox Muslims understand the passage. For them, the passage states that Jesus was not crucified; it was only his appearance. Docetism (from the

Greek for 'appearance') had affirmed this in earlier centuries, though for the vastly different reason that Docetics could not envisage God involved (in Christ) in death. Even unorthodox Muslims, in the form of the Ahmadiyya movement (which orthodox Muslims do not regard as having any part in Islam) believe that Jesus did not die, but went to North India, where he taught and healed for a further period until he died a natural death; and the Ahmadiyya can even take you to his grave.

But even short of that, there is, in Islam, a deep denial of the Christian understanding of what has been done by God, in Christ, for human redemption. For Muslims, Isa is, like Muhammad, one sent by God to warn people of the account they will have to render. There cannot be any ransom of one by another – nor even of oneself; even if one brought the whole earth as a down-payment on salvation, it would not be accepted:

Surely, those who reject God [*kafaru*] and die while they are still rejecting, never would there be accepted from anyone of them all the gold the earth contains, even if they brought it as a ransom. For those people there is a grievous penalty, and they do not have helpers. (iii.85/91; cf. x.55–8/54–7, xxxix.48/7)

The Quran even comes close to denying the efficacy of inter-cession for others, at least on the Day of Resurrection:

Ha! you are the ones who contend on their behalf in the present world. But who will contend with God on their behalf on the day of Resur-rection, or who will be a guardian on their behalf? Whoever does evil or wrongs his own *nafs*, then seeks God's forgiveness, he will find God forgiving, merciful. And whoever earns a sin, earns it against his own *nafs*; and God is knowing, wise. And whoever earns a fault or a sin, then throws it on to one who is innocent, he has burdened himself with a falsehood and an open sin. (iv.109–12)

The Quran clearly warns against relying on anyone's inter-cession on the Day of Judgement: vi.51 (cf. vi.69/70, xl.14–19, ix.81/80) says bluntly, 'Warn by it [what is revealed] those who fear that they will be gathered to their Lord: beside him they have no protector, no intercessor.' However, the Quran allows some exceptions, to Abraham, to the angels and evidently to Muhammad. The efficacy of intercession is undoubtedly restricted, but exactly *how* it is restricted is unclear, because of an ambiguity in the Arabic: the preposition *l* can mean either 'to' or 'for'. Hence the Quran says, 'On that day, intercession will not be any use except to/for him to whom the Merciful One allows it'; 'Intercession will not be any use with him except to/for whomsoever God allows it' (xx.108/9; xxxiv.22; cf. xxi.26–9, liii.26). The restriction is either to some particular intercessor, or to the category of those for whom it will be efficacious (for example, for those who have repented, that they may be guarded from lapsing, xl.7ff, iv.144f.). In the latter case, it has been understood as tipping the balance when the scales are equal (and traditionally it has been restricted to believers); in the former, it has been understood of Muhammad, who does function as an intercessor in Islam, in a very extensive and popular way, and it is extended also to other categories such as prophets and martyrs. Indeed, the Hadith collector Muslim recorded the tradition that if forty men who are not *mushrikun* (those who associate anything with God as equal to God) stand over the bier of a Muslim, God will accept them as intercessors for him (according to Aisha, it has to be one hundred men). Such intercession is efficacious for believers on the Day of Judgement who would otherwise have attained the Garden only after punishment; and it is also efficacious in shortening the punishment of believers in the Fire. It was thus possible for abu Huraira to describe his prayer over a dead person as follows:

I follow the bier from the house and, when it is put down, I say the *takbir* and praise the Lord and send blessings on the messenger of Allah, and then say: 'O Lord, your creature and your creature's son and the son of your hand-maid used to witness that there is no true God but you, and that truly Muhammad is your servant and your messenger, and you know well his state: if he is righteous, increase his reward; and if he is sinful, forgive him his sins. O Lord, do not deprive us of our reward, and do not put us on trial after him.' (Malik, *Muwatta*, 2.135.529)

There is one other way in which it is possible to create a good consequence which reaches into the period after death: though it is too late to do new works which might help the dead person, once he or she has gone into the *barzakh* ('the barrier', beyond which or in which lies the period in the grave), it is possible for some works which were done *before* death to continue to have a good effect. In Hadith, these are specified as a charity which continues (such as building a mosque, building an irrigation canal, planting a tree), ensuring the diffusion of knowledge (by, for example, endowing schools or providing for the distribution of the Quran), and leaving on earth (after one's death) God-fearing and God-following children who pray for the individual's forgiveness.

But despite those marginal exceptions of continuing works and of intercession, the constant theme of the Quran is one of division, ultimately between those who enter the Garden of reward and those who enter the Fire of Jahannam, and more immediately between those who turn themselves to God in *islam* in this life, and those who do not. The ultimate divide is graphically described in vii.38 – 49, where (as in the parable of Dives and Lazarus, Luke xvi.20ff.) the companions of the Garden and of the Fire can call to each other, but cannot reach each other. In the antiphonal 'psalm', lv.35 – 78, the descriptions of the two outcomes are built up in contrast, verse by verse. Over and over again, the Quran describes the contrast between the two final states (for example, ii.22ff., iii.194 – 7, iv.59f., 120f., v.88, ix.68ff., xv.43, xvi.28ff., xviii.99ff., xxi.94ff., xxv.10ff., 21ff.), and the states are final at least in the sense that the fire of Jahannam is *not* a purging or purifying fire; in other words, it is not a purgatory. This claim on the part (probably) of Christians (who say 'The fire will not touch us except for a limited number of days') is rejected as a corruption of their own religion (iii.23/24), as it is in ii.74/80:

They say, 'The fire will not touch us except for a limited number of days.' Say: Have you taken up a covenant with God – since God never breaks his covenant? Or are you saying of God what you do not know? No, but those who earn evil and are surrounded by their sins, they are companions of the fire, they are the ones who dwell in it. And those who believe and do righteousness, those are the companions of the Garden.

On the other hand, the condition of those in the Garden or in the Fire is still contained within the will of God, and one passage *may* imply that God can change the status originally allocated:

As for those who are wretched, they will be in the fire (there will be for them in it groaning and sighs), dwellers in it for all the time that the heavens and the earth endure, except as your Lord wishes. Surely, your Lord is the one who does what he wills. And as for those who are well-favoured, they will be in the Garden, dwellers in it for all the time that the heavens and the earth endure, except as your Lord wishes – a gift without interruption. (xi. 108 – 10/106 – 8)

The meaning of this verse has been vigorously debated: on one side, the argument has been that these heavens and this earth are *not* eternal, so the punishment will not be eternal. This was the view adopted by a Muslim in *Worlds of Faith* (p. 300). He said:

Whatever is the will of Allah, I'll be pleased to go wherever he wants me to be. If it is his will that I shall go to the Fire, then I shall enjoy the Fire. If it is his will that I should go to Janna [the Garden], then I will enjoy the Janna – wherever is his pleasure.' So I asked him: 'Supposing you went to the Fire, would it be for ever?' He replied: 'Not necessarily so. Punishment is only temporary, according to the preponderance of good over evil; and that's true for everybody, every-one … He didn't create us to punish, he created us to love.'

That is certainly an orthodox view, though the Quranic verses to which appeal is made are by no means unequivocal in its support. Thus M. A. Quasem (*Salvation of the Soul*, p. 25) says, of the records which will be allocated on the Day of Judgement to the left hands (pp. 109f., 120), that these belong to 'those who will be damned, even though temporarily'. A footnote refers to lxxxiv.7, 10, lxix.19, 25, xlv.28, xvii.13; but none of them says anything explicitly about the punishment being temporary.

The argument, therefore, on the other side has been that the heavens and the earth referred to are new and eternal creations, and that the clause about the will of God is simply a reminder that that will is indeed unlimited, but that he happens to have willed that the rewards and punishments will be *abadan*, for ever. It is, in its way, a counterpart to the universalist debate in Christianity, and it was once one of the issues in contention, in early theology, between the Mutazilites (who were ready to admit reason into the evaluation of Quran and tradition) and the Asharites, who resisted what they regarded as the subordination of revelation to reason. It was the Asharites who prevailed and who established that there may be release from Jahannam for believers when they have been punished for such sins as have outweighed the good they have done. It is the *kafirun* and the *mushrikun* (those who have compromised the absolute unity and sovereignty of God) who will be punished for ever.

But while they last, whether for ever or for a long period, the punishments are vividly described – as are the delights of the Garden. So far as Jahannam is concerned the penalties are severe:

Surely the tree of Zaqqum [xxxvii.62 – 8] will be the food of the offenders; like molten metal it will boil in their insides, like the boiling of scalding water. Seize him and drag him into the midst of the blaze, then pour over his head from the penalty of boiling water: taste! surely, you once were mighty, honoured. Surely, this is what you used to call in question. (xliv.43 – 50)

In contrast, the Sura continues with a description of the rewards of the Garden:

Surely, the righteous will be in a secure place, among gardens and springs. Dressed in silks and embroidered garments, they will enjoy each other's company – like that. And we will unite them with companions of wide eyes [*huri*]. They will ask there for every fruit, confidently. They will not taste death there, except the first death, and he will preserve them from the penalty of the blaze.

These descriptions are repeated and extended in many passages in the Quran, and it is their repetition which makes so powerful an impression. The important point to remember is that these descriptions, for the vast majority of Muslims, are not metaphorical: they describe literally (since the Quran is the word coming down directly from God) a part of his creation; if we could search diligently enough, we could find these Gardens and the Fire, and we could find them in the created order (though some Muslims believe that the Garden and the Fire will be created only at the final Day). Heaven for the Muslim is not, as it was for one Christian in *Worlds of Faith*, 'to be with God, to live with him … to be absent from life and to be present with God' (p. 269). A Muslim is already present with God, as much now as in the future. It is a matter of extreme passion in Islam that the descriptions it offers of the Garden and of the Fire are not metaphorical or mythical. To give a recent example, Abd alQadi asSufi repudiated any non-literal interpretation in these words:

From the perspective of the science of Revelation it would not be acceptable to reduce the descriptive content of the after-death states to the realm of myth, simply because built into the whole anthropological approach to the zone of what they call religion is a – quite metaphysical – claim to be examining it from a superior standpoint that is above the 'relativism' of the source of the myth geographically and historically. This magical standpoint which from the start declares itself superior to the material it is examining also lays down that what will be deduced from its ritual examination and analysis will invalidate the mythic material once it has seen the clear magical light of scientific method which reduces all that comes into its scope to the dust of primitivism and pre-scientific ignorance ... It is this utterly spurious but brilliant intricate illusion system that has barred millions of 'educated' Muslims, to say nothing of genuine seekers of knowledge among the *kafirun* [unbelievers], from access to the great body of wisdom books in Islam. (in alQadi, *The Islamic Book of the Dead*, pp. 9f.)

Consequently, for a Muslim to be in the Garden or in the Fire is simply to be in another part of God's creation. And God continues to create the means of their perpetuation. Thus, in the Fire, skins are rapidly burnt off; but new ones are created to replace them:

Surely, those who reject our signs we will soon roast at the fire. As often as their skins are burnt through, we change them for other skins, that they may taste the penalty. Surely, God is powerful, wise. And those who believe and do deeds of righteousness we will cause to enter gardens with rivers flowing beneath, dwellers there for ever. There they will have companions unsullied, and we will bring them into the shade of shades. (iv.59f/56f.; cf. xx.20ff.)

So the Day of Judgement (*yaum udDin*) is also the *yaum ulFasl*, the day of Discrimination (xxxvii.20f., xliv.40f., lxxvii.3f., lxxviii.17) when there will be an exchange of (for the righteous) the ills of this world for the good of the next (lxiv.9). On the day of discrimination, all the disputes on earth which seem to have been left undecided, will *be* decided, both in general (vi.164) and in particular – for example, the disputes between Jews and Christians (ii.107, xvi.125, over observing the sabbath) between Christians and unbelievers (iii.48), among the children of Israel (x.93, xlv.17), among Muslims (xvi.94) and among his servants (xxxix.47). These matters *could* have been decided earlier, but the decision has been postponed until the last day, to preserve the time of testing and probation:

Mankind was nothing but a single community. Then they fell into disputes. If a Word [*kalimat*] had not gone forth from your Lord, what was an issue between them would have been settled. And they say, 'Why has a sign [*ayat*] not been sent upon him from his Lord?' So say: The hidden is only for God. So wait: surely I am with you. (x.20f.; in xlii.20, the Word is described as *kalimat ulfasl*)

On the day of discrimination, the two parties will be sorted out: those to whom their written account is given in their right hand will be going to the Garden, but those to whom it is given in their left hand will say, '"Oh, would that it [death] had been a complete end ... my control has perished from me!" and he is taken to the fire' (lxix.18 – 37). Again, there are only marginal exceptions, all of them doubtful, to this absolute division into two parties: the first concerns 'those who are foremost' or pre-eminent (*asSabiqun*), who are a third party (in addition to those on the right and on the left) in lvi.10; they are not in an intermediate state, but are 'the closest to God' (verse 11). The second are 'the men on the heights' (or battlements), who have been taken by some commentators to be those in an intermediate state (vii.44). The third are the *munafiq*, those whose religion is for show, who are 'not for this, nor for that' (iv.142): 'They are in the lowest depths of the fire: you will certainly not find any helper for them – except for those who repent, make amends and hold fast to God, and purify their *din* [religion or lifeway] for God: those ones are with the believers, and God will indeed give to the believers a vast reward' (iv.144). But even though they are at present on the point of balance, it is not envisaged that they will remain so.

The power of the Quran, therefore, lies in the simplicity of its appeal to all people to recognise the issues that lie before them and their own accountability for every action of their lives. *AlWaqia*, the Event, the Day of Resurrection, will certainly happen (lvi.1). The emphasis on this in the Quran corresponds to the fact that many of those whom Muhammad encountered clearly did not believe it. The Quran makes it clear that many of his contemporaries found the idea of resurrection ludicrous, because it conflicts with the clear observation of what happens when people die. This scepticism is recorded sufficiently often in the Quran (eg. xiii.5, xvii.100, xix.66f., xxxiv.7f., xxxvi.78, xxxvii.16) to make it clear that it was not an isolated opinion. Muhammad undoubtedly confronted people who believed that there is nothing beyond this life (vi.29f., xxii.10), and xxiii.3 – 43 makes it clear that this is a central issue for the prophets before Muhammad. Where he is concerned, the sceptics claim that even if bodies *were* reassembled, it could only be by a kind of magic (xi.10; cf. the response in lii.11 – 15), and they challenge him to restore their forefathers as a demonstration:

And they say; 'What is there but our life in this world? We die and we live, and the thing that destroys us is time'. And in that they have nothing in the way of knowledge, but only guesswork. And when our clear signs [*ayat*] are displayed to them, their argument is nothing but to say, 'Bring your fathers if you are truthful'. Say: It is God who gives you life, then gives you death, then assembles you for the day of Resurrection. There is no doubt about it. But most men do not know. (xlv.23 – 5/24 – 6; cf. the opening verses of the Sura entitled Qiyamat, Resurrection, lxxv)

But those are not the only doubts or queries concerning the resurrection. The Quran also had to face questions raised by believers. What, for example, is the status of those who have been killed in the service of God?

Do not say of those who are killed in the way of God, They are dead. No, they are living, but you do not perceive. Certainly we will test you with something of fear, and hunger, and loss of goods and lives and fruits; but give good news to those who are patient, who say, when afflicted with calamity, 'Surely to God we belong, and to him is our return'. (ii.149)

From this and from the many verses commending the *shahid* (the witness), Muslims concluded that those who bear this *ultimate* witness to the truth of God and of his Apostle are given a specially privileged place in the Garden, nearest to the Throne of God; and in the grave they are exempted from the interogation by Munkar and Nakir (p.105). They are freed from the weight of their sins and therefore do not need the intercession of Muhammad (indeed, in later belief they themselves become intercessors), and since they are already purified, their bodies do not have to be washed before burial; they should be buried in the clothes in which they were martyred. With such rewards held out before them, it is not surprising that *talab ashShahada*, the longing for the status of a witness, developed on occasion into a deeply determined quest for death in the way of God, especially in *jihad*. As I have pointed out and described in *Problems of Suffering* (pp. 130 – 3), this quest for martyrdom was taken even further in Shia Islam, because of the way in which the first three legitimate (from the Shiite point of view) successors of Muhammad, Ali and his two sons, were killed. The acceptance of bloodshed and death in the defence of Islam has been more than evident in recent years.

Short of death in battle, many *ahadith* extend the notion of *shahid* to other ways of accepting or performing the will of Allah with patience (for example, accepting the death of three sons with patience is sufficient to count; and, when pressed, Muhammad said that even two would suffice). Thus in his response to a question about why an epidemic of plague had spread in the community, alBukhari recorded the reply of Muhammad:

God sent it as a punishment to whom he would, and he made it a blessing to the believers; for any servant [of God] in any place who remained there and was patient, reflecting only that what God has written will befall him, will receive the same reward as for witness [involving death].

Elsewhere the category of martyr is even further extended:

The Apostle of God said; 'There are seven martyrs other than those killed in the way of God; those struck down by plague; those who are drowned; those who die of diseases of lungs, or of stomach; those who are burnt to death; those who are buried under anything; women who die in childbirth [or while pregnant].' (Malik, *Muwatta*, 2, 141, 548)

But what about the *exceptionally* faithful in their witness? Might they perhaps be exempted from death altogether? This was a troublesome question, focused on Muhammad himself. After all, the Quran states that this is what happened to Jesus (see p. 113):

God said: Isa, I will receive you and raise you to myself and clear you from those who reject [*kafaru*]. I will make those who follow you superior to those who reject, until the day of Resurrection. Then you will all be returned to me and I will decide between you of the matters concerning which you are in dispute. (iii.48/55)

If this is true of Jesus, then should it not, *a fortiori*, be true of Muhammad? Clearly, this was a question that could only be asked while Muhammad was still alive, but it was a serious question for the first Muslims, as can be seen from the final pages of ibn Ishaq's *Life*, where the fact that Muhammad *did* die was disturbing to at least some of his close followers.

The Quran had, in fact, already met this question (showing how seriously at least some believed that the real vindication of Muhammad would lie in his being exempted, like Jesus, from death):

Muhammad is only an apostle. The apostles before him passed away. If he died or were killed, would you turn on your heels? Whoever turns on his heel does no harm in any way to God, but God will reward those who are grateful. And it does not belong to a *nafs* to die except with the permission of God at a term written down. (iii.138f./144f.)

In the end, the question is resolved, in Hadith, by the saying reported from Aisha that no prophet or messenger of God dies until he has been given the option; Muhammad therefore chose the moment when he would join 'the exalted companions'.

To all these questions, whether from within the community or from the outside, the Quran constantly reiterates the great theme of creation: since all things are derived from God and only exist as a consequence of his will, the disposal of life and death are entirely his (xxii.66/5); and any who doubt the resurrection and the reuniting of soul and body for judgement are advised to consider the miracles and wonders of the *first* creation (lvi.57–62): if God can do *that*, in the first creation, is it really so remarkable if he continues that work in the reassembling of individuals after death? The sequence is continuous, as it is stated in xxii.12–16:

We created man from an extraction from clay, then we placed him as a sperm-drop in a secure place, then we fashioned the clot into a lump and we fashioned the lump into bones, and we clothed the bones with flesh. Then we developed him as a different creature. So blessed be God, the best of creators! Then surely after that you will die. Then surely on *yaum alQiyama*, you will be brought back.

And if the miracle of human birth is not enough, consider, the Quran suggests, the constant renewal of the dead earth, or of inert seeds with the fall of rain; and this again is an extremely common theme in the Quran:

God it is who sends out the winds and they raise up the clouds, and we drive them to a dead land, and we give life thereby to the earth after her death. Like that is the resurrection. (xxxv.10/9)

Vivid though many of the details are in the Quran, of the process from life through the grave to the resurrection and judgement, they are even more vivid in Hadith, and in Hadith the brief allusions in the Quran are considerably expanded. Thus in the Quran, the angel of death, who comes to gather in those due to die, is mentioned only once, in xxxii.10/9 – 11, without description. In Hadith, both his appearance and his role are elaborately described. These and other Hadith are gathered, but without references, in *Islamic Book of the Dead*, and, more extensively, though again without precise references, in K. M. Islam, *The Spectacle of Death*.

But there is another exegesis of the Quran, the practical exegesis in mourning and burial custom. The Arabic word, *janaza* or *jinaza* refers to both the corpse and bier, and also to the burial rites. All collections of Hadith record fundamental practices and prayers (the collections of Muslim and alBukhari are translated into English, as is the *Muwatta* of Imam Malik and the late anthology, *Mishkat alMasabih*). Burial and mourning customs (which again are very extensively described in K. M. Islam, *Spectacle of Death*) must be grounded in Quran and Hadith, though particular practices vary in different communities. What is certainly essential is that the body must be washed and buried as quickly as possible, preferably on the same day, but not later than eight hours after death, as a Muslim makes clear in *Worlds of Faith*:

When the Muslim person, the woman or man, dies, it is immediate that we should hide him. We should hide him: that means, we should send him into the grave as soon as possible. So, once the soul is away from the body, we bring the body home. In our country when the person dies quickly we try to make arrangements to wash him and then take him to the *salat aljinaza* which is the last prayer; and as many Muslims as can get together, they try to get together for his *jinaza*. And then we say the last prayer and bury him in the grave with the face facing Mecca. The imam must be the person to lead the prayers of the *jinaza*, but if there isn't any imam at the time, anybody can stand. (p. 247)

The body *must* be respected, because it is to be restored on *yaum alQiyama*. Aisha said that to break a bone of a Muslim's corpse is as bad as to break the bone of one still alive (Malik, 2.144.557). It must be respected also in the sense that it is an act of great virtue to accompany the bier to the burial, as it is also to visit the sick.

Prayers should be said over the dead, particularly four *takbirs* (proclamations of the greatness of God), and if possible there should be a recitation of the whole Quran, or at least of s.vi. Awf b. Malik remembered something of Muhammad's own prayer over a dead person:

God's messenger prayed at a funeral and I have retained in my memory some of his supplication. He was saying, 'Oh God, forgive him, show him mercy, grant him security, pardon him, grant him a noble provision and a spacious lodging, wash him with water, snow and ice, purify him from sins as thou hast purified the white garment from filth, give him a better abode in place of his present one, a better family in place of his present one, and a better spouse in place of his present one, cause him to enter paradise and preserve him from the trial in the grave and the punishment in hell.' A version has, 'And guard him from the trial in the grave and the punishment in hell.' He added that the result was that he wished he had been that dead man. (*Mishkat* I, p. 348)

Mourning itself should not be excessive. According to Jabir b. Atik, Muhammad allowed lamentation until the moment of death. He visited Abdullah ibn Thabit when he (Abdullah) was seriously ill, and when Abdullah made no response to him, he said: 'Surely we belong to God, and surely to him we are returning' (see p. 107). When the women began to weep, Jabir tried to silence them, but Muhammad said; 'Let them weep now. When the time comes, none should weep.' Asked what he meant by 'when the time comes', Muhammad replied, 'When death occurs'. There is a deep tradition in Islam that crying for the dead disturbs them in the grave – which is clearly possible, given Muslim beliefs about 'the period in the grave'. That was eloquently expressed by a Muslim in *Worlds of Faith*:

When Muslims die, we mustn't cry. People can't help it, crying, because it's something you can't control. But we mustn't cry, because if we do – well, the person to *us* is dead, but to Allah, he is not dead. So we try to bury the person quickly, because in a way it's torturing him: he can hear the people crying for him. So we try to bury him quickly for his own good. (p. 248)

In fact, what is really forbidden is excessive weeping, since that contradicts acceptance of God's way and will in creation. Muhammad is thus reported as saying, 'Anyone who beats the cheeks, tears the front of the garments, and laments as people did in the Jahiliyya [the period of ignorance before the advent of Islam] does not belong to us.' This prohibition of *niyaha* (lamentation) together with a related tradition which repudiates (to hell) anyone who tells a lie deliberately concerning the Prophet, are *mutawatir* traditions in Islam, traditions so revered that Juynboll said of them, 'one can almost speak of an aura of holiness'. Yet the paradox is exactly as Juynboll observes: 'Although this custom [of *niyaha*] is found in practically the entire Muslim world, in one form or another, there are many sayings attributed to the prophet and various important contemporaries in which it is officially forbidden' (*Muslim Tradition*, p. 96). It is an instance of local custom clothing, or colouring, the expression of Islam. Granqvist's description of Muslim death and burial in a village in Jordan records exactly that tension between what was actually done and what the official religion allowed.

In general, therefore, the Muslim understanding of death contradicts many of the accounts of death put forward for exploration earlier in this book. Thus Islam ought, certainly, to exemplify the importance of liminality (pp. 21–2): of all the major religions, Islam is the most specific and literal in describing an interim stage, the period in the grave; yet it certainly does not provide rituals to help the transition of those in the interim condition into their final state. In fact, exactly the reverse; any such 'interference' would be to resist the *qadr*, or final determination, of God. This is a reminder that theology can construct, from its own resources and from attention to its own subject matter, contradictions of what might otherwise seem too well established in traditional behaviours to be changed; folk-religion, in contrast, clearly retains those actions, of which official religion disapproves.

Islam also appears to contradict a basic point put forward at the outset, that religions in their early histories explore the meaning and significance of death far more through sacrifice than through speculations about life after death; but clearly the Quran is extremely specific and literal in its map of the Garden and the Fire, and in its account of how to make sure of getting to the former and not the latter. But this is not surprising, since Islam is a *late*, not an early, form of religious tradition (the Judaeo-Christian). Consequently, what had before been tentative and diverse (working out the detail of how there will be a continuity of life with God beyond death) now became explicit; and this means that, whereas Jews and Christians *may* (some do not) regard particular imaginations of heaven and hell as conceptual episodes, whose rise and fall can be traced, Muslims cannot do so: the descriptions of the Garden and the Fire are not conceptual episodes – they are not even concepts: they are places and circumstances, the reality of which will be eschatologically verified, as the Quran frequently reminds us, though it does not use that language!

Conversely, the theme of sacrifice is diminished; or, perhaps more accurately, it is formalised. The offering of one's own life in generosity far beyond the requirement of *zakat* is one obvious way in which the theme of 'living sacrifice' can be kept in play. 'It is not their flesh, nor their blood, which reaches Allah, but to him what is acceptable is righteousness on your part' (xxii.37). Islam does retain sacrifice as a literal religious duty, but in specific and restricted circumstances, especially the sacrifice during the pilgrimage to Mecca, and the corresponding Id alAdha which takes place throughout the Islamic world – a goat or a sheep for one man or one household, a cow or a camel for up to seven men. But that sacrifice is not applied to the understanding of death; it is embraced in the duties which, if undertaken, allow a Muslim to approach death without fear.

Islam, therefore, represents the understanding of death, in the western religious history and tradition, at its furthest extreme of formalisation. Later developments in Judaism and Christianity (and in sectarian offshoots from the latter) have rivalled Islam in the formality of their detail and in the literalness of their descriptions of heaven and hell. But in Judaism and in Christianity it has been possible for individuals to recognise that much of the accumulated detail is a pictorial and imaginative exercise which can be abandoned without (at least in their own view) abandoning the faith. There is a winnowing of tradition which is a still-continuing process. That process is more problematic – and certainly more suspect – in Islam, because of the status of Quran as revelation.

In the three connected western religions we can therefore see a history moving towards the points which Marx and Freud and many others have made about the religious exploitations of death: the more literal the beliefs became, the more explicit become also the appeal to change one's behaviours for prudential reasons. Thus, to give but one example (already referred to), K. M. Islam's book, *The Spectacle of Death*, begins:

In the Name of God, the Most Beneficent and Merciful

BEWARE

God alone is worthy of all Praise, Who sent down death upon the greatest oppressors and the mightiest of men and wrigged their necks; and broke the backs of the greatest kings; and extinguished the hopes, the aspirations of the possessors of enormous hordes and treasures by putting an end to their lives, but when the promise of the Almighty (the time of death) came to pass, they were thrown into a pit and tumbled from their high palaces to the depths of the earth, they were lifted from their soft beds under the sparkle and glare of electric lights and were hurled into the darkness of the grave. They were engaged in dalliance with their slaves and handmaids when they were given over to the worms and insects, and instead of enjoying the delights of eating and drinking they were rolling in the dust; and they became lonely prisoners in the wilderness instead of enjoying the convivial society of friends. (p. iii)

A consequence of this is that Islam must necessarily reject any attempt to interpret its language as provisional, approximate or corrigible, despite the fact that it has had to recognise (after major conflict in its early history) that much language in the Quran is analogical or metaphorical – God does not sit, even for a Muslim, spatially on a throne. Nevertheless, Islam rests, as the other major religions do not, on one literal and inerrant picture of the final outcome of human lives beyond death. Very different is the religious imagination of Hinduism.

CHAPTER 5

Hinduism

All extensive and enduring religions are coalitions of beliefs, practices and traditions. It may be desirable, for the sake of good order and statistics, to define the boundary of a religion as 'quod semper, quod ubique, quod ab omnibus creditum est' ('that which is always, that which is everywhere, that which is by all people believed'), but such a condition never has and never will exist. In the coalition which constitutes any religion, there are certainly common elements, but even these are differently interpreted. Different religions, and different organisations within a religion, then interpret the *fact* of diversity differently. At one extreme, there may be an insistence within a religion that only one particular interpretation is authentic, and that all others, while parasitic on the true, are nevertheless defective: the polychaete worm takes up residence on a hermit crab and depends upon it, ultimately, for its food; but it remains a worm and not a crab; and that (to give an example) is the attitude of Vatican Catholicism to other Christians.

At the other extreme, there may be a highly positive evaluation of diversity, on the grounds that no single organisation, whether individual or social, can embrace all valid possibilities, nor (even more to the point) can it exist in isolation from its environment. In that case, diversity is not an ornament but a necessity. This is to evaluate an ecosystem (say, a woodland or a coral reef) as a single unit, in which all the parts are superficially independent, but in which they enable each other's possibility: the parts do not make up the whole: the parts *are* the whole. This interpretation gives a positive evaluation to diversity as *necessary*. To revert to the parasites: the parasitic relation *may* be what is known as

129

commensal symbiosis, as opposed to being simply neutral: the relation may be one of mutual dependence, as, for example, in the case of the micro-organism, *Mixotricha paradoxa*, which lives in the hindgut of dry wood termites, ingesting pieces of wood and digesting the cellulose; without its wood-digesting competence, wood-eating termites could not survive, since only a few bacteria, fungi and protists contain the celluloses and enzymes needed to digest wood.

In the religious case, this 'welcome to diversity' appears most obviously in Hinduism, where it is accepted that people with different histories and different circumstances require correspondingly different opportunities to convert those histories and circumstances to a more desirable outcome. Or, to put it more colloquially, there are many paths to the same goal, many routes by which the same mountain can be climbed.

The coalition of 'ways to the goal' which is known now (but only since the nineteenth century) as Hinduism adds to all this the further consideration that no one person can ever see, still less understand, the whole of any object. Picasso attempted to represent the three dimensions of a violin on the one dimension of a rectangular canvas, but even he did not deny that there was yet more to be seen. We can certainly get further by co-operation – by adding our individual and inadequate perceptions together. But even at the end of that process, the result will remain inadequate. The story of the blind men trying to describe an elephant has become a cliché, but it does at least make the point with a light touch – that to each, as he touches a different part, the 'object' appears to be a tree, a spear, a snake, a fan, a rope. In the version of J. G. Saxe ('The Blind Men and the Elephant'):

> And so these men of Hindostan
> Disputed loud and long,
> Each of his own opinion
> Exceeding stiff and strong,
> Though each was partly in the right,
> And all were in the wrong!

None of this prevents subsystems within the Indian coalition from maintaining their own boundaries and insisting on them with, on occasion, ferocious determination: Gandhi was, after all, assassinated by a *devoted* Hindu.

So one Hindu may be to another 'a violent friend, a brimstone enemy', as Robert Louis Stevenson described his wife. And that may be a necessity, not a treachery, in the sense that each living appearance, whether human or not, must live in the way that is appropriate for it, according to its own *dharma*. An Indian name for what in the west is called Hinduism is *sanatana dharma*, eternal *dharma*. Hinduism is the map of how to live appropriately: it is the description and the evocation of the ways in which to live, in whatever circumstances one finds oneself, in order to move towards (and perhaps attain) the goal.

This theme is central to the Bhagavad Gita, The Song of the Lord, the sacred text of greatest importance to most Hindus. Hindu scripture is made up of two parts, Sruti (texts recording revelation heard by the *rsis* of old and transmitted orally) and Smriti (the 'remembered' texts, which may be attached to Sruti texts, but may also extend them). Thus the main components of Hindu scripture are the four Vedas (mainly chants, hymns and songs), the Brahmanas attached to the Vedas (mainly concerned with the rituals to which the Vedic chants etc., belong), and the Aranyakas and the Upanishads (recording and expressing the search for knowledge, insight and understanding). The Gita is closest in content and concern to the Upanishads, but it is not a part of them. It is a text which occurs within the long epic, the Mahabharata. It was regarded early as having spiritual authority, at least formally in the sense that it was regarded as one of the three texts or group of texts which required commentary – the others being the Upanishads and the Vedanta Sutras of Badarayana. These three form the *prasthana-traya* which are the basis of those interpretations of the Indian tradition which are known as Vedanta, the 'end of the Vedas'. Among these, the Gita occupies the central place in the formation of Indian life. As a Hindu put it in *Worlds of Faith*: 'Our Holy Book is the Gita; and if you read it, and if you can understand it, you'll find the answer to all of your questions. The only question is, whether you can understand what is written there' (p.131).

So the Gita is in any case a wise point at which to begin in attempting to understand the Hindu religion. But in the case of death, it is particularly important because the fundamental issue in the Gita of *dharma* is focused on death. In the Mahabharata, the story is told of a war between two branches of the Kaurava family, the hundred sons of Dhritarashtra, led by the eldest brother, Duryodhana, and on the other side, their cousins, the Pandavas, led by their eldest brother, Yudhishthira. Yudhishthira, who has been cheated and wronged by Duryodhana, goes to the limit to avoid war, but Duryodhana militantly refuses his overtures, even to the extent of defying the manifestation (*avatara*, or incarnation) of the god Vishnu in the form of Krishna: offered the choice of his army or of Krishna alone, Duryodhana chose his army. But Yudhishthira's younger brother, Arjuna, offered the same choice, chose Krishna, who agrees to serve as his charioteer. At this point – the moment when the Gita begins – Arjuna has a crisis of conscience, and refuses to fight. In the second of two accounts of this crisis, Arjuna says that he cannot bring himself to kill his revered teachers and members of his own family.

The main part of the Gita is made up of Krishna's response to Arjuna's paralysis. There is an initial response in ch. ii, parts of which are then unpacked or extended in the rest of the Gita. In the initial response, Krishna (somewhat like Weiss' de Sade, p. 9, but for utterly different reasons) argues that Arjuna is giving a false importance to death, because the selves which are embodied are eternal and cannot therefore die when the body dies:

The Blessed Lord said: ... Those who are truly wise do not mourn for the dead any more than they do for the living. Never was there a time when I did not exist – or you or these princes; nor will there be a time when any of us shall cease to be hereafter. Just as embodied selves [*dehin*] pass through childhood, youth and old age in their bodies, so too there is a passing [at death] to another body. (ii. 12)

The argument of Krishna then follows that, if the embodied selves which are the true person (in contrast to the material constituents which are transient) cannot be affected by contingent accidents or even by death, then Arjuna should not hesitate to fight:

Fight, then, son of Bharata. Whoever thinks that the embodied self can be the one who kills, or can be killed, has no sound understanding. It does not kill nor can it be killed. It is not born, it does not die ... It is not killed when the body is killed ... As a person throws away his clothes when they are worn out and puts on other new ones, so does the embodied self cast off its old bodies and enters new ones. Weapons cannot cut it, nor can fire burn it. Water does not make it wet, nor does the wind dry it. It cannot be cut or burned or made wet or dried. It is undying, flowing everywhere, stable, unmoved, eternal ... And just as the death of all that is born is certain, so is the birth of that which has known death. Therefore, since this is something that no one can prevent, it should not be a cause of grief for you. (ii.18ff.)

To these arguments, Krishna then adds three further considerations. The first is that, since Arjuna is a warrior, he must fulfill the *dharma* of being a warrior: he must act in the ways laid down as being appropriate for a warrior, since otherwise he will create a far greater disorder than the relatively small episode of death: 'Give thought to your duty [*dharma*], then you will have no reason to hesitate ... But if you will not engage in this battle which your duty requires, then, by discarding both duty and honour, you will bring evil on yourself' (ii.33).

But the fulfilment of *svadharma* (his own *dharma*) is not a matter of setting sails and drifting before the wind. It requires appropriation by acts of intention and will: 'The essence of the soul [*buddhi*, concentrated mental attitude] is single-minded resolution' (ii.41). So the second point that Krishna adds is that action according to *dharma* must be cultivated, but without attachment to, or concern about, the consequences. Thus, if it is his *dharma* to be a warrior, he must indeed be that, but without getting preoccupied in an evaluation of that activity in terms of its immediate results: 'Work alone is your proper business, and not the fruits of it. Do not allow the fruit of your works to be the motive, but on the other hand, do not seek to avoid acting altogether. Stand fast in Yoga, giving up all attachment' (ii.47f.). In practice, this involves drawing in one's senses as a tortoise withdraws into its shell.

There is clearly an inconsistency in the Gita at this point, because, despite this emphasis on non-attachment, Krishna has been advancing arguments which depend on consequences for their appeal: thus a war justly fought in accordance with one's *dharma* 'opens the door to heaven' (ii.32); not to fight would break up the *dharma* of society on which order depends; and if he does not fight, he will lose face and be accused of cowardice (ii.34). But these arguments can be understood as examples of what is known in Eastern religions as *upaya-kausilya*, skill in means: a teacher will use arguments that will ultimately be transcended, because the pupil is at a level of understanding which requires such preliminary instruction in order to make that transcendental move. The overall picture of the Gita is not in doubt (which is not to say that it is not open to diverse and conflicting interpretation, as we shall see): reflection of a well-informed and well-intended kind (*samkhya*, ii.39, not here in its technical sense of a school of Indian philosophy) leads to the realisation of the distinction between the true self (*atman*) and all that is not self (*prakrti*); the correct mental attitude (*buddhi*) which leads to this realisation involves non-attachment to all or anything that happens; however, disciplined effort and striving to be yoked to *buddhi* is entirely necessary; and this is the meaning of yoga in the Gita (not, as is sometimes supposed, yoked to, or united with, God), as in ii.39.

The point of that argument is then unfolded in the third of Krishna's additional points: the true objective is to become so detached from the transient appearances in the world that the self is no longer bound to this or any other world by its desires for things (including states) within the worlds of appearance. This is to realise that one's self is undying, eternal, immortal. To realise this and to attain this condition of wisdom is to attain *brahman*:

Whoever forsakes all objects of desire and goes about without cravings or possessiveness or self-preoccupation becomes serene [*santi*]. This is the state of *brahman* [*brahmi stitih*], Partha. Whoever achieves it is not deceived. Maintaining this state even in his last hour, he attains to the *nirvana* which is *brahman*. (ii.71f.)

The earliest meaning of *brahman* seems to have been connected with 'power', and especially with the power inherent in the words and chants of the Rgveda, as Gonda (1950) has argued. In the Upanishads, attempts are made to determine what that power essentially is. Although the Upanishads can be read as suggesting that Brahman is the Absolute source of all manifestation, the unproduced Producer of all that is, a less partisan reading indicates that there are several candidates for understanding what *brahman* is: speech, mind, breath, space, sight, and so on, as well as the Absolute source. Equally, the meaning of *brahman* was not fixed by the time of the Mahabharata, where it refers to time, seasons, fire, even the god Prajapati. In the Gita, *brahman* may refer to Krishna himself (vi.28, x.12, xiii.12, 62), or to the Veda (vi.44), or to the offering in the ritual (iv.24). But in this passage (ii.72) and elsewhere, *brahman* is the state experienced in liberation, both in this life and after death. Thus it cannot be absorption into the Absolute, since consciousness of this state continues. Equally, the attainment of *brahman-nirvana* after death is not cessation, but rather the state in which the freed self abides eternally.

Thus *nirvana* is not at all like the Buddhist *nibbana/nirvana* (to be discussed later). At death, according to the Gita, the freed selves go to be with Krishna, and are in the same state of being as he is, but remain distinct from him. Nirvana is the state of happiness and peace of one who is eternally with Krishna. Far from it being 'the blowing out of a candle', the Gita describes the condition of the yogin as being like 'a candle flame away from a draught which does not flicker' (vi.19).

But what of the unfreed self, the one who remains attached and entangled in appearance? The self remains immutable but is reborn repeatedly, until it finds its way to liberation – and the Gita exists to indicate the paths to follow. In moral life a law exists which is as impersonal and inevitable in the consistency of its outcomes as gravity. It is the law of *karma*. *Karma* means both action and the consequence of action. According to the Gita, as we have already seen, the way to overcome the accumulation of bad *karma* is not to withdraw from all life and action, but to engage in appropriate action without attachment. Otherwise, the long continuation of rebirth (*samsara*) will continue.

In this way, the Gita contains all the main elements of the Hindu scheme of the self and its salvation. Can one say, then, that the Gita *is* the Hindu understanding of death? Clearly not, because the Gita itself is open to very different interpretations. Thus although the Gita seems to envisage the final state as a relation with Krishna, and not as a union with Brahman understood as the Absolute and undifferentiated source of all appearance, that other interpretation nevertheless appears in both ancient (such as the philosopher Sankara) and modern (such as Zaehner) guise.

This understanding of reality and appearance is known as Advaita, or non-dualism. In this understanding, Brahman lies behind all appearance as its source, bringing things into appearance through *maya*. *Maya* is frequently translated as 'illusion', and that translation does at least make the point that what presents itself to observation is not Brahman itself. Brahman is the guarantor of all appearance, subsisting beneath it and able to be discerned through it. *Maya* is thus the capacity of Brahman to bring all forms of appearance into their manifest being. Those forms include the forms of appearance which can rightly be called theistic (that is, the gods and goddesses, of which Vishnu is an example), but in this perspective the gods are clearly subordinate to Brahman; thus the ultimate state cannot be union with Krishna, unless one sees that Krishna/Vishnu is one of the outer forms of appearance which is a consequence of Brahman and that Brahman is the Truth underlying them – and *maya* may also mean exactly that, the outward form of manifestation. In this perspective, the worlds of *maya* and *prakrti* (p.134) are worlds of movement and change – hence the extreme importance of the dance in the Hindu religion. As such they are characterised by action (*karma*), and they are in a constant process of change. That necessarily involves death. The changeless is Brahman alone, and only Brahman is deathless.

In this understanding of the Gita, Brahman is present within the human appearance as *atman*, as the real and continuing identity persisting through the transient appearance of human form – 'indestructible (alone) is That – know this – by which this whole universe was spun' (Gita ii.17). But insofar as the self attaches its desire to the transient manifestations of appearance, it projects itself as *jiva*. *Jiva* is the temporal projection of *atman*, and the more it gets entangled in the world of sense and appearance, the more it forgets its source (and liberation) in *atman* and identifies itself increasingly with this complex but nevertheless transient human form. *Atman* can therefore be considered under two aspects, the one in its true nature as the unchanging, un-changeable Brahman, but the other in its attachment to the world of sense and change:

Verily, this self [*atman*], the seers declare, wanders here on earth in every body [from body to body] unaffected, as it seems, by the light or the dark fruits of action ... As an enjoyer of righteous work he covers himself with a veil made of qualities, but he remains fixed, yea, he remains fixed. They said, Bhagavan, if you thus indicate the greatness of this self, then there is that other, different, one also called self, who, affected by the bright or dark fruits of action, enters a good or an evil womb, so that his course is downward or upward and he wanders about, affected by the pairs [of opposites like pleasure and pain]. (Maitri Up. ii.7, iii.1)

In a famous image, the two truths of *atman* (its independence, as Brahman, from transience; and its transience from form to form as it makes itself dependent on appearance) are seen as two birds sitting on a single branch:

Two birds, companions [who are] always united, cling to the self-same tree. Of these two the one eats the sweet fruit, and the other looks on without eating. (Svet. Up. iv.6)

While *atman* remains attached to *maya*, to the worlds of manifestation, it continues as *jiva-bhuta*, as living self. And the word 'continues' is correct, because the *jiva*, so long as it remains attached to the objects of its experience, will necessarily reappear, or be reborn, in countless new forms of appearance. That must be so, because the true self, Brahman, is deathless, and cannot be destroyed. Therefore, in a continuing flow of rebirth (*samsara*), the *jiva* will reappear. Traditionally, the self may be reborn as many as 84,000,000 times, perhaps as an animal or perhaps as a divine being, sometimes in heaven, sometimes in hell:

Desire – Anger – Greed: this is the triple gate of hell, destruction of the self [*atman*]: therefore avoid these three. When once a man is freed from these three gates of darkness, then can he work for [his] self's salvation, thence tread the highest way. (Gita xvi.21f.)

None of the states of rebirth, however long enduring, is per-manent. Release from the endless chain of rebirth (*samsara*) is possible. But how to attain it? The Gita states (xvi.24) that the guidance is already supplied in the *Sastras*, the post-Vedic compilations which gather together 'the rules of the road', and which are therefore known, most usually as *Dharmasastra*. The following of *dharma* is the *sine qua non*; and indeed, Arjuna's *first* objection to fighting against his own kinsmen rested on this ground: the quickest way to hell (to a rebirth in that uncomfortable condition) is to disrupt the obligations within a family – and if, as in this case, the disruption involves *killing* members of the family, then other members of the family *already dead* may be precipitated into hell, because their successors are no longer alive to keep them afloat in a better circumstance by the appropriate sacrifices. Just as hazardous, the boundaries of caste would be confused, which makes the following of *dharma* impossible. (Caste is the formalisation of *dharma*, in the sense that it marks the boundaries within which particular life-ways can be pursued appropriately. The four original groups, Brahmans, Kshatriyas, Vaisyas and Sudras, were more divisions of occupation, but from those four classes, the multiplicity of castes eventually derived.)

What, then, determines whether one's rebirth is in a higher or lower outcome? Ultimately, it is *karma*. We have already encountered *karma* as action (p. 135), but it is also action with the implication of consequence. Every action throws forward its long shadow of subsequent effect: what we are is a consequence of what we have done (or failed to do) in the past – not as a matter of crude reward or punishment, but as a simple matter of consequence. *Karma* is an impersonal law of the universe, much as gravity is. By that impersonal law of consequence, what we do now will create the circumstance that the *jiva* will inhabit at some future date – not necessarily in this birth, but in some future form beyond rebirth. A person's basic character is thus the accumulated integration of good and evil actions in past lives which are now manifested in this present circumstance, which in turn is setting forward further consequence in the indefinite future horizon of rebirth.

So to live according to the *dharma* of one's present circumstance is to make a start in altering the future – that is, in moving the stream of rebirth toward more desirable outcomes. But it is not in itself enough. So Krishna, in the Gita, corrects Arjuna's rather rudimentary understanding of obligation expressed in his *first* objection to fighting. The effects of karma only operate on the self (*atman*) insofar as it attaches itself (binds itself) to consequence within the world of *maya* (of appearance and change) as *jiva*. Humans then make the mistake of thinking that the Self is *jiva*, that that self is the agent of *karma* (of future consequence), and that consequently they must commit themselves with even greater energy to the works of this world and their fruit. But that in fact is driving the spiral of entanglement and attachment deeper and deeper down – as when a screw is deeply embedded in a piece of wood and one seeks to release it, not by *un*screwing it, but screwing it farther into the wood in the hope that it may perhaps be driven through and out the other side. But the 'wood', the *prakrti*, of this universe – and the next and the next, since universes are 'spun out' indefinitely (Gita ii.17) – has no 'other side'. There is *no* release by a deeper and deeper commitment to the constituents and to action upon them: 'By the constituents of Nature [*prakrti*], fooled are men attached to the constituents' works. Such men, dull-witted, only know in part' (Gita iii.29).

To be 'the knower of the whole' is to realise that one can never stop the endless process of *karma* and cause by throwing oneself ever more deeply into it. To gain release (*moksha*) is to become completely disentangled from that process, even though the constituents of appearance – the form of the body – persist, at least for a while. Action (*karma*) continues, but without any investment in the outcome:

Work alone is *your* proper business, never the fruits [it may produce]: let not your motive be the fruit of works nor your attachment be to [mere] worklessness. Stand fast in Yoga, surrendering attachment, in success and failure be the same, and then get busy within your works. Yoga means 'sameness-and-indifference'. (Gita ii.47f.)

The meaning of Yoga in the Gita has already been considered. In a more general way Yoga, which means literally 'the act of yoking together' (or conceivably from the root *yuj*, to contemplate), is part of the coalition of Hinduism understood as ways of approach toward *moksha*. It is classified as one of the six orthodox (*astika*) darsanas, or interpretations (the others being the Vaiseshika, Nyaya, Samkhya, Purva-Mimamsa and

Uttara-Mimamsa). Yoga takes many forms, but it is essentially the recovery of the scattered self (divided in its functions and interests) as Self, as co-ordinated and integrated and at one: the yogi and the 'object' of his attention fuse into a single field, where distinction between subject and object is transcended. Yoga is atonement, not by the action of another to do what we cannot do for ourselves (cf. p. 98), but by the disposition of our own available energies in a particular exercise, which calms the raging sea by discipline, if not by a word. Thus *hatha* yoga seeks integration through control of the body and its functions, *bhakti* through absolute devotion and love, addressed to God, *mantra* through penetration of symbols and sounds into an interior and sounding silence, *jnana* through knowledge as wisdom, *karma* through action as Scripture lays it out; and the culmination, built on the foundation of those and many other forms of yoga, *raja* yoga, the royal yoga through which, when all buzz and business in the mind and body have been brought to a dynamic rest, the integration of the perceptions beyond the ordinary occurs and the underlying unity of all that exists is known. And that is Brahman. And that *is* one's self: *Sa va ayam atma brahma*: it, this *atman*, is most truly Brahman.

Yoga is thus a means towards, not an end, but *the* End which is also beginning – and neither. Brahman is outside the phenomenal world of *maya*, appearance and change, although it is the guarantor of such a promiscuous loan. Release is to realise (and to live *as* the realisation) that the persistence and subsistence in oneself is not the *atman* in its temporal projection as *jiva*, attached to the world and its actions, but, in the other direction, that *atman* is Brahman: already within us *is* the imperturbable, unchanging 'isness' of what there is, even when it is not. All we have to do, to become exempt from consequence, change and rebirth, is to become what we already are, the vehicle of Brahman as *atman*, as the Self which enables the self. *Atman* is always the source and subsistent guarantee of *jiva* in its attachment to the world of *maya*. But *atman* as Brahman is not involved in the phenomenal enterprise of *jiva* – it is the second bird in the tree (p. 137). But *jiva* can wither on the branch precisely as you realise that you already *are* the unchanging, unchangeable. Already, 'you are that' (*tat tvam asi*), the famous formula, that *atman* is Brahman. *Moksha* is to turn a formula into a fact:

Hard to attain is true renunciation without karma-yoga. The sage well-versed in yoga [*yoga-yukta*] soon attains to Brahman. Well-versed in yoga, his self [*atman*] made pure, in control of self and senses, identifying his self with the selves of all creatures, he is not tainted although he is active still. (v.6f.)

Thus Brahman is not only the unproduced Producer of all that is, unchanged by the changes and chances of any fleeting world (and if conceived theistically, then also 'the Divine Person who is beyond the beyond', Mund. Up. iii.2.8), it/he is also the entire totality of all souls or selves, either absolutely or in a continuing relational network.

From that allusive hint in the last paragraph ('if conceived theistically'), it can be seen that the issue remains unresolved in Hinduism, whether to understand Brahman non-dualistically as the impersonal, Absolute source of all appearance, or to affirm the nature of Brahman as personal and theistic. If it is the former, then Brahman may manifest itself in the form of Isvara, as *purusottama*, Supreme Person, God; and then God may be regarded as the intermediate creator of this particular cosmos, to whom devotion may well be appropriate. But if it is the latter, then the theistic character of Brahman is fundamental, and in that case it is God, not impersonal Brahman, which is the subsisting, persisting truth with which we have to deal. What perhaps unifies the divergent interpretations of ultimate reality in Hinduism is the realisation that *however* Brahman is conceived, what must be cultivated, if the *jiva* is to become *jivanmukti*, the liberated self, is the right way of 'seeing'. Since Brahman is that which truly is, underlying the fleeting appearances of *maya*, Brahman can be discerned, by those who have eyes to see, under the forms of *all* appearance, even those of disorder and death. The eyes required are not those on each side of the nose, but the inner eye, a literal sixth sense, the eye, as it is called, between the eyebrows. It is what William Johnston called, as the title of a book, *The Inner Eye of Love*; and in explaining that title (p. 8), he makes clear why this is a point of unity in the Hindu understandings of the way to Truth:

The title, I believe, touches a chord in the great religions of East and West. All are aware that man born of woman is somehow in ignorance but that redemption is at hand. For he has a third eye, an inner eye, the eye of the heart, the eye of wisdom, the eye of love. When this inner eye is awakened, man, blind from birth, sees the real glory and beauty and meaning of the universe. 'The eye is the lamp of your body. So if your eye is sound, your whole body will be full of light; but if your eye is not sound, your whole body will be full of darkness' (Matthew 6:22, 23). Surely these enigmatic words remind us that the important thing in human life is to *see*, to be full of light, not to walk in the dark.

In that perspective, it can be seen that death should never be a matter of great moment. In the long sequence of *samsara* (rebirth) death will happen many times; and one should not be involved in it in any anxious way. The incident of death is a staging-post in a long process. In that way, it is reminiscent of Islam (p. 105); but whereas in Islam there is but one 'first death' and then the judgement, in Hinduism there is a seemingly endless repetition of deaths as the *jiva* moves on from one birth to another, and it is the form of the next birth which is the dispassionate judgement on what has gone before – so far as 'judgement' is the right word: it is really the impersonal manifestation of consequence. The belief that the continuing self has already, literally, passed on when a person dies (or is cremated) is reflected in the fact that Hindus should not persist in their mourning or grief, though they can assist the soul on its journey by the appropriate rituals and prayers. As a Hindu told me in *Worlds of Faith*:

At death we believe that the soul goes, and we shouldn't disturb the soul by crying a lot. So we have a ceremony, called *shraddh* ceremony, where we invite people and entertain them, and ask them to pray for the soul. (p. 241)

Nevertheless, the moment or incident of death *does* have importance, because the soul can actually help itself and be helped at the moment of death. Just at the moment when in the graphic image of the Upanishad (Brh. Up. iv.4.3), the caterpillar is hunching itself up and swaying forward in order to transfer itself from one blade of grass to the next, so the self, as it is about to leave this body and launch itself into the next-state, can influence what the eventual next form will be, by its concentration on what it most desires – usually on Brahman as manifest in a particular form of God, as Krishna says of himself in the Gita:

Whoever, at the hour of death, when abandoning his body bears me in mind, rejoins my being: there is no doubt of this at all. Whatever state a person bears in mind when in the end he abandons his body, even to that state he comes, because one is given being from its being. So think of me at all times; and fight. For if you fix your mind and spirit on me, you will undoubtedly come to me. If a person's thoughts are integrated in yoga [*yoga-yukta*], not straying to anything else at all, while meditating on the divine Supreme Person [*purusha*], to him, Partha, he goes. The ancient seer, governor of all things, smaller than the smallest, creator of all, in form unthinkable, sun-coloured, beyond the darkness, whoever meditates on him with mind unmoving at the hour of death, by devotion [*bhakti*] and discipline [*yoga*] integrated, forcing the breath entirely between the eyebrows, so will that person attain to that divine Supreme Person. (viii.6–10)

The ability to concentrate, *in extremis*, on God is clearly much helped if it is preceded by a life-time of practice in yoga. The most concentrated form of that concentration is in the *namakirtana*, the constant repetition of the name of a god until all else falls away and only the identity expressed in the chant endures. But in any case those who surround a dying person can build a raft of recollection for the departing soul, as another Hindu told me, when I asked him what happens to a person when he or she dies:

What we believe is that the soul inside, the *atman*, never dies. Just as – I give you an example: when my clothes become old, I bring new ones and put on new ones instead of the old ones. The same happens to the *atman*: it just changes the body; it goes from one person to the other person.

I asked him at that point whether it could be reborn as an animal. He replied:

Yes, yes, it could; it depends what he was thinking at the end of his life. So that is why, when we know that he is about to go, about to finish, we say, 'Ram, Ram', in the ears, so that he can concentrate on that word [Ram(a) is another *avatara* (incarnate appearance) of Vishnu]. (pp. 241f.)

Anyone who dies in this *dharana*, single-pointed concentration on the god, does more than help his own self: according to the

Agni Purana, he does indeed attain the god, but he also helps onward and upward the souls of his relatives. At the moment of death, his soul escapes through the *brahmarandhra*, the Brahma-gap, a minute opening in the crown of the head (or, some say, between the eyebrows in the forehead). This escape may be assisted by the practice of breaking the skull of the body that has been burning on the pyre (see also Chan. Up. viii.6.6, Katha Up. ii.3.16). In contrast, the entrance through which *atman* gains access to the body is known as *siman* or *vidrti*. But the escape through the *brahmarandhra* occurs only if he has not been evil or depraved in his life: in that case, his soul would be expelled through the anus. William Blake, in contrast, when his brother Robert died, saw his brother's spirit escape from the body and pass through the ceiling 'clapping its hands for joy'. The soul does not, though, go unaccompanied. It must have *some* support until it is reborn, and that support is the *lingasarira*, the subtle body which accompanies the *jiva* after cremation and gives it its subsistent support, until it recovers its identity as *atman* with Brahman. The subtle (intangible) body is also known as *suksmarsarira*, in contrast to the tangible body (*sthulasarira*) which is dispersed in cremation.

Thus far it must seem, to the sceptic, that Hinduism comes as close to exemplifying Marx's observations about the uses and functions of religion, as Islam comes to exemplifying Freud's description of religion as deriving its power from the offer of compensation after death. In the caste-system, justified by *dharma* and by the promise of better things to come in rebirth for those who maintain the *dharma*, Hinduism appears to have created a social structure of extremely formal alienation and exploitation, and to have maintained it through the belief system which the Brahmins (the custodians of the rituals and the traditions) have successfully perpetuated for their own benefit. Here at least, it would seem, we can say that death is the origin of religion.

But we cannot; or at least, we cannot say it of the Indian tradition, because the earliest records of that tradition, especially in the Vedas, show very little trace of that pattern of cosmology and anthropology which we have just been exploring through the Gita. In particular, there is very little trace, if any, of that understanding, vital to a Marxist analysis concerned with universal laws of historical occurrence, of the immortal *atman*, identical with Brahman, projecting itself into time and attachment as *jiva*, and being reborn millions of times until and unless it recovers its identity with Brahman by withdrawing from its entanglement in the worlds of *maya*. The earliest records have a very different exploration of death.

The earliest records of the Indian religious tradition in addition to archaeology are the Vedas, which themselves have different layers of development. The earliest are the four *samhitas*, the Rg-, Sama-, Yajur- and Atharva-Vedas, which are collections of hymns, chants and formulae particularly for the proper performance of sacrifices. To these were attached the Brahmanas, Aranyakas and some Upanishads. The material thus covers many centuries; and even the four *samhitas*, the foundation of Hindu scripture as *sruti* (that which was heard by the *rshis*, and not composed by them), were collected over a long period. So there is certainly no consistent or even single doctrine to be found in them. Nor are they easy to interpret. As David Knipe observed:

The poets of the Rgvedic hymns did not frequently chant on death and the afterlife. Most of their funerary verses are collected in an early section of the tenth mandala; these hymns to Yama, Agni as the cremation fire, and the ancestors are just as obscure as those on other subjects addressed to other beings. ('Sapindikarana', p. 112)

The meaning of Yama and Agni we will come to in due course. Rohde reinforces the quantitative point, that even the main word for death appears infrequently: 'The normal word for death is *mrtyu*, which has clear Indo-European relations: Lat. *morior*, etc. This word appears only in eleven RV-hymns. Furthermore, we find *mrtyu-bandhu*, "subject to death", in two hymns. Of these thirteen hymns all but two are found in the tenth mandala' (*Deliver Us From Evil*, p. 81) – the exceptions being 7.59.12 and 8.18.22. Where death is concerned, the picture of rebirth does not appear. As Wendy O'Flaherty says flatly (*Karma and Rebirth*, p. 3): 'The theory of rebirth does not appear in the Vedas; but the theory of re-*death* appears at a very early stage.'

So what *does* appear in the early Vedas is an imagination of death very similar to the one which, as we have seen, was prevalent in the Mediterranean world. Death is most emphatically *not* something to be looked forward to as the gateway to some better life, still less as leading to a compensation for the ills of this life. The Aryan invaders (from whom, as they settled in north-west India from the second millennium BCE onward, the *samhitas* essentially derive) found plenty to enjoy in *this* life. Indeed, they are often portrayed as a kind of preincarnation of G. K. Chesterton and Hilaire Belloc in their more rumbustious moods – praising 'the rolling English drunkard who made the rolling English road', or conversely condemning, in Belloc's case, the filthy horde who refuse to seize hold of life – or more literally, of the cup:

> Bootless for such as these the mighty task
> Of bottling God the Father in a flask
> And leading all Creation down distilled
> To one small ardent sphere immensely filled.

'This lust for life', as Organ described it,

is found particularly in the early *mantras* [roughly, chants or formulae which possess or manifest the power they involve], such as this one to Ushas, the goddess of dawn: 'The divine Ushas lights up with her beams the quarters of the heavens; she has thrown off her gloomy form, and, awaking those who sleep, comes in her car drawn by purple steeds. Bringing with her life-sustaining blessings, and giving consciousness to the unconscious, she imparts to the world her wonderful radiance ... Arise; inspiring life revives; darkness has departed; light approaches'. (RV 1.16.8.14–16, cf. also 1.48)

This enthusiasm for what life offers and each dawn renews is summarised in the fact that the Rg Veda portrays Usas as a young woman who repeatedly uncovers her breast for men to admire. Organ continues:

The predominantly cheerful religion of the Vedics has led some students to conclude that these people were completely hedonistic, consuming great quantities of *ghee* and *soma* [see below, p. 154], sporting continually with women, and having no thoughts more serious than the procurement of a wide variety of amusements. (*The Self in Indian Philosophy*, pp. 29f.)

Organ then corrects that oversimplified picture; but insofar as there is some justification for it, it is not surprising that the Vedas

regard death as something to be postponed for as long as pos
– very much as we saw also in the Jewish Psalms, a differe
being that the Vedic 'psalmist' can address Mrtyu directly:

> Go hence, O Death, pursue thy special pathway
> apart from that which Gods are wont to travel.
> To thee I say it who hast eyes and hearest: Touch
> not our offspring, injure not our heroes.
>
> Divided from the dead are these, the living: now
> be our calling on the Gods successful.
> We have gone forth for dancing and for laughter,
> to further times prolonging our existence.
>
> Here I erect this rampart for the living; let none
> of these, none other, reach this limit.
> May they survive a hundred lengthened autumns,
> and may they bury Death beneath this mountain.
>
> (RV 10.18.1, 3–4)

The characteristic prayer is: 'We human beings, who are subject to death [*mrtyubandhu*], O Adityas [sons of Aditi who personify aspects of nature], lengthen graciously our lives that we may live' (RV 8.18.22; cf. 10.59.4 addressed to Soma). In the funeral hymn recorded in AV 18.3, the mourners pray: 'Let Vivasrat [father of Yama, who is the Lord of the realms of the dead] separate us from death [*amrtatva*]. Let death [*mrtyu*] go away. Let not-dying [*amrta*] abide with us. Let it protect these men till old age. Let not their life-breaths go to Yama.'

In the hymn addressed to Mrtyu, the ideal to be aimed for is a life of 100 years. Amrta, which could literally be translated as 'im-mortality', refers, in these early texts, to the postponement of death, not to a condition where death does not obtain. Thus, when a boy is born, the Veda supplies a blessing:

> This child, Old Age! shall grow to meet thee only:
> none of the hundred other deaths shall harm him …
> Let not breath drawn or breath emitted fail him.
> Let not his friends, let not his foemen slay him.
> Let Heaven thy father and let Earth thy mother,
> accordant, give thee death in course of nature,
> that thou mayest live on Aditi's bosom, guarded,
> a hundred winters, through thy respirations.

Much as we found in the case of early Israel, there is a kind of 'outreach' beyond one's own death, in one's children. This is specific in the prayer addressed to Agni (Fire) in RV 5.4.10, 'May I, a mortal, calling with might on thee, Immortal, be immortal (*amrtatva*) in my children.'

Wendy O'Flaherty makes the same point about *tapas*, contrasting the kind of 'immortality' that *tapas* aims for in the Vedas and in the Upanishads: 'In the Vedas, *tapas* is able to accomplish the chief desideratum, fertility; in the Upanishads, *tapas* is the means to the new goal, Release' (*Siva*, p. 76). *Tapas* means 'warmth' or 'heat', and hence 'potential power' or 'action'. In the characteristic Indian way of combining paradox, the Indians realised that abstention or asceticism creates the greatest potency: so *tapas* is the 'heat' or potency created through ascetic practices – the greatest possible potency, since (according to AV 2.5.5 and 19) it was through *tapas* that the gods secured their own deathlessness:

Prior to the *brahma* the *brahmacarin* was born; clothed in heat, by creative fervour he arose. From him sprung the *brahmanam* and the highest *brahma*, and all the gods together with *amrta* ... Through holy disciplehood, through creative fervour, the gods drove away death.

But in the end, in the Vedic view, even if death is postponed for a hundred years, it cannot be postponed for ever; and its action is radical: the elements which have constituted an individual are returned to their source. In RV 10.16.3 the dead person on the cremation pyre is ritually returned in this way, the eye to the sun, the breath (*atman*) to the wind, the body to the earth-plants. Book 18 of the Atharva Veda gathers material concerned with funeral ceremonies (see also Taittiriya Aranyaka 6), which illustrates this concern to make sure that nothing remains at the end of the ceremony: 'Let nothing whatever of your mind, nor of your life (*asu*), nor of your members, nor of your sap, nor of your body, be left here' (AV 18.2.24).

At this early stage, *atman* and *jiva* bear scarcely any trace of the meanings associated with them in the Gita or the later philosophical or meditative texts. According to Narahari (pp. 5ff), *atman* occurs about 30 times in the Rg Veda (and its abbreviated form, *tman*, 78 times, generally as a reflexive pronoun), meaning 'breath', as above, or the whole body as opposed to particular parts, or simply 'being animate' (e.g., 1.1.11.8). In this last sense, *atman* is the invisible support of life, and this certainly anticipates or comes close to a subsistent reality: 'Who has seen the primeval being at the time of his being born? What is that, endowed with substance, which the unsubstantial sustains? From earth are the breath and blood, but where is the *atman*? Who may repair to the sage to ask this?' (RV 1.22.8.4). But on this basis, *atman* is identified as the source from which a human's activity derives – and this of course allows the speculative possibility that that resource of activity is not itself subject to change, or to the cessation of activity. RV 1.12.9.2 says of Agni: 'He who is like the divine Sun, who knows the truth of things, preserves by his actions his votaries in all encounters; like nature, he is unchangeable, and, like *atman*, is the source of happiness.'

But even without that later speculation, the Vedas do not believe that *everything* disappears in death. *Some* trace of the dead continues, in the form, immediately, of a *preta*. The *preta* is a classic example of 'autonomous liminality' (see p. 21), and of the importance of the rites concerned with this transitional phase: the *preta* is in a half-way condition, possibly threatening to survivors (unless the correct rituals are observed), and certainly vulnerable to a great variety of 'alarums and excursions' – again, unless helped by the appropriate rituals, the *ekoddista* and the *sraddha*.

The word *eka* means 'one', so that technically the ekoddistasraddha is a rite focused on a single dead person. The *sraddha* rites may have that single reference, but they also embrace groups of ancestors, at least as far back as the great grandfather. The *sraddha* rites move through a sequence, traditionally of sixteen stages: the 'new' or *nava-sraddhas* take place in the first ten (or, according to some, eleven) days after death, and their main purpose (in post-Vedic times) is to construct through the rituals a temporary body for the otherwise disembodied *preta*. There then follow the 'mixed' or *misra-sraddhas*, which establish the *preta* in its new location and which also make payment to the *brahmanas* who represent both the deceased and the ancestors. The *misrasraddhas* used to last for a whole year, but they are now often compressed

into a single day. The culminating rite of *sapindikarana* marks the
transfer of the *preta* into the world of the ancestors, the *pitrloka*.

Pindas are balls of white rice containing at least *tila* (sesame
seeds) and perhaps such things as milk or honey. Accompanied
by an offering of water, they both form the new body piece by
piece and also nourish it. Ideally, a bull known as *anustarani* should
be sacrificed for the same purpose – and also, the Puranas add,
so that the *preta* as it crosses the dread river, Vaitarani, into the
domain of Yama, can hang on to its tail. It is still the case in India
that a cow may be given away as an equivalent to the ancient
vrsotsarga, offering of the bull. Until the new body is formed, the
preta necessarily lingers around – in Indian villages, usually near
a particular *pipal* tree on which two clay pots are suspended, one
containing water and the other a *ghee* lamp to give light to the *preta*
in its darkness. On the tenth day, the *preta* is fully sustained in
the new body, and the two pots are smashed. All the male
members of the family will then bathe and be shaved, and will
thus be released from the impurity and dangers associated with
death. The dissociation from death and the dead is a strong
constraint in Hinduism in any case. Cremation and burial
grounds (*smasana*) are unclean and contaminating, as are corpses;
and the *navasraddhas* are at least as much for the living (to purify
them) as for the *preta* (to form its body). But with the *sraddhas*
completed, it is at this point that the *brahmana* who has represented
the dead person in the rituals is 'paid off' – 'one of the most
extraordinary roles', as David Knipe observes, 'in all of Hindu
ritualism'. The *brahmana*, who is known as *mahopatra*, represents
the *preta*. He is thus so closely associated with death and its
threatening defilements, that he is frequently regarded as virtually
outside the respected castes. Among the poor, he will perform only
residual parts of the *navasraddhas*, but for the wealthy, his role is
more elaborate. As the representative of the *preta*, he says and does
nothing, but he receives gifts to sustain the *preta* during the
subsequent year: utensils, money and food. Ten days after death,
the most dangerous impurity ceases, and on the eleventh day,
eleven *mahapatras* are entertained and fed. The eleven represent
the eleven Rudras, and hence they stand in for the ancestors of
the dead person. The meal is again another way of sustaining

the ancestors. On the twelfth day, the dead person is ritually joined to the ancestors.

The transfer of the *preta* to the *pitrs* (ancestors) is marked by the ceremony known as *sapindikarana*. It is described by Gonda (*Vedic Ritual*, p. 443), and it shifts the four remembered generations, so that the great-great-grandfather is no longer sustained in the *sraddha* ritual. The shift is literal, because the preceding generations move through three different domains to a fourth and remote domain, each of which is associated with a different group of gods. There is thus (as Knipe, 'Sapindikarana', p. 119, lays it out in diagrammatic form) a progression with corresponding cosmic and divine triads. At the *sapindikarana*, the *preta* becomes dependent on *his* son to maintain his position by sacrifice. After the fourth level, the ancestors receive far less ritual attention, because they have moved into the furthest domain, no longer dependent in the same way on the living here on earth:

4	Transcendent	Visvedevah	Remote ancestors
3	heaven	Adityas	great grandfather
2	midspace	Rudras	grandfather
1	earth	Vasus	father
			son

It is in this context that one has to understand *sati*, transliterated in earlier days as *suttee*, and taken to mean 'the self-immolation of a widow on her late husband's funeral pyre'. In fact *sati* comes from the same root as *sat* (as in the famous and fundamental formula *sat – cit – ananda*, 'being – consciousness – bliss'); and it therefore relates in meaning to something like 'true' or 'real', and thus (via the route of *dharma*) 'good' or 'virtuous': the term was therefore applied to a widow who demonstrated her devotion to her husband by being burned with him; it is only by transference that the term came to be used, particularly during the British occupation, for the act itself.

So it follows that marriage in Hinduism, from the *woman's* point of view, is not until 'death us do part', nor even, as the original words put it, ''til death us depart'. The man has an obligation to remarry, especially if the union had been childless. The woman could *only* (in the earliest period) remarry if the union had been childless, by assignation (*niyoga*) to the late husband's closest relative, usually his brother. In that respect, an attitude to continuity in children clearly prevailed comparable to the one in early Israel which produced the Levirate law (see p. 50). In any case, the widow came under the authority of the eldest son, and remained bound in fidelity to the man who had died, living a life of extreme simplicity and restriction. In a sense, therefore, she became a 'living sacrifice', because her continuing fidelity was believed to help her husband in whatever circumstance he now found himself; and as beliefs in heavens and hells elaborated, so the importance of this self-sacrifice became increasingly obvious. The demonstration of *sati* in self-immolation summarised the point in a dramatic way; and by the nineteenth century, the time of the greatest British indignation against it (it was declared illegal in 1829), it was being summarised in this way:

There are ... 85,000,000 hairs on the human body. The woman who ascends the pile with her husband will remain so many years in heaven. As the snake-catcher draws the serpent from its hole so she rescuing her husband from hell, rejoices with him. The woman who expires on the funeral pile with her husband purifies the family of her mother, her father, and her husband. If the husband be a Brahminicide, an ungrateful person, or a murderer of his friend, the wife by burning with him purges away his sins. There is no virtue greater than a virtuous woman's burning herself with her husband. No other effectual duty is known for virtuous women, at any time after the death of their lords, except casting themselves into the same fire. As long as a woman, in her successive transmigrations, shall decline burning herself, like a faithful wife, on the same fire with her deceased lord, so long shall she not be exempted from springing again to life in the body of some female animal. (Ward, *A View of the History, Literature and Mythology of the Hindoos*, III, p. 308)

But even without the consummation of *sati* in self-immolation (in any case, in the Vedic period, the commitment seems to have been symbolised by the widow lying beside her husband on the pyre, but then being taken away before the fire was lit, RV 10.18.8, AV 18.3.1), the sense of the living continuing to assist the dead is clearly strong. It assisted the transfer of the deceased person to a secure outcome.

This 'transfer' is already apparent in the Rg Veda, where one of the cremation prayers intercedes: 'Agni [Fire], consume him not entirely; afflict him not; scatter not here and there his skin and his body; when, Jatavedas [fire], thou hast rendered him mature, then send him to the Pitrs' (RV 10.1.16.1).

But where are the *pitrs*? Most usually, in the *pitrloka*, that part of the cosmos which is their realm or domain. There is no suggestion in the early texts that they have entered an unchanging paradise where their life is eternal (i.e., 'immortal' in the strong sense, of *never* dying again). It is true that they may (particularly if well supported by sacrifices) go to the *devaloka*, or domain of the gods; and in that sense, there are, as RV 10.88.15 says, two possibilities after death, 'two paths for mortals, that of the *pitaras* and that of the gods'. But even the gods are not necessarily immortal in the strong sense. They are indeed described (e.g., RV 10.72.5) as *amrta-bandhu*, not bound by death, in contrast to humans who are *mrtabandhu* (see p.147). But that freedom from death has to be maintained; and it is part of the function of sacrifice to maintain that condition and at the same time to incorporate the sacrificer (and/or those for whom it is offered) in it, with the effect of attaining the condition of *amrta* at least in the limited sense of postponing death and of serving the full term of life appropriate for a *pitr* or for a human. Thus Satapatha Brahmana 2.1.3.4 says of the ritual of Agnyadhana, the establishing of the sacred fires in the north (where the domain of the gods is located) and in the south (the domain of the *pitaras*):

When the sun moves northwards, then one may set up his fires. The gods have evil dispelled from them. He [the sacrificer] therefore dispels evil from himself. The gods are *amrta*. He, therefore, though there is for him no prospect of freedom from death [*amrtatva*], attains the full life [*sarvamayus*], whosoever sets up his fires during that time. Whoever, on the other hand, sets up his fires, when (the sun) moves southwards, he does not dispel evil from him, since the *pitaras* do not have evil dispelled from them. The *pitaras* are mortal [*martya*]. Hence he dies before [the full] life, whosoever sets up his fires during that time. (Rodhe, *Deliver Us From Evil*, pp. 90f.)

It follows that the gods themselves have to work hard in order to keep death at bay, and to sustain their own immortality. Many myths explore this theme of the gods in conflict with death, as equally they give many and varying accounts of how and why death was introduced into the cosmos – for example, because, without death, heaven would become too crowded (for a summary and discussion of these myths, see O'Flaherty, *Origins*). In this quest for their own resistance to death, the gods have powerful assistance through their control and use of *soma*. *Soma* (usually identified with the Avestan *haoma*) was an essential libation in Vedic sacrifices, offered to the gods and drunk by the sacrificers, with powerful, probably hallucinogenic, effects. The identity of *soma* is now lost (though some Parsis – descendants of the Zoroastrians – claim that the juice they obtain from the *hum* shrub is the *haoma* of the Avesta), but it is frequently identified with the fly agaric toadstool. In Vedic belief, *soma* is, quite literally, the medicine of immortality (see p. 96): it is the drink of the gods which helps them to postpone the death that would otherwise assail them, and it is known as exactly that, *amrta*, but here in the sense of constant rejuvenation.

As with all things of any importance in India, Soma is personified as a god – and not just as *a* god, but as one of the most important in the Vedas – the 'one small ardent sphere immensely filled' (see p. 146). The Sama Veda is offered to him, and the whole of the Ninth Book of Rg Veda is made up of hymns addressed to Soma:

> Soma, you give powerful defence
> Against the hate of strangers,
> The hate that weakens and wastes us.
>
> ...
>
> Soma, King, do not terrify us;
> Do not strike us with panic;
> Do not wound our heart with confusing flames.
>
> King, Generous One, when in your hands,
> If I see your enemies raise their heads,
> Chase the fear away, dispel the host.
> (RV 8.68, trans. de Nicolas)

By *soma* and by other endeavours (for example, *tapas* in AV 11.5.19) the gods hold death at bay. A 'full life' for the gods is a thousand years, ten times as long as for a human. But there is a possibility that the gods might achieve complete immortality, and that humans eventually, by the way of sacrifice, might be carried into the same goal. There is thus a pattern of increasing disconnection from the *mrtyubandu* (the death-bound), effected through sacrifice and through the proper utterance of the breath as Word: 'In the beginning Prajapati [Lord of creation, eventually merged with Brahma] was both mortal and immortal [*amrta*]: his breaths [*prana*, in the Upanishads equated with *atman*] were immortal, his body mortal. By the sacrifice [*karman*] properly performed he made his body undecaying and immortal [*ajara*, *amrta*]: by the sacrifice properly performed, the sacrificer makes his body undecaying and immortal' (Sata. Br. 10.1.4.1). Sacrifice properly performed includes word or chant as well as action. So there is a sense in which one can say that 'in the ending was the Word, and the Word was with God, and the Word reunites with God'. This is particularly clear in the hymn addressed to Vac (speech eventually personified as a goddess), which reiterates many of these points:

> I am the queen, the gatherer of wealth,
> I know knowledge, the first to be sacrificed.
> The gods have scattered me to all places;
> I have many homes, [for] I have scattered the chants in many places.
>
> Through my power, he eats and sees,
> Breathes and hears, who hears me as *Vac*.
> Even if they do not know, they dwell in me.
> In truth I speak: hear me, famous men.
>
> I, and no other, utter the word that brings joy to gods and men.
> The man I favour, to him I give my power;
> I make him like a god,
> The seer, a perfect sacrificer.

In the earliest period, therefore, there is little sense of immortality as the Gita and Upanishads understand it. Equally, there is no great emphasis on there being compensation, by way of reward or punishment, for the *preta* or *pitr*. The Vedas envisage sacrifice leading to the domain of Yama, not, as it later became, a terrifying place, but a place where family relations are continued, and the aches and pains of this life are healed. 'Having gone to my relatives [not *pitara* but *jami*], let me not fall down from their world. Where the well-hearted, the well-doing revel, having abandoned disease of their own selves, not lame with their limbs, undamaged in heaven, there may we see our parents and sons' (AV 6.120.2; cf. 12.3.17, RV 9.113.7 – 11, 10.14.8). It is the place where 'the wishes of the wisher are obtained' (RV 9.7.10.7ff.).

Conversely, the Rg Veda does envisage a deep pit for evildoers who 'false, untrue, go about like women without brothers, like wicked females hostile to their husbands' (RV 4.15.5; CF. 7.89.1, 7.104.3, 10.12.1.4). But it is only in the later and post-Vedic literature that the imagination of hell (or of places of torment and punishment after death) took off and produced descriptions as vivid and literal as those of the Muslims, but (in typical Hindu style) with many more of them: there are not less than 6, but perhaps as many as 28, each with 144 sections; they are situated beneath the seventh, or lowest world. In these *narakas*, the punishments fit the crimes: thus the *asipattra* is a forest in which the leaves of the trees are sharp swords (*asi*): those who needlessly cut down trees go to this hell to be cut by the swords (so, admittedly, do slaughterers of camels, where the connection is not so obvious; for further descriptions, see Shinn, 'Death and the Puranas').

To incorporate punishment after death, into the scheme of *preta* transferring into *pitr*, was relatively easy: it simply meant splicing in a twelve day journey of the *preta* to the domain of Yama (hence the coming of the dark river Vaitarani; see p.150), before a further progress to whatever *lokas* (places, mainly, of reward) or *narakas* have been earned by the individual concerned. But even here, in this early period, there is no sense of *eternal* punishment and reward. The frame of reference is still the same: what has to be avoided or postponed for as long as possible is the repetition of death.

It is the repetition of death which is the primary fact about death. It is *punarmrtyu*, repeated death, which distinguishes the *pitrs* from the gods, once the gods have succeeded in postponing their own repeated deaths indefinitely (see, e.g., Sata. Br. 2.1.3.4). As Holck observes, this brings us very close to the later doctrine of *samsara* and rebirth, though 'redeath' is not yet a statement of it:

Man is the architect of his own future. 'He is born into the world made by him' [Sata. Br. 6.2.2.27]. This idea does not yet constitute the famous Hindu doctrine of transmigration, as rebirth takes place not in this world, only in the next. But the thought of appropriate punishment or reward, together with the possibility of recurring deaths and consequent births, needed only a minor shift of emphasis to develop into the Upanisadic theory of Karma-Samsara. (*Death and Eastern Thought*, p. 41)

That scheme also requires a continuing subject of the experience, *atman* not simply as breath but as subsistent self; or at least as that part of life conferred directly by the creator, Prajapati, and remaining connected with him instead of with the death-bound aspects of human life, as AV 10.8.13f., 25–8, 43f., suggests:

Prajapati goes about within the womb; not being seen, he is manifoldly born ... This beautiful one [is] unaging, an immortal in the house of a mortal ... Free from desire, wise, immortal, self-existent, satisfied with sap, not deficient in any respect – knowing that wise, unaging, young soul, one is not afraid of death.

But these hints are very rare in the Vedas. The *real* link between the Vedic and the later understanding of death is not in anticipations of *atman* identified with Brahman, but in ritual and sacrifice, both literally (in the sense that the *sraddha* and *ekodistta* rites continue, modified but not broken, despite a total transformation in the concept of continuity) and theoretically, because death continues to be understood as the necessary and indispensable condition of life. Death is necessarily sacrificial, because without it, no life can happen. As Daniélou put it:

The universe appeared to the Vedic Aryan as a constant ritual of sacrifice. The strange destiny which compels every living thing to kill, to devour other things so as to exist, struck him with awe and wonder. The transformation of life into life seemed the very nature of the universe. 'To live is to devour life'. All existence could be brought back to the fundamental dualism of two factors: food (*anna*) and the devourer (*annada*). Every creature is the devourer of another and is the food of some other. Existing means devouring and being devoured. (*Hindu Polytheism*, p. 63)

This process of devouring and of being devoured is epitomised in fire, Agni:

All the aspects of combustion, of digestion, are subtle forms of fire. The relation of food and eater, of fire and offering (*soma*), or fuel, is the visible form of an all-pervading divinity. 'I am food, I am food, I am food! I am the eater, I am the eater ... the first born,' claims the divinity of the Taittiriya Upanisad (3.10.6). The same teaching appears in other Scriptures. 'This whole world, verily, is just food and the eater of food'. (Brhadaranyaka Up. 1.4.6.) 'All this universe, conscious and unconscious, is made of *agni* and *soma*' (Mahabharata, Santi parvan, 338.52).

According to the Purusa Sukta, all living creatures, including humans, are derived from the sacrifice of Purusa (primordial potency) by his first offspring, the gods and *rshis* (an understanding of the total cosmos as a process of sacrifice which was recapitulated in Asvamedha, the horse sacrifice, which lasted two years and rivalled the pyramid builders and the funeral directors of California in tying up vast capital and expenditure in death (see especially Brhad. Up. 1.1.1. for the description of the world as the sacrificial horse; and also Sata. Br. 13.5, Ait. Br. 2.6.13, Tait. Sam. 5.7.25)). Here, supremely, the theme of sacrificial death, as the necessary condition of life, is made clear. By application, and in a later text (Chandogya Up. 5.4–8), the birth of a child is the culminating consequence of a five-stage ritual (and that is why, in every ritual, the fifth offering is called 'man'):

> The world is a [sacrificial] fire, the sun is
> the fuel, the rays the smoke, day the flame,
> the moon the embers, the stars the sparks.
> In this fire the gods offer devotion,
>   and from this offering arises Soma, the royal offering.
> The god of rain [Parjanya] is the fire, the wind
> is the fuel, the clouds the smoke, the lightning
> the flame, the thunder the embers, the roar of
> thunder the sparks.
> In this fire the gods offer soma, the royal offering,
>   and from this offering arises rain.
> The earth is the fire, the year is the fuel, space
> the smoke, night the flame, the four quarters the
> embers, the intermediate points the sparks.
> In this fire the gods offer the rain,
>   and from this offering arises food.

Purusa is the fire, his speech is the fuel, breath
the smoke, his tongue the flame, his eyes
the embers, his ears the sparks.
In this fire the gods offer the food
    and from this offering arises semen.
Woman is the fire, the penis is the fuel, attraction
the smoke, the vulva the flame,
penetration the embers, pleasure the spark,
In this fire the gods offer semen,
    and from this offering arises the embryo.

By the time of the Brahmanas, Prajapati has displaced Purusa as the source through sacrifice of the entire cosmos, and, as Bruce Long observes, he is simultaneously the sacrificer (Ait. Br. 7.8.2; Tait. Br. 2.1.2.1), the sacrifice (Tand. Br. 7.2.1), the victim (Sata. Br. 11.1.8.5) and the recipient of the fruits of the sacrifice (Sata. Br. 10.2.2.1):

He *is* the entire universe ... The central message of this myth is that the person who perceives the mystical identification between Prajapati, Kala [Time], and Mrtyu and gives public demonstration to this knowledge by faithfully performing his sacrificial duties will survive for a full term of life. Persons who succumb to a premature death, before their lifetime has run its normal course, must be presumed to have been ignorant of the ontological identity between creator (*srasta, dhata*) and destroyer (*antaka, vinasaka*) and, as a consequence, to have failed in the performance of their ritual duties.

Into this whole perspective, death fits naturally as a necessary means of creation and process. That is not to say that death is so natural that it should not be resisted. However, one should go with the grain of death *when and while it is still appropriate*, because there is no other way to attain those circumstances which are not 'death-bound'. Therefore, to hasten death, as Sata. Br. 10.2.19 emphasises, is to stay death-bound:

Whosoever builds a 101-fold [altar], or whosoever lives a hundred years, he indeed obtains that freedom from death [*amrta*]. Therefore, whether they know it, or whether they do not, people say, 'The life of a hundred years makes for heaven [*lokya*]'. Hence one ought not to yield to his own desire and pass away before [attaining] the full life, for that does not make for the heavenly world.

Nor is *every* death natural in that sense. Death enters by a hundred doors: it is only the 101st, the death at the end of the full term of 100 years, that is natural: 'You gods that are in the heaven, on the earth, in the air, in the plants, in the cattle, within the waters, may you make old age the length of life for this man, and let him avoid the hundred other deaths' (AV 1.30.3; cf. 3.11.5–7, 7.2.27, 11.6.16). When a child is born, this prayer is said over him:

> For you only, old age, let this one grow. Let not
> the other deaths, which are a hundred, harm him.
> As a caring mother with her son in her lap, so let
> Mitra protect him from distress that comes from
> a friend [*mitriya*].
>
> ...
>
> Let Heaven your father and Earth your mother,
> in agreement together, make you one that dies of
> old age, that you may live in the lap of Aditi,
> ، guarded by breath and breathing out, a hundred winters
> (AV 2.28.1–4)

This impressive Vedic vision of the entire universe constituted by death as sacrifice (by life yielding, not simply *to* other life, but *for* other life, to enable its possibility) has its most immediate expression in the personification of the dynamic forces in the universe as gods; and also in the many myths which recount their adventures. The different aspects of death appear as Antaka (the Ender), Krtanta (the Finisher), Kala (Time), Mrtyu (Death itself) – though all these are also regarded as names of Yama. The miseries associated with death are summarised in Nirriti, the associate of Disruption (Adharma) and the mother of Death (Mrtyu), Fear (Bhaya) and Terror (Mahabhaya): 'Embodiment of all sins, she appeared at the time of the churning of the oceans before the goddess of good fortune, Lakshmi ... To her realm belong dice, women, sleep, poverty, disease and all the forms of trouble' (Mahabh, 1.67.52).

But the three major representatives of death are Yama, Kali and Siva. In the Vedas, Yama was the first to die and is therefore *pitr-raja*, ruler of the ancestors, who conducts the dead to their realm. The verb *yam* means to restrain, so Yama is the one who keeps the human population in check. His two four-eyed dogs keep charge of the path of the dead, and when the *preta* leaves the body, the messengers of Yama escort the thin and weary ghost to the domain of Yama where he acts as judge. How he appears depends on whether the individual has been virtuous or not. To the virtuous he appears like Vishnu:

He has four arms, a dark complexion. His eyes resemble open lotuses, he holds a conch, a discus, a mace and a lotus. He rides on Garuda. His sacred string is of gold. His face is charming, smiling. He wears a crown, earrings and a garland of wild flowers. But to the sinner his limbs appear 300 leagues long. His eyes are deep wells. His lips are thin, the colour of smoke, fierce. He roars like the ocean of destruction. His hairs are gigantic reeds, his crown a burning flame. The breath from his wide nostrils blows off the forest fires. He has long teeth. His nails are like winnowing flails. Stick in hand, clad in skins, he has a frowning brow. (Padma Purana, Kryayogasara, 22, in Daniélou, *Hindu Polytheism*, p. 133)

The dual aspect of Yama is deeply fundamental to other Hindu characterisations of appearance in the form of gods. All things have entirely opposite characters, depending on the standpoint from which anyone views them. Thus, time is threatening when it brings nearer some catastrophe, but beneficent when it removes us from it. When Krishna, in the Gita (II.32), reveals himself as Kala, Time, in order to encourage Arjuna, he says: 'Time am I, wreaker of the world's destruction, matured, resolved here to swallow up the worlds. Do what you will [or, 'except you'] all these warriors shall cease to be, drawn up in these opposing ranks.'

This dynamic energy of time is personified as Kali, the consort of Siva. In her destructive mode (see especially Kali Tantra), she appears 'naked, clad only in space ... Her tongue hangs out, she wears a garland of skulls ... and she dwells near the funeral pyres'. That one does not tangle lightly with Kali was made very clear by a Hindu mother and daughter in *Worlds of Faith*:

It is believed that if you do not offer in worship by sacrificing the animal, then she takes somebody from the family. Believe me or not, it has happened in two families. It has happened in my family: I lost a sister, and everybody told my father he should give up worshipping goddess Kali, and he didn't. He said, 'No. If Kali likes that, I wouldn't stop' -- because he didn't sacrifice any animals. And it happened in one of our friend's family as well. She lives in Delhi, and she prayed to goddess Kali, and she lost her daughter not very long ago. And then she was told the same thing, that if you pray to goddess Kali, she wants sacrifice. If you don't give anything as a sacrifice, then she takes somebody from the family. (p.166)

So if Kali has this terrifying aspect, as remorseless and all-consuming Time, why get involved with her as the focus of one's devotion? The answer is that, at some point in the long sequence of rebirths, we all have to come to terms with the process of Time. If we hate it (when it hurries us toward our own death) or if we welcome it (when it brings a loved one back to us after some absence), then in both cases, we are involved emotionally in Time. That would be the contradiction of the detachment which is the necessary precondition of *moksha*, release. Therefore, as Daniélou makes clear, Kali, the power of destruction, has a dual aspect.

She is, from the point of view of finite existence, the fearful destroyer of all that exists. As such she is known as the Power of Time and her male counterpart, known as Kala in cosmology, is called Rudra, the lord of tears, or Bhairava, 'the wrathful', in the religious scriptures. But when all is destroyed and the Power of Time is appeased, the true nature of the eternal night reveals itself as limitless joy, as eternal peace. In this respect Kali is known as the Transcendent-Night (Maharatri) or as the Power-of-Ether (Parvati). Her counterpart is known as the auspicious lord-of-sleep (Siva) or the Abode-of-Joy (Sambhu). (pp.273ff.)

The dual aspect of all appearance is equally manifest in the case of Siva, whom (to make the point) Wendy O'Flaherty has called (as the subtitle of her book, *Siva*, when it was reissued in 1981) 'the erotic ascetic'. In the Vedas (and sometimes later), *siva* is an epithet applied to the storm-god, Rudra (meaning 'auspicious'):

Rudra, your body which is auspicious [*siva*], unterrifying, showing no evil -- with that most benign body, O dweller in the mountains, look upon us. O dweller among the mountains, make auspicious the arrow which you hold in your hand to throw. O protector of the mountain, injure not man or beast. (Svet.Up.3.5)

But Siva became eventually distinct, the Lord of Sleep, one of the great Trinity with Vishnu and Brahma, and the focus of the devotional cults of Saivism – part of the heterogeneous coalition of beliefs and practices which constitute 'Hinduism', but itself a coalition of extremely diverse beliefs. Siva is basically the embodiment of *tamas*, the tendency of all things to dissipate and fall apart into inertia. Yet at the same time he inaugurates – and he is – the resulting condition, one of equilibrium, albeit still latently dynamic, 'the changeless state, the undisturbed joy [*sambhu*], in whom the universe comes to rest and sleeps' – 'still to his beloved he gives sleep' (p. 14): and Saivism is a cult of extreme devotion and love.

Sometimes the two aspects of *tamas* are separated out and ascribed to Rudra (as destructive) and Siva (as the peace-maker). But more often the duality is embraced in the single figure of Siva, the Creator *and* the Destroyer, the Lord of Death by which he can also be the guarantor of life. As O'Flaherty concludes (*Siva*, p. 318): 'By refusing to modify its component elements in order to force them into a synthesis, Indian mythology celebrates the idea that the universe is boundlessly various, that everything occurs simultaneously, that all possibilities may exist without excluding each other.' The unity lies in the underlying importance of *dharma*, of each appearance pursuing, so far as it can, the way that is appropriate for it. The wolf can here lie down with the lamb, without waiting for a messianic age (Is. xi.6); and it will eat it. So the lamb will no longer pursue its dharmic way and 'safely graze' as, in one sense, it should; yet it *is* fulfilling its (provisional) *dharma* in becoming the devoured in relation to the whole cosmic sacrifice; and the wolf is certainly fulfilling its own *dharma*: death has its *dharma*.

It is this theme, so fundamental to the Indian way, which underlies Tantric Hinduism. Tantra is a complex subject. But in extremely broad terms, it cultivates participation in, along with absolute detachment from, whatever is going on. Left-hand Tantrism applies to things that would normally (i.e., following the norms of *dharma*) be regarded as defiling or dangerous. It is one thing to learn to participate in the pleasurable with detachment; it is another, and different, thing to participate in the repulsive and defiling – with equal detachment. An example of what this involves has been described by Parry, in the case of the

Aghori cult, who use the rite of *cakrapuja*. This requires the ritual involvement of the *pancanmakara*, five forbidden 'Ms': these include *maithuna*, sexual intercourse, preferably with a corpse or a prostitute, either of which would be defiling.

In this, as in every other way, the Hindu must not be disturbed by death. It is this which underlies the apparent contradiction between *ahimsa* ('not causing harm or injury') which is a fundamental virtue and demand of Hinduism, and the *dharma* of taking life for some people (for example, Arjuna, because he belongs to the warrior caste). It was a conflict which exercised Gandhi greatly. Equally, many Hindus take life in order to eat, but in theory they ought not to eat meat. In an explanation which bears some relation to the Jewish understanding of life residing in the blood, a Hindu *pandit* (expert in religious matters), told me, in *Worlds of Faith*, what he teaches when people come to him for instruction:

I explain our way, and sometimes they accept, but not always. Let me give you the example: drinking alcohol and eating meat is prohibited according to Hindu religion. Whoever comes round here, I explain to them, 'You are eating the meat at the cost of the death of somebody – killing somebody. And whenever anybody kills anybody, chopping them, it hurts: the voice comes out from the body, "Oh, Oh!", like that. So the life comes in the blood, and when you eat that type of flesh, meat, it will come in you also … Whatever we eat, our brain and our thoughts become like that also' (pp. 137f.)

But the reconciliation of these apparent contradictions lies in the fact that humans must learn, in all circumstances, to go with the grain of the universe. What is appropriate to one, in one circumstance, is not necessarily so to another in another. Death has to be seen and evaluated as it occurs, as a part of the profound *rta*, or order, of the universe. In the hymn to Yama (RV 10.14), those who act in accordance with *rta* are promised a secure place in the domain of Yama and the *pirloka*.

But the supreme safety is offered to those who make their final pilgrimage to Kashi (Varanasi, Banaras), the City of Light. To die in Kashi is to achieve liberation (*moksha*) almost, one might say, despite *karma*. Kashi is the place (*the* place) where Siva himself whispers the final guidance in the ear of the dying person, the *taraka mantra*, the ferryboat *mantra*, the '*mantra* of the great crossing over'. In general, it is a *guru* who bestows a *mantra* upon a qualified student. To the pilgrim in Kashi, it is Siva himself who is the *guru*:

> Where else does a creature obtain liberation as he does
> here, simply by yielding up the body, with very little
> effort at all?
> Not by asceticism, not by donations, not by lavish
> sacrifices can liberation be obtained elsewhere, as it
> can in Kashi simply by yielding up the body.
> Even the yogis practising yoga with minds controlled are not
> liberated in one life-time, but they are liberated in
> Kashi simply by dying. (Kashi Khanda)

Diana Eck, whose book *Banaras, City of Light*, is one of the finest studies of Indian religion and its practice, concludes:

Kashi promises much more than a good life. This city promises a good death. Here death comes as no surprise. Every day the processions pass, bearing a corpse toward Manikarnika [the cremation ground]. Every night the fires burn on the river bank ... Here death is not denied. Perhaps that is why they can say that death is not feared, but welcomed as a long-awaited guest. (pp. 343f.)

Perhaps all this seems a long way from the cosmology and anthropology envisaged by the Gita and the Upanishads – to say nothing of some of the later schools of philosophy. But it is (at least so far as the Upanishads seem to understand the matter) a matter of extension, not of contradiction. Of the famous 'three requests' of Naciketas, in the Katha Upanishad, the first two can be understood well within the Vedic framework (even though the Upanishad, as a whole, assumes the truth of *samsara*). Naciketas is given, by his angered father, to death (*mrtyu*). When he appears before Yama, Yama offers him three gifts: for his first, Naciketas asks to be restored to and reconciled with his father – it is granted; for his second, Naciketas asks how the dwellers in the *svarga-loka* (the domain or heaven, of Indra, of full life) manage to keep death at bay, through the fire sacrifice: Yama tells him how the altar is made and the sacrifice is performed.

It is the third request which takes us onto new ground, because Naciketas asks what the final state of a man who has departed is, 'some holding that he is and some that he is not' (1.1.20). Yama offers to give him all manner of Vedic alternatives, in order to avoid answering the question – 'sons and grandsons that shall live a hundred years, cattle in plenty, elephants, gold and horses ... vast expanses of land, and life for yourself as many years as you will' (1.1.23). But Naciketas persists; and the rest of the Upanishad delivers the answer, that *atman* is Brahman; and it summarises the way to realise that truth, in terms often reminiscent of the Gita:

The knowing self is never born, nor does he die at any time. He sprang from nothing, and nothing sprang from him. He is unborn, eternal, abiding and primeval. He is not slain when the body is slain. If the slayer thinks that he slays, or if the slain thinks that he is slain, both of them do not understand. He neither slays nor is he slain. (1.2.18f.)

So the Upanishad concludes: 'Then Naciketas, having gained this knowledge declared by death [*mrtyu*] and the whole rule of Yoga, attained Brahman and became freed from passion and from death. And so may any other who knows this in regard to the self [*atman*]' (2.3.18). This means that the Upanishads approach the Vedas as indeed true (as Scripture) but as a special limiting case in its own perspective: there is a wider and more liberating perspective to be gained. The vast majority of Hindus live in a world of myth, ritual and sacrifice, far more than they live in the Upanishads. If there *is* a contradiction, it is one of emphasis, since the pursuit of *moksha* (a union with the changeless) implies something unsatisfactory in the condition of change – which life necessarily is; whereas the Vedic view appears to have been not unlike that of Browning's 'Confessions':

> What is he buzzing in my ears?
>   'Now that I come to die,
> Do I view the world as a vale of tears?'
>   Ah, reverend sir, not I: ...
>   Alas,
>   We loved, sir, used to meet:
> How sad and mad and bad it was –
>   But then, how it was sweet.

In contrast, as Rodhe puts the point, 'In Katha [Upanishad] the new life is regarded as a new evil. Consequently, deliverance from death means deliverance from life as characterized by birth and death' (*Deliver Us From Evil*, pp. 102f.).

But even this is a matter of perspective: for how else, in the end, could the evil of the Vedas, *punarmrtyu* (repeated death) be escaped unless that escape went beyond even the furthest outreach of Yama's ranging hounds? The *real* contradictions lie elsewhere. Neither Vedas nor Upanishads, neither the myths nor the sacrifices, stand up, if one believes that there is nothing but this body or this life, or that the whole apparatus is illusory – the apparatus of sacrifice, and of *atman* or *jiva* being constantly reborn. But to take that view would be to revise the whole meaning of the repetition of death. Those criticisms *did* arise, and they arose within the Indian coalition itself: they arose especially in the emergence of Buddhism.

CHAPTER 6

Buddhism

Buddhism, like every other major religion, is no simple phenomenon. From a single source, the life of Gautama who became known from his Enlightenment as the Buddha, Buddhism has flowed into countless different forms of expression. Theravadin Buddhism (mainly in Sri Lanka and South East Asia) claims to have stayed closer to the teaching of the Buddha. Its texts (in the Pali Canon) are briefly described in my *Problems of Suffering*, and more fully, with details of translations, in A. K. Warder, *Indian Buddhism*. Mahayana Buddhism took root mainly in Tibet, Korea, China and Japan. The account in this book concentrates mainly on Theravadin Buddhism, although some of the developments in Mahayana are indicated.

The Buddhist understanding of death begins with the familiar story of Gautama's childhood and youth. He who in later life became the Buddha (the Enlightened One) when he saw the entire truth of all things, was born in a palace protected from the experience of anything which his father thought might be disturbing or threatening. His father kept him in the palace, in the midst of beauty and delight. But then one day, Gautama ordered a carriage-driver to take him out into the countryside, and there, on his drive, he saw beside the road a sick person. That was the first disturbance. So twice more he ordered the carriage, and on the next occasion he saw an old person, on the third a dead body, prepared for cremation. In contrast to the pleasures of the palace, he could not suppress the disconcerting thought that all this might happen also to him. Desperate to find some remedy, or some resistance to disease and death, he went out a fourth time. On this occasion, he saw 'a shaven-headed man, a Wanderer, wearing the saffron robe'. In other words, he saw an ascetic, one of those who anticipates death by practising detachment from all worldly entanglements in this life. Gautama immediately left his palaces, abandoned his wife and son, Rahula, and threw himself into the practice of many of the methods of austerity and detachment which were available in the Indian religion of the time (c. 6th century BCE). In the Majjhima Nikaya (1.77–9), the extreme severity of those methods is graphically described, along with the unremitting commitment of Gautama to this way of escape:

Then again, Sariputta, in a charnel-field I lay down to rest upon bones of corpses. And the cowherds came up to me, even spat upon me and even made water upon me, spattered me with mud, even poked straws into my ears. Yet Sariputta, I cannot call to mind that a single evil thought against them arose in me. Thus far was I gone in forbearance, Sariputta.

Even all this was not enough, Gautama went on to even more extreme practices, in his attempt to disentangle some absolute reality in himself which would not be touched by the process of decay and death. In the end, he realised that none of these practices could rescue him from death. Even so, he did not find these endeavours wholly useless: the Buddhist critique of Hinduism is not as radical as that. He found experimentally that such practices attain the goals appropriate for them; but the goals, in his view, were too limited. Later on he commented to Kassapa, a naked ascetic, who had come to him to find out whether he rejected the value of asceticism:

Kassapa, I know well, with absolute clarity and seeing beyond what men can see, how some men given to asceticism, living a hard life, are reborn, on the dissolution of the body, after death, some into an unhappy ... others into a happy state, or into a heavenly world. How then, Kassapa, could I who know all this, thus aware, as they really are, of the states whence men have come, and whither they will go, as they pass away from one form of existence, and take shape in another, – how could I deride all penance, or bluntly revile and find fault with every ascetic, with every one who lives a life that is hard? (Dial. 1.224)

But what Gautama also found was that these practices cannot achieve *more* than their appropriate goals: they may indeed carry the process of rebirth into a delighting heaven, but that condition itself does not endure. It may *postpone* death, exactly as the early Vedas has said (p.147), but it cannot rescue some inner reality, *atman* or even *jiva*, into a condition immune from death. So Gautama found himself in the position of the Dutch boy who realises that the water is seeping through the dyke and who, with heroic determination, attempts to stem the flood by pushing his finger in the hole, only to find that the floods have already poured through a breach elsewhere and are now rising all around him.

It was at this point, on the night of his Enlightenment, that Gautama moved, in reflection on all this experience, through the four *jhanas* (the stages of movement from ordinary consciousness to the complete transcendence of it), and came to the realisation that there is nothing – no thing – which is not subject to transience (*anicca*), change and dissolution. There is not even a self, an *atman*, which continues from life to life through the repetition of death: there is no-self (*anatta*); there is only the process of change which produces apparent forms. But none of these can endure, not even the forms of the gods, though they endure longer than most.

So the truth that the Buddha realised is the fourfold nature of *dukkha*, which is the subjection of all things to change and impermanence, and the suffering that inevitably accompanies this. But of course, to realise that transience is the truth about all things, without any exception, is to see at once how *dukkha* arises; and if you see how *dukkha* arises, you can discern what would have to be involved for *dukkha* to cease; and once you see *that*, then you can see immediately the path that leads to the cessation of *dukkha*: you can discern the release and disentanglement which the ascetics had sought in vain, because their efforts were, paradoxically, tying them ever more securely to the present order of things, which is *dukkha*; they were operating *on* the system in order to get out of the system. Equally unavailing was the attempt to hide from impermanence in sensual delight, for that certainly cannot endure. There is only *dukkha*, of which death is an epitome. The Enlightenment of the Buddha was the realisation, profoundly and deeply within him, of this truth:

I knew as it really is: this is *dukkha*; this is the arising of *dukkha*; this is the cessation of *dukkha*; this is the course leading to the cessation of *dukkha*. I knew as it really is … Ignorance was dispelled, knowledge arose, darkness was dispelled, light arose, even as I abided zealous, ardent, with a self that has striven. (Vin. P. 1.1.7)

Initially, immediately after his Enlightenment, the Buddha rested in this condition of detachment from the whole process of transience, impermanence and change. That is the condition of *nibbana* (*nirvana*), though in his case (as we shall see) it has a different status from the prevailing Indian understanding of *nirvana* (p. 135). The Buddha was reluctant to share his new-found truth with others, because he could see nothing coming to him but abuse if he tried to share with others an evangelical report (a 'good news') which tells them that there is nothing about them which is permanently real, not even a self or a soul to give permanence to *them* through the process of death; for that sounds like *bad* news:

Then to Vipassi the Exalted One, Arahant, Buddha Supreme, this occurred: 'What if I were now to teach the Dhamma [the true and appropriate way]?' Then to him this occurred: 'I have penetrated this Dhamma, deep, hard to perceive, hard to understand, calm, sublime, not to be grasped by logic alone, elusive, intelligible only to the wise. But here we have the human race, attaching itself to the things to which it clings, holding on to them, taking delight in them. And for such a race, attaching itself to the things to which it clings, holding on to them, taking delight in them, it is far too hard for them to realise that one thing is conditioned by another, and that everything which happens is constrained into its outcome by preceding cause. Far too hard, also, is the bringing to rest of the activities of life, the renouncing of all that flows into rebirth, the destruction of craving and the extinction of passion, the perfect cessation, *nirvana*. And if I were to teach the Dhamma, and those who heard did not respond to it with assent, that would be a heavy weariness to me and a deep hurt.'

And then to Vipassi the Exalted One, Arahant, Buddha Supreme, were revealed all at once these lines never heard before:

> All this which I have gained through arduous toil,
> Why should I try to make it further known?
> How can this Dhamma be, by men, absorbed,
> Who in their lives are seized by lust and hate?
> It is too difficult, too subtle, too profound,

Too much against the grain of common sense.
By those in bondage to desire, in shrouding mists of ignorance,
It cannot be discerned.

Thinking about it, with these words in mind, Vipassi turned away
from making any effort, and away from declaring Dhamma openly.
(Dig. N. 2.35f.)

Yet in the end the Buddha *was* prevailed upon to share his
insight with others, at least some of whom would respond and
would therefore be helped. In the first sermon of the Buddha
at Banaras (Sam. Nik. 56.ii) a summary is made of the Middle
Way between the two extremes which he had explored to their
limits; and in that sermon is the effective summary of Buddhism,
including a description of the Eightfold Path to enlightenment
(see my *Problems of Suffering*, pp. 239ff.).

From first sermon to last words, the Buddha emphasised
the same message, that nothing is permanent, not even a self
or soul. According to the Maha Parinibbana Sutta (Dig.N.
2.156), the last words of the Buddha before he died were: 'Decay
is inherent in all compounded things [*samkhara*]: so continue
in watchfulness.' The formula of Majjhima Nikaya 1.128 becomes
a familiar friend to Buddhists: *sabbe samkhara anicca*: all *samkharas*
are impermanent – and that includes every aspect of one's
own being. It is relatively easy to imagine the end of this or
any other cosmos, as a passage in the Mahavagga (4.100) makes
clear: 'In the course of time, even such great mountains as
the Sineru, even this wide earth, will begin to smoke and be
burnt up in a great and universal fire.' Much harder to imagine
is the complete cessation of oneself – of one's self. Yet that
is precisely why the breakthrough to the cessation of *dukkha*
must achieve the realisation that there is no self and that every
aspect of this appearance which I regard as myself is subject
in the end to change and death:

There is no materiality whatever, O monks, no feeling, no perception,
no formations, no consciousness whatever that is permanent, everlasting, eternal, changeless, identically abiding for ever. Then the
Blessed One took a bit of cowdung in his hand and he spoke to the
monks: 'Monks, if even that much of permanent, everlasting, eternal,
changeless, individual selfhood [*attabhava*], identically abiding for

ever, could be found, then this living of a life of purity for the complete eradication of *dukkha* would not be feasible' (Sam. Nik. 22.96).

What, then, *is* the human appearance? It is the aggregation, or coalescing together, of the five *khandhas*, the five components of the human form of appearance: *rupa*, the basic materials of construction; *vedana*, sensation, which involves the six (not five) organs of sense, sight, hearing, smell, touch, taste and interior perception (*manas*); *sanna*, perceptions, the means to receive and organise sensation; *samkhara*, the composition of mental states; *vinnana*, persistent consciousness, unattached sensation without content. The human appearance or person (*puggala*) is thus a compound of *nama-rupa*, with *nama* (lit. 'name') representing those mental formations and functions. There is no dualism here: *nama-rupa* is the single form of human appearance with its varying capacities and functions – not the least important of which is the capacity to move one's contemplation or consciousness (*citta*) into the realm of pure form (*rupadhatu*), where it has lost all sense of 'I' being my self. Thus the aggregation which constitutes human appearance can operate in the immediate and available domain of ordinary experience, which is the *kamadhatu*, the domain of attachment and craving. At the opposite extreme is the domain where there is no form (*arupadhatu*) and thus no craving. Between the two are domains of pure form, which can be realised by that stream of continuity which constitutes human appearance, provided it has abandoned all sense of being 'I' or a self. This is pure consciousness without attachment, which, at its highest level (still short of *nibbana*) is without content.

So the Buddha's view that *citta* can live in a realm of pure form or formlessness, unattached to *rupa*, is not in any way like a dualistic emancipation of the *jiva*. *Rupa* is not in itself a bondage or captivity. In a famous phrase, *rupam sanyojaniyo dhammo*, '*rupa* is conducive to fetters', or 'productive of them'. It is easy to be captivated by material pleasures of *rupa*; but it is the 'laying hold of' (*upadana*) the material enticements of *rupa*, not *rupa* itself, which constitutes the chain of captivity.

So *nama-rupa* is a single (though constantly shifting and changing) form of appearance, constituted by the five *khandhas*, but not containing a continuing or persisting 'I' as soul or self:

When one says 'I', what is happening is that one refers to all the *khandhas* combined, or to any one of them, and deludes oneself that was 'I'. Just as one cannot say that the fragrance of the lotus belongs to the petals, the colour or the pollen, so one cannot say that the *rupa* is 'I', or the *vedana* is 'I' or any other of the *khandhas* is 'I'. There is nowhere to be found in the *khandhas* 'I am'. (*Sam. Nik.* 3.130)

It follows that when the *khandhas* fall apart, death occurs; and because there is nothing but the *khandhas*, there is no self to be reborn. As Buddhaghosa observed in the *Visuddimagga* (III, p. 665), 'Whoever has no clear idea of death and does not master the fact that death everywhere consists in the dissolution of the *khandhas*, comes to a variety of conclusions, such as "A living reality dies and transmigrates to another body".'

Does this, then, mean that death is extinction or oblivion, the end of a living form of appearance without further consequence? The Buddha's teaching is emphatically, No. There *is* continuity of consequence, even though there is no self or soul being reborn through the process. The Buddha in fact specifically repudiated *both* the eternalists (those who maintained that there is an undying, unchanging soul) *and* the annihilationists (those who held that nothing continues from this present life), offering a middle way between the two. The Brahmajala Sutta surveys the proliferation of those views, culminating in the 'recluses and Brahmans who arrange the future, and who on forty-four grounds put forward various assertions regarding the future' (Dig.N. 1.30), and others who 'in sixty-two ways put forward propositions with regard to the past and to the future' (Dig.N. 1.39). But despite the sophistication of these arguments, they cannot establish the case against each other, nor even for themselves.

What, then, continues in the Buddhist case, if there is no self being reborn? It is karmic, or kammic, consequence, which flows on from life to life. The aggregates of any form of living appearance are the expression and manifestation of a long previous history, governed by the law of *karma*. Thus here again we find, not a rejection of the prevailing Indian understanding of *karma* and *samsara*, but an adaptation of their accepted truth to the realisation that there is *anatta*. But certainly *karma* prevails: 'All that we are is the result of what we have thought; it is founded on our thoughts, it is made up of our thoughts. If a man speaks or acts with an evil thought, pain follows him, as the wheel follows the foot of the ox that draws the cart … If a man speaks or acts with a pure thought, happiness follows, like a shadow that never leaves him' (Dhammapada 1.1f.). Every consequence, good and ill, has to be worked out, not as punishment or reward (which might be, perhaps, remitted), but simply *as* consequence: 'Brethren, of deeds done and accumulated with deliberate intent I declare there is no wiping out. That wiping out has to come to pass either in this life or in some other life at its proper occasion. Without experiencing the result of deeds so done, I declare there is no making an end of *dukkha*' (Ang. Nik. 5.292). The only slight modification of this appears in the later collection of stories concerning the future outcomes that may await us (the Vimanavatthu and the Petavatthu, discussed on pp. 198 – 9) where it is stressed (no doubt *pour encourager les autres*) that a single action, good or bad, may have amplified consequences in some future state. Thus failure to give food to a hungry *bhikkhu* (member of the Buddhist *sangha*, or community of monks) will result in becoming a wretched, hungry *peta* (cf. Hindu *preta*, p.149) for many years in a future life, whereas to give a single, beautiful lotus to a *bhikkhu* will result in a future life in a blissful paradise surrounded by pools of lotuses.

It follows, as Govinda (*The Psychological Attitude of Early Buddist Philosophy*, p.109) summarises the point, that the aggregates which constitute human appearance are 'just materialised *karma*, the consciousness of past moments made visible. *Karma* is nothing else but the acting principle of consciousness which, as effect (*vipaka*), also steps into visible appearance. The appearing form is thus essentially "past", and therefore, for him who has mentally developed out of and beyond it, is felt as something alien'. It follows that the Buddhist Middle Way must be to stop the on-going karmic construction of new forms of appearance. The Eightfold Path (p.172) is the briefest summary of the route to follow, and it includes, necessarily, the cultivation of awareness of the transient nature of *nama-rupa* as the manifestation of *karma*. That explains, as Govinda goes on to make clear, why particular ways of concentration on breathing are a decisive point of access:

This hybrid position of the body as a product of a long past consciousness and the basis of a present one, finds expression also in the fact that a part of its functions are conscious and subject to the will, as, for example, the movements of our limbs, while another part runs its course unconsciously, or at least subconsciously (subliminal), and is not subject to the will, that is, to the present, as, for example, the circulation of the blood, digestion, internal secretions, the integration and disintegration of cells, and the like. Breathing holds a middle place which out of an unconscious, can be raised to a conscious, function, and can proceed just as well by deliberate volition as automatically. Thus it is breathing that combines the present with the past, the mental with the corporeal, the consciousness with the unconscious. It is the mediator, the point of departure from which we lay hold of what has become and what is becoming, and can become master of the past and the future; it is therefore the starting point of creative meditation. (*The Psychological Attitude of Early Buddhist Philosophy*, p. 110)

Yet still the question obviously remains: if there is no self or soul going on from one life to another, how can 'I' be the subject of any future consequence? And if 'I' am not, why should it be any concern of mine (i.e., of my self, which is also not-self) now? To put it more crudely, *what* is going on from life to life? Certainly not a self, in the sense of a single continuing subject of experience which goes from life to life, as a man might go from one room to another, or, having worn out one set of clothes, might get dressed in another:

Suppose that a man who is not blind were to behold the many bubbles on the Ganges as they are driving along, and should watch them and carefully examine them. After carefully examining them, however, they will appear to him empty, unreal and unsubstantial. In exactly the same way does the monk behold all the corporeal phenomena ... feelings ... perceptions ... mental formations ... states of consciousness, whether they be of the past, present or future, ... far or near. And he watches them and examines them carefully: and after carefully examining them they appear to him empty, unreal and unsubstantial. (Sam. Nik. 22.95)

Nevertheless, it is certainly possible to *refer* to a particular aggregation as John Smith; and this particular aggregation, which constitutes the *human* form of appearance, constitutes it in such a way that it is conscious of itself, and can therefore refer to itself as 'I'. Furthermore, it is constituted in such a way that it also has memory of its previous condition (including, at least potentially, memory of its condition in forms of appearance previous to this particular life). Even so, this sense, of being myself, and of being a continuing identity through time, does *not* create or constitute a self sustained by the aggregates: it simply points to the complex phenomena thrown up by this (human) kind of aggregation, which has these properties of self-reference and persistent (but not eternal) identity. It is perfectly proper, from the Buddhist point of view, to refer to an aggregation of poles, wheels, yoke, framework, reins as 'a chariot'; but the chariot does not exist apart from its aggregates: a chariot has properties which are more than the sum of its parts; but 'it' is not projected into some independent existence by those parts being aggregated into the appearance to which we refer as 'a chariot'. So also, Nagasena replies to King Milinda (since this is the famous illustration in *The Questions of King Milinda*),

The same is true with me. In dependence on the 32 parts of the body and the five *skandhas*, there takes place this denomination 'Nagasena', this designation, this conceptual term, a current appellation, and a mere name. In ultimate reality, however, this person cannot be apprehended. And this has been said by our sister Vajira when she was face to face with the Lord:

> 'Where all constituent parts are present,
> The word "a chariot" is applied.
> So likewise where the *skandhas* are,
> The term a "being" commonly is used.'

This means, as the Buddha answered Citta (in the Potthapada Sutta, which is a long discussion of various soul-theories), that it is perfectly sensible to regard the aggregation in the past or in the future as a real, identifiable person, without inferring a substantial (subsistingly permanent) self, linking the two:

'If people should ask you, Citta, thus: "Were you in the past, or not? Will you be in the future, or not? Are you now, or not?" – How would you answer?'

'I should say that I was in the past, and not not; that I shall be in the future, and not not; that I am now, and not not.'

'Then if they rejoined: "Well! that past personality that you had, is that real to you; and the future personality, and the present, unreal?

The future personality that you will have, is that real to you; and the past personality, and the present, unreal? The personality that you have now, in the present, is that real to you; and the past personality, and the future, unreal?'' – How would you answer?'

'I should say that the past personality that I had was real to me at the time when I had it; and the others unreal. And so also in the other two cases.'

'Well! Just so, Citta, when any one of the three modes of personality is going on, then it does not come under the category of either of the other two.'

There is, therefore, continuity of karmic consequence and manifestation, with each formation giving immediate rise to the next, with long, over-arching continuities reaching through the process – although, as the *Visuddimagga* 8 puts it,

strictly speaking, the duration of the life of a living being is exceedingly brief, lasting only while a thought lasts. Just as a chariot-wheel in rolling rolls only at one point of the tyre, and in resting rests only at one point; exactly in the same way, the life of a living being lasts only for the period of one thought. As soon as that thought has ceased the being is said to have ceased. As it has been said, 'The being of a past moment of thought has lived, but does not live, nor will it live. The being of a future moment of thought will live, but has not lived, nor does it live. The being of the present moment of thought does live, but has not lived, nor will it live.'

And not only is the moment of existence extremely brief (the 'thought-moment' or *cittakkhana* lasts less than a billionth part of the time it takes to blink an eye-lid), it is divided into its own three stages, the moment of its initiation (*uppada*), the moment of its relative stability (*thiti*) and the moment of its dissolution (*bhanga*); the longest endurance of a moment of consciousness is seventeen *cittakkhanas*. Yet out of these flickering moments is built up a stream of continuous connection (*bhavanga-sota*) which allows karmic consequence to be worked out.

Not *everything* that occurs to or within consciousness is conditional from or by *karma*. Some causes (*hetu*) of occurrence in consciousness are coincidental – such as hearing a car-door slam in the street outside. Such occurrences, when consciousness is passively receptive and simply receives impressions through the senses are known as *ahetuka*, not linked to root causes – and although innocent in themselves, the Buddhist is encouraged to learn to concentrate that they have no effect – as a Buddhist describes in *Worlds of Faith* (p. 87). In the Mahaparinibbana Sutta (Dig.N.2.130–3), the Buddha is described as being fully conscious and yet failing to hear 500 carts roll past him, or even to notice a violent thunderstorm in which two villagers and four oxen were struck by lightning and killed.

In contrast to *ahetuka* are *sahetuka*, those appearances in consciousness which are conditioned by root-causes. The three general characteristics of *hetu* (fundamental causes) are (in the case of bad *karma*) *lobha* (greed), *dosa* (hatred), and *moha* (delusion), with their opposites, *alobha*, *adosa* and *amoha*, in the case of good *karma*. Thus at any moment an individual represents the manifestation of *karma* in two modes, either without further effect (when it is known as *kriya*, exhausted), or in the process of creating further consequence (*vipaka*): if it is initiating the first moment of new consequence, it is known as *kusala* (if that consequence is for good) or *akusala* if it is the reverse.

Yet for all this emphasis on the analysis of each moment, so that the process of life is like the frames of a film, with each individual frame giving rise to the next, it is perfectly well realised that there *is* a continuous story being told; and this story continues from life to life. That is why the Buddha (and others) can remember their experiences in previous existences, even though the consciousness which is remembering was not present as the same consciousness or self in that previous life. Indeed, it is precisely because individuals *can* remember previous existences that (according to the Buddha) they rush to the erroneous conclusion that there must have been a self in those previous lives to be the subject of those events and (now) memories (see, for example, Dig.N.3.103f.). But in fact all that has been demonstrated here is that this particular aggregation is constituted in such a way that it is able to remember its previous sequences including (at least potentially and sometimes actually) those which occurred in earlier lives – hence the many Jataka stories, the stories of what happened to the Buddha in previous lives, and the claim of the Buddha to be able to 'call to mind my various states of birth: for instance, one birth, two births, five, ten ... a hundred thousand births' (Sam.Nik.2.213).

What, then (if there is no self), is the nature of the continuity which enables this kind of memory? A main candidate here is that aggregation of overall consciousness known as *vinnana*, to which the discrete modes of awareness, such as *vedana*, contribute. In later Buddhism, the *vinnana* which carries on the process of karmic manifestations from one life to another becomes known as *alaya vinnana*, 'storehouse consciousness', the persistent subsistence which underlies particular events in consciousness, as water underlies the manifestation of waves on the surface; but even so, it is not eternal: it too will eventually cease (see Griffiths, pp. 93ff.).

For other Buddhists, that development of *alaya vinnana* was pressing too far in the direction of *atman*; furthermore, it lacked the component of agency – of the continuity being the agent of its own acts and thoughts. For this emphasis, the term *citta* seemed more appropriate – though the distinction between *vinnana* and *citta* is by no means absolute, as Sam. Nik. 2.24 (*cittan iti pi mano iti pi vinnanan*) indicates. On this basis, Shwe Zan Aung (*Compendium of Philosophy*, p. 234) has claimed that the 'two terms, *citta* and *vinnana*, are synonymous, and that they are used interchangeably, in psychological discussion'. However, Johansson, in contrast, identified *citta* as the persisting continuity:

Citta is the core of personality, the centre of purposiveness, activity, continuity and emotionality. It is not a 'soul' (*atta*) but it is the empirical functional self. It is mainly conscious but not restricted to the momentary conscious contents and processes. On the contrary, it includes all the layers of consciousness, even the unconscious; by it the continuity and identity are safeguarded. It has a distinctly individual form. (*The Psychology of Nirvana*, p. 30)

If, then, there is no self continuing, but only the continuity itself, it becomes clear why Buddhists cannot really speak of 'rebirth' because there is no entity, no self or soul, to be reborn. But they do speak of *punabbhava*, 'again-becoming'. At death, the karmic consequence which is not yet exhausted gathers itself and passes into its next stage of appropriate manifestation – appropriate, that is, to the accumulated karma, good or bad. This process is described in many similes and metaphors: of a flame passing from one candle to another; of a seal impressed on wax; of waves on the surface of an ocean; of the passing of wisdom from a teacher to a pupil; of a chrysalis transforming into a butterfly. From those and many other illustrations, it is obvious why Buddhists have, in general, opted for *vinnana* and *citta* as the means through which karmic consequence continues through death, since death, as we have seen (p. 174), is the dissolution of the *khandhas*, which, in the case of *rupa*, visibly dissolves. Yet there is a paradox here, which the Buddha had already pointed out to his followers: the body is actually a *stronger* candidate for continuity, since it persists longer than moments of consciousness (p. 178):

It would be better for an untaught ordinary man to treat as self [*atta*] this body, which is constructed upon the four great elements [see p. 192], than *citta*. Why? Because this body can last one year, two years ... even a hundred years; but what is called *citta* and *mano* ['mind'] and *vinnana* arises and ceases differently through night and day, just as a monkey ranging through a forest seizes a branch, and, letting that go, seizes another. (Sam.Nik.2.94f.)

For this reason, it may be wiser to think of continuity simply as the whole stream of being, which is known as *bhavanga*: 'By *bhavanga* we mean the cause, reason, indispensable condition, of our being regarded subjectively as continuous; the *sine qua non* of our existence, that without which one cannot subsist or exist' (Aung, *Compendium of Philosophy*, p. 265). But that of course is simply to name what the problem is (*what* is it that persists which allows us to regard ourselves as subjectively continuous?) rather than to solve it; and by the time (5th century CE) Buddhaghosa came to analyse *bhavanga*, he made it virtually synonymous with *vinnana*. This can be seen if one considers the problem from the point of view, not of the end of life, but of the beginning of life, birth: when a new life is conceived, the total 'life-set' (*bhavanga*) which obtained in a previous individual at the moment of death (*cuti*) is formed in direct sequence in the embryo as *patisandhi vinnana*, rebirth consciousness. This is the direct result of previous *janaka* (generating) *kamma*. This rebirth consciousness is, therefore, already endowed with *hetus* both good and bad (pp. 178f.), but it is not actively conscious: it is more like the state of *bhavanga* consciousness of an adult in a deep and dreamless sleep. Buddhaghosa then describes the ensuing process:

As soon as rebirth-consciousness [in the embryo at the time of conception] has ceased, there arises a similar subconsciousness with exactly the same object, following immediately upon rebirth-consciousness and being the result of this or that *karma*. And again a further similar state of subconsciousness arises. Now, as long as no other consciousness arises to interrupt the continuity of the life-stream, so long the life-stream, like the flow of a river, rises in the same way again and again, even during dreamless sleep and at other times. In this way one has to understand the continuous arising of those states of consciousness in the life-stream. (*Visuddimagga* XIV)

In all this discussion, Buddhists are facing a problem somewhat comparable to the one which faced the post-Vedic Indians. The Indians had to consider what (if the *jiva* escapes from the body as it crumbles on the funeral pyre, p. 144) there is which can now give the *jiva* some support, given that it has lost the support of the body. Since they evidently found it hard to imagine completely disembodied souls (i.e., souls without a body of some sort to act upon as agent or through which to be acted upon as subject), they proposed the subtle body (p. 144). Buddhists did not have the problem of support for a *jiva*, still less for an *atman*, but they did have the problem of how, given the interaction of *nama-rupa*, anything can be carried over into a new outcome when the *rupa* ceases and dissolves. In the earlier Dialogues, the problem is solved ingeniously, though mythologically, by locating the guarantee of support in another form of karmic manifestation, a *gandharva*, a form of being in a heavenly realm who has to be present for conception to occur, since they themselves are seeking rebirth (Majj.Nik.1.265). But the question would only be postponed, since there would have to be some support for 'again-becoming' in the manifestation of a *gandharva*.

In the end, Buddhism had no option but to affirm a direct and immediate continuity without substance. Anything else ends up in annihilationism (that there may be consequences flowing on from an individual's life, since anything we do 'disturbs the universe', but no persistent, conscious continuity into another life) or the postulation of a persistent *and* subsistent agent of its own activity in karmic manifestation which could therefore survive the cessation of the karmic process.

Some Buddhists, the Puggalavadins, were undoubtedly pulled in that latter direction, since to them it seemed illogical to point to the goal of the cessation of *dukkha* (the cessation of the karmic process in my own particular 'stream of being') without there being any subject of that condition, beyond-cessation, which is known as *nirvana*. This argument created the so-called Personalist controversy in Buddhism, which lasted at least a thousand years. The term *puggala* is a way of referring to the whole intelligent person as the union of the *khandhas*. The Puggalavadins argued that that union is a reality which appropriates the *khandhas* and makes them its own:

We claim that there is a Person; but we do not say that he is an entity. Nor do we believe that he exists merely as a designation for the *skandhas*. What we say is that the word 'Person' denotes a kind of structural unity which is found in correlation with the skandhas of one individual, i.e., with those elements which are actually present, internal to him, and appropriated by him. (Vasubandhu, *Abhidharmakosha*, 9)

But the main streams of Buddhism kept well away from that conclusion, insisting that there is a middle way between the two extremes of annihilation at death or the endurance of an immortal soul. For that reason, the Buddha refused to give a direct answer when he was asked whether there is (or is not) an eternal soul: any answer, particularly a contradiction, might imply an affirmation of the opposite. But the Buddha was pointing in an utterly different direction. It is the reason why, also, the Buddha refused to answer when asked whether the Tathagatha (the one who has arrived) is, or is not, after death. This is one of the *avyakatani*, unprofitable, questions, which distract from, rather than help, the real issue. Two of the Buddha's followers, Kassapa and Sariputta, discussed this question after the Buddha's death: does he still exist in the final attainment of *nibbana*? Sariputta replies that it has not been stated. Can we then say that the Buddha does not exist? Sariputta makes the same reply. Perhaps, then, he both does and yet does not exist? The same reply. It is not that Sariputta says that it has been left uncertain, but rather that the Buddha deliberately refused to give *any* answer, yes or no, since it takes the discussion onto the misleading ground of debates about existence:

This is a question not concerned with profit or with the first principles of the holy life. It does not conduce to aversion, disgust, cessation, calm, to supernormal powers, nor yet to perfect wisdom nor to Nibbana. That, friend, is why it is not declared by the Exalted One. (Sam.Nik.2.222–3)

The Buddha, then, pointed to the way of realisation as a matter of practice, not as a solution to intellectual puzzles. To realise that one's sense of being one's self does not constitute a self or soul, but is simply one moment in a flickering sequence of moments, is to move beyond the clinging thirst which attaches itself to appearances as though they are permanent. In that context, the moment of death, *cuti*, is clearly one fleeting moment among many in the long sequence of change. But it does have a particular importance, because it is the moment beyond which there will be a reorganisation of appearance into an entirely different outcome – or into the cessation of reappearance, if the existing appearance has attained that condition of enlightenment. Death can occur for four reasons: because the natural term for the continuity of the five *khandhas* has been reached (*karma* is neutral); because the *karma* which has created this particular consequence has reached the point of being exhausted (*karma* is extinguished); because both the first and the second obtain; because destructive *karma* demands this consequence of death (*karma* is cause).

The moment of death is extremely important, as it is in Hinduism, because there comes into the awareness of the dying individual some indication of what the next outcome, after death, is going to be. This indication may be a manifestation of what, in the past, has accumulated good or bad karma, or it may be an anticipation of the next state.

At the moment of death, the power of *karma* brings into consciousness an image of whatever in past experience is bringing about reappearance, or it brings a sign of what is about to become the next outcome beyond this death. When the person then concentrates on what is thus presented, the consciousness becomes filled with the good or evil according to the *karma* that is being matured. Only such *karma* as is capable of producing a new outcome presents itself in the dying process.

It is then a disputed issue how immediately, or with what kind of interval, the new form of the continuity appears. At one extreme (to give a practical example), Mikkoyen Buddhism in Japan insists that the continuity is immediate, and that since it *is* a continuity, the zygote should be accorded the respect and rights – and rites – due to a person. An aborted foetus is known as *mizugo*, and Mikkoyen supplies both prayer and ritual to remove the shadow and to improve the good fortune of one's own family. But the relation, comparable in its way to the relations with the ancestors, is initiated even earlier: 'A *mizugo*'s existence begins at the "membrane stage" produced by conception, which in modern parlance means that life is seen to start from the instant the sperm joins with the egg' (Miura, *The Forgotten Child*, p. 27).

But in many forms of Buddhism (for an example in China, see p. 202), the transition is not immediate. There is an interval during which the stream of continuity gathers itself for its new appearance. The living can therefore help the dying, and the immediately dead, by surrounding their mental formation with supporting images, readings and chants. This became dramatic and detailed when Buddhism spread into Tibet, with its existing traditions of assisting the souls of the dead. The resulting fusion produced the Tibetan Book of the Dead (for translations and introductions, see Evans-Wentz, *The Tibetan Book of the Dead*; Fremantle and Trungpa, *The Tibetan Book of the Dead*; Lauf, *Secret Doctrines of the Tibetan Books of the Dead*).

The title, though, gives a misleading impression, if it suggests that there is a single work of that name. The *bar-do'i-thos-grol* is a widely diffused stream of practised traditions which (a bit like the *targumim* in early Judaism) was occasionally 'frozen' into written (or block printed) forms: those forms have obvious connections with each other but they are not identical. So what is the point of this tradition and with what is it concerned?

Fundamentally, it is concerned with the *bardo*, the intermediate state which follows death – though the two words mean more literally 'between' and 'island': the *bardo* is that metaphorical stepping-stone, from the accumulation of what one has acquired by way of *karma*, into a new resolution. Therefore, in this interval all manner of possibilities and consequences will present themselves – in particular, the four realms (p. 198) in which the continuity of consequence may reappear, ranging from the

depths of torment in hell to the *devaloka*, the domains of the gods
or of those who maintain themselves in a constant condition of
samadhi (of peace and absorption) until the time for reappearance
even from that condition comes. Equally, there will appear the
agents of punishment and of reward, Dharmaraja and the wrathful
deities, so graphically portrayed in Tibetan art, and also the
Bodhisattvas and the forty-two peaceful deities, above all Adibud-
dha, the source and creator of all *mandalas* (active creations of
spiritual space into which we enter through their re-creation), the
Buddhas Vairocana, Amitabha of the Sukhavati, the 'Western
Paradise' (p. 197), and the six incarnated Buddhas who are
emanations from the supremely compassionate bodhisattva,
Avalokitesvara. The purpose of the Tibetan Books of the Dead
is to bring into present awareness the whole range of consequence
which lies before us – and which lies before us not only in the
bardo and beyond, but is already a *present* reality, if we will only
open up our awareness to it.

Even from those extremely brief comments, it will be obvious
that the Tibetan imagination of gods and goddesss, of demons
and devils, is extraordinarily rich; and indeed, nothing but an
attention to the traditions themselves will even begin to illustrate
how immensely complex the Tibetan universe of states and
appearances is. But do any of them actually *exist*? The answer is
both yes and no. They have exactly that degree of reality which
we confer on them from our ignorance or from our enlightenment.
They cannot, after all, have more reality than any other form of
appearance, which is ultimately none, since there is no assured
foundation of knowledge on which we can stand in order to assess
how correspondent or otherwise our descriptive languages are,
when they attempt to talk about 'what is'. To put it in more
Buddhist language, appearance arises within *sunyata*, emptiness,
the void. Appearances gain the reality we confer on them: if from
ignorance we cling (*tanha*) to appearance as immune from
transience, it will act upon us with precisely that character,
although in fact it has neither that particular essence nor that
substance (to revert to the language of western analysis). This
means that hells and heavens are 'figments of imagination', but
of imagination which experiences them as real – as in a prolonged

dream. They are thus projections of inner states: all hells and all heavens already exist within, but we may nevertheless experience them as external and objectively real to ourselves until we overcome our ignorance.

It is in this context that a Tibetan Buddhist could describe hell as both existing and yet not existing except in his own imagination:

A lot of these pictures are for the purpose of visualisation. I mean, presumably we want to have some sort of concept of hell, and therefore one has to have some sort of ghastly picture of a physical environment ... I think there are two levels: if one is at a very elementary level, then one really needs to be frightened of doing something. And therefore there must be some sort of penal restriction. But if one's ideas are slightly more developed, then I think hell itself is a creation of the mind. I would like to think that it really doesn't exist – it's a creation of one's own *karma*, or lack of understanding, or ignorance. (*Worlds of Faith*, p. 278)

But even in that explicitly demythologised form, it is still an important part of the preparation for death. So also are two major parts of Buddhist meditation, the meditation on death, and the meditation on the transient nature of this body. Both these are summarised in Buddhaghosa's *Visuddhimagga* (VIII, 1–41, The Mindfulness of Death, and VIII, 42–144, The Mindfulness of the Body).

The Mindfulness of Death is a concentration, undertaken in solitary retreat, on the fact that death (*marana*) is approaching *me*. It is not meditation on death in general, but on its application to me. It therefore begins with thinking of death in eight ways:

1 As appearing like a murderer, sword in hand: death comes with the fact of birth – 'as budding toadstools always come up lifting dust on their tops, so beings are born along with ageing and death'.
2 As the ruin of success: 'all health ends in sickness, all youth ends in ageing, all life ends in death'.
3 By comparison with those who appear to have been great in the world; but all are dead.
4 By reflecting on the deaths already occurring in the human body which is shared as a habitation by many parasites:

Here they are born, grow old and die, evacuate and make water; and the body is their maternity home, their hospital, their charnel ground, their privy and their urinal. The body can also be brought to death with the upsetting of these worms.

5 As constantly close because of the extreme frailty, or vulnerability, of life in this body.

6 As not giving clear signs in advance of when it will come:

> For in the case of all beings,
> The span, the sickness, and the time, and where
> The body will be laid, the destiny:
> The living world can never know these things
> There is no sign foretells when they will be.

7 As putting a short limit on even the longest human life – accepted still, as with the Vedic Indians, as being about 100 years at most.

8 As in any case being related to the fact that each *moment* of human appearance is all that ever exists, and it is no more than the point where the rim of a wheel briefly touches the ground before rolling on.

That kind of *memento mori*, through which all attachment to life is conquered, is reinforced by the second related meditation, Mindfulness of the Body. This is a review of 'the repulsiveness and foulness' of the body, in thirty-two stages, from the soles of the feet to the top of the hair. It is a deliberate attempt to realise how filthy, ugly, frail and disgusting each part of the body is, in order to sever even the least temptation to cling to the flesh or its appearance.

The contemplation of death is important in all forms of Buddhism. But it received dramatic reinforcement in Japan, when the Chan/Zen form of Buddhism attached itself to the *bushi-do* ideal – *bushi* meaning 'warrior', and *do* meaning 'way'. For the Samurai warrior, life is a preparation for dying in such a way that the nature of death is made clear. The way in which one dies relativises death in relation to other goals and concerns, just as it demonstrates the truth or otherwise of what one asserts to be the case. Zen reinforced the *bushi*'s determination to remove what Suzuki has called 'encumbrances', or, in other words, residual fears or inhibitions. Thus 'Bushido means the determined will to die: when you are at the parting of the ways, do not hesitate to choose the way to death' (Yamamoto Jocho, quoted in Suzuki, *Zen and Japanese Culture*, p. 73). The Zen interpretation of Buddhism powerfully reinforced this attitude to death.

It was in that way that *budo*, the martial way, could become a *religious* way towards enlightenment. Zen in any case requires effort on the part of its practitioners, and above all of its pupils. To place this effort in the context of the immediacy of death was a powerful way of learning to master oneself and one's attachment to life. As the Zen teacher, Takuan (17th century CE) explained, the natural tendency has to be overcome:

In the case of learning to use the sword, when the opponent tries to strike you, your eyes at once catch the movement of the sword, and your eyes strive to follow it. But as soon as this happens, you have ceased to be master of yourself, and you are sure to be beaten.

In contrast, Zen inculcates perfect control, even in the face of violent death: death is seen in its relative context, as one event among many. But it is regarded in that way, not simply with passive resignation, but with active control. The so-called martial arts, *kendo* (fencing) and *kyudo* (archery), are designed to create exactly this effortless concentration in a freed and pure state of mind. In that way, Zen was able to make death, including violent death, an aesthetic event: it is deliberately 'placed' in context. In a famous proverb, this placing of death is summarised: among flowers it is the cherry blossom, among men it is the samurai. The blossom of the cherry is the controlling metaphor because its scent can scarcely be detected, and its colour is delicate; but above all because it falls in full bloom and does not resist its own death. So also the ideals of the samurai are simplicity, modesty and death in the bloom of life.

The connection of this with the *kamikazi* pilots of the Second World War is not difficult to see, though here again the contribution of the indigenous Shinto tradition is fundamental. However, a problem in engaging with the Japanese understanding of death lies in the fact that our knowledge of pre-Buddhist Shinto is extremely limited. But at least a basic sense of impermanence and transience was prominent, with 'transience' understood as literal movement: hence the importance of festivals of leave-taking and of welcome to the dead on their return.

Equally clear is the association of the dead with *kami*. The term *kami* is fundamental to understanding Japanese religion: the indigenous folk religion is known as *kami no michi*, the way of the kami, corresponding to the Chinese *shen-tao*, hence Shinto. But the term cannot be translated in any simple way. The word is both singular and plural, and it refers to the sacred and numinous character of virtually all appearance which can be focused in particular objects (such as mountains or animals) or people. It thus refers to personal or personified powers, but also to impersonal but power-possessed objects. So far as death is concerned, to die is to die into the sacred process of the cosmos, so the dead could easily be thought of as *kami*, as continuing cosmic beings with enhanced capacity for good or evil. The extensive worship of the *kami* then actualises that relationship, bringing humans into connection with the life-power which generates and sustains the cosmos.

The arrival of Buddhism, with its emphasis on *anicca* (p.170), simply made transience less literal and more metaphorical, and it thereby made central the Japanese concept of *mujo*, 'impermanence'. That impermanence can be observed in virtually every aspect of life, so that *mujo-kan*, the observation and contemplation of death, becomes in Japan a vastly extended practice of that *memento mori*, or 'mindfulness of death', which is in any case so central to Buddhism.

Ars moriendi then follows naturally – as naturally as some deaths are effortless, while others are resisting and distressed. That becomes an aesthetic observation which flows into Japanese art and poetry. Things can even gain in beauty by being transitory and brief, in line as much as in life. Terms like *aware*, *hakanai* and *akirame* resonate with this observation of the transitory life-process being manifested as beauty (on this see especially S. Hisamatsu, *The Vocabulary of Japanese Aesthetics*).

The fusion of indigenous traditions with Buddhism occurred particularly through the Chan/Zen schools (from the 12th century CE on). For Dogen (founder of the Soto school), *mujo* lost all note

of deprivation or absence. The condition of *mujo* is the totality
of all appearance – so much so that *mujo-bussho* is the Buddha-
nature realised as impermanence, into which the truly focused
disciple can enter with great immediacy, especially through
appropriate death. The fusion of that understanding with the
training of warriors in the 13th century then transformed the 'Great
Death' of the Buddhist monks into something more active and
charismatic; and it was that which produced *bushido*.

There is a comparable fusion of traditions in the other most
obvious way in which Japanese demonstrate mastery of death,
namely, *seppuku* – more popularly known as *hara-kiri*, since this
form of volunteered death involves cutting into the abdomen or
hara, which was believed to be the vital centre of life and control
(see von Durckheim-Montmartin, *Hara*). The point of the action
has been summarised by Michael Reich (in Lifton, *Six Lives, Six
Deaths*, p. 37) as the ultimate demonstration of feudal loyalties,
whose ritualisation made it available to religious ideation as well.

In all this, it follows that all styles and developments of
Buddhism, however remote they sometimes seem from the Pali
Canon, insist that the root of the root-causes of *dukkha* and of *tanha*
(clinging) is the attachment to the sense of a permanent self:
'"I am" is a vain thought; "I am not" is a vain thought; "I shall
be" is a vain thought. Vain thoughts are a sickness, an ulcer, a
thorn. But after overcoming all vain thoughts one is called a silent
thinker. And the thinker, the Silent One, does no more arise, no
more pass away, no more tremble, no more desire' (Majj.
Nik.140). On this basis, Buddhists can recognise continuity of
consequence without an ontologically independent identity of the
subject of the successive, connected experiences:

The king asked: 'Is there, Nagasena, any being which passes on from
this body to another body?' – 'No, your majesty!' – 'If there were
no passing on from this body to another, would not one then in one's
next life be freed from the evil deeds committed in the past?' – 'Yes,
that would be so if one were not linked once again with a new organism.
But since, your majesty, one is linked once again with a new organism,
therefore one is not freed from one's evil deeds.' – 'Give me a simile!'
– 'If a man should steal another man's mangoes, would he deserve a
thrashing for that?' – 'Yes, of course!' – 'But he would not have stolen

the very same mangoes as the other one had planted. Why then should he deserve a thrashing?' – 'For the reason that the stolen mangoes had grown because of those that were planted.' – 'Just so, your majesty, it is because of the deeds one does, whether pure or impure, by means of this psycho-physical organism, that one is once again linked with another psycho-physical organism, and is not freed from one's evil deeds.' – 'Very good, Nagasena!'

With all this emphasis on *anicca*, *dukkha*, *anatta*, it might seem that the Buddhist imagination sees nothing but ceaseless change. But change is *not* unceasable – the Four Noble Truths (p.170) are truths of importance because they make that point. The purpose of Buddhism is that it offers the *dhamma*, the appropriate guidance or way, which will enable any particular manifestation of *karma* to act within the flow of change, in order to direct it to a condition where it ceases – a condition which is not subject to process, to continuity, to again-becoming. If this were not so, then clearly there could be no cessation of *dukkha*:

Bhikkhus, there is [*atthi*] a not-born [*ajatam*], a not-become [*abhutam*], a not-made [*akatam*], a not-compounded [*asamkhatam*]. If that unborn, not-become, not-made, not-compounded, were not, there would be apparent no escape from this here, that is born, become, made, compounded. But since, bhikkhus, there is an unborn, unbecome, unmade, uncompounded, therefore is apparent the escape from this here, that is born, become, made, compounded. (Khuddaka Nik. 1.3.8.)

This condition has no involvement any more in the flow of change. It is the ultimate consequence of bringing the constant transformations of energy into a kind of dynamic equilibrium: it is, and yet it is not, since 'it', being in this stateless state, is not in interaction of any kind:

Bhikkhus, there exists that condition wherein is neither earth, nor water, nor fire, nor air [the four *mahabhutas*]; wherein is neither the sphere of infinite space nor of infinite consciousness nor of nothingness nor of neither-consciousness-nor-unconsciousness; where there is neither this world nor a world beyond nor both together nor moon-and-sun. Thence, Bhikkhus, I declare is no coming to life; thither is no going from life; therein is no duration; thence is no falling; there is no arising. It is not something fixed, it moves not on, it is not based on anything. That indeed is the end of *dukkha*. (Udana 8.1)

This condition is *nibbana* (*nirvana*). Strictly speaking, no one can 'enter' *nirvana*, because that would imply that it is a place, such as a paradise or heaven. There are plenty of heavens in Buddhist belief, as we shall see. But *nirvana* is not one of them. It is a condition/non-condition where karmic flow has ceased: it *is* that cessation. That is why the image most often used of the attainment of *nirvana* is that of the blowing out, or extinction, of a flame: 'To him who has won freedom through the cessation of *vinnana* [p.180] and the destruction of *tanha*, the liberation of mind is [like] extinction [*parinibbahi*] of a lamp' (Ang.Nik.1.236). hen the Buddha died, Anuruddha proclaimed:

> When he who from all craving want was free,
> Who to Nirvana's tranquil state had reached,
> When the great sage finished his span of life,
> No gasping struggle vexed that steadfast heart!
> All resolute, and with unshaken mind,
> He calmly triumphed o'er the pain of death.
> E'en as a bright flame dies away, so was
> The last emancipation of his heart.   (Dig.N.2.157)

Etymologically, *nirvana* was taken to mean 'the negation of lust': 'It is called *nibbana*, in that it is a departure from that craving which is called *vana* (lusting)' (Aung, *Compendium of Philosophy*, p.168). Humans at present are like children absorbed in their games, building sand-castles and delighting in them:

So long as they are not rid of lust, not rid of desire, not rid of affection, thirst, feverish longing and craving for those little sand-castles, just so long do they delight in them, are amused by them, set store by them, are jealous of them. But as soon as those boys or girls are rid of lust, of desire and affection, are rid of thirst, feverish longing, and craving for those little sand-castles, straightaway with hand and foot they scatter them, break them up, knock them down, cease to play with them ... The destruction of craving is *nibbana*. (Sam.Nik.3.188)

To press further (as the brahmin Unnabha did on one occasion) and to ask what exactly *nirvana* is like, is to ask the impossible: 'That question, brahmin, goes too far. You cannot get an answer to encompass that question. Plunged in *nibbana*, brahmin, is the holy life lived, with *nibbana* for its goal, and ending in *nibbana*' (Sam.Nik.5.218). It is therefore much easier to say

what *nirvana* is *not* (the *via negativa* of Buddhism) than to say what
it *is*; but since it is the cessation of all that is unpleasant, it does
receive positive descriptions as well (for a summary of these, see
my *Problems of Suffering*, pp. 253ff.).

But whether the attempted descriptions are negative or positive,
they are definitely approximate and incomplete. *Nirvana* cannot
be described because it is a contentless state of cessation.

Not surprisingly, therefore, the Dhammapada (§203) simply
and elliptically states, *nibbana paramam sukham*, 'Nirvana is the
highest happiness' – *sukha* being the opposite of *dukkha*, a
reminder that Buddhism perfectly well accepts that within the
overall context of *dukkha*, there are many experiences which are
pleasing and delightful. Nevertheless, to attain *nirvana* is to be
disentangled from those as well as from particular experiences of
dukkha.

But given this emphasis on the impossibility of describing
nirvana, and given also that it is a stability in which all connection
with the worlds of karmic manifestation is severed, how can we,
who are still manifestations in those worlds, know anything about
it, or even that it is? The main answer is, because those who *have*
attained *nirvana* maintain connection with us long enough to let
us know. When King Milinda asked how those who have not
attained *nirvana* can know anything about it, Nagasena replied:

'Now what do you think, your majesty? Do those who have not had their
hands and feet cut off know how bad it is to have them cut off?' – 'Yes,
they do.' 'And how do they know it?' – 'From hearing the sound of
the lamentations of those whose hands and feet have been cut off.' –
'So it is by hearing the words of those who have seen Nirvana that one
knows it to be a happy state.' – 'Very good, Nagasena!'

This must, obviously, mean that it is possible to attain *nirvana*
in this life: it must be possible to stop the karmic flow even though
the *khandhas* still hold together, so that the human appearance
continues, running through its remaining time before its dissolution in death. This, indeed, is what is believed to have
happened to the Buddha: he attained *nirvana* in his Enlightenment,
yet he remained, without attachment, in his earthly appearance
helping others by his teaching: 'Searching after the unsurpassed

state of security, that is *nibbana*, free from the impurities, I attained the utter peace that is *nibbana*, that is free from impurities, so that the knowledge arose in me, the Insight arose in me thus: "Sure is my release, This is my last birth. There is no more birth for me"' (Majj.Nik.1.166). Then, at his death, the Buddha-appearance ceased into that condition completely.

Those who attain *nirvana* are therefore able to be and not to be at one and the same time. There is no question about it. What *is* a question (and it was one of the earliest questions in Buddhist philosophy) is to decide *what* has attained *nirvana* if the constituents of human appearance still continue to eat and teach and contemplate and have provisional and nominal identity. The question is raised in Majj.Nik.1.296: what is the difference between a dead person who has passed away and a *bhikkhu* who has attained the cessation of sensation and conceptualisation? A distinction is drawn between physical, verbal and mental functions on the one hand, and on the other *ayu* ('vitality') and *usma* ('heat'). The former cease while the latter continue – rather as the light from a star may continue to travel and give the impression of a star when it falls on a retina, although the star itself exploded and disappeared long ago. *Nirvana* is not cessation/annihilation, but infinite (to continue the illustration) transmission. What came to be known as '*nirvana* without remainder' is attained at death, but *nirvana* as such can be attained before. But this was only the beginning of debate in Buddhism, not the conclusion of it, as Griffiths' admirably lucid account makes clear (*On Being Mindless*; see especially pp. 29f.).

The *nirvana* with the life-complexes still remaining is known as exactly that, *sa upadi sesa nibbana*. This is *nirvana* visible in this life, as the Buddha explained to the brahmin, Janussoni (Ang. Nik 1 158f.). The final *nirvana* without life-complexes remaining is absolute: there cannot be any return from it. But what *may* happen is that Enlightened beings, on the edge of the final realisation of *nirvana*, turn back and return out of compassion for those still trapped in ignorance and *karma*, in order to help them. These are the bodhisattvas.

The full elaboration of bodhisattva belief occurred in the developed forms of Buddhism, known as Mahayana, but the root of it can already be seen in the many conflicts of the Buddha with Mara, the personification of destructive evil, whose very name (Zendavestan *mar*, Latin *mors*, French *mort*) means Death. Mari in India was a goddess who personified pestilence and disease, and who came to be identified with the terrifying goddess, Durga. From the time of the Buddha's Enlightenment to his death, Mara attempts to dissuade the Buddha from sharing his teaching with others, because they would thus escape. But in accord with the bodhisattva compassion, the Buddha refused to realise the absolute condition of *nirvana* until both the *sangha* (p.175) and the *dhamma* are established (see, e.g., Mahaparinibbana Sut.2.34f.).

So the bodhisattva belief, and particularly the compassion which turns back from its own fulfilment for the assistance of others, is already well established in the Pali canon. But it developed much further in the many interpretations of Buddhism known collectively as the Mahayana, the Great Vehicle. In relation to death, the Bodhisattva comes as close as is possible in Buddhism to the concept of a saviour bringing salvation. So much is this so that Conze, writing of 'Buddhist Saviours', drew attention to the conviction of some early Christian missionaries that these beliefs were 'a counterfeit gospel, deliberately created by the Devil to deceive the faithful' (*Thirty Years of Buddhist Studies*, p.33). Of great importance in helping Buddhists (particularly in Tibet) is Tara, whose cult is now the subject of a fine and detailed study by Meyer. She is the goddess who 'ferries across' [*tarayati*] those on their way to *nirvana*, and who, in one account, emerged from a tear shed by Avalokitesvara when he looked on the misery of this world. The repetition of her 108 names 'destroys all evil, heals all sickness and brings ease to all beings':

Whoever meditates on our Blessed Lady in a lonely mountain cave, he will behold her face to face with his own eyes. And the Blessed Lady herself bestows upon him his very respiration, and all else. Not to say any more, she puts the very Buddhahood, so hard to win, in the very palm of his hand.

Salvation by devotion reaches its culmination in the commitment to the perfectly enlightened Amitabha Buddha. When he was the monk Darmakara, he undertook forty-eight vows before the Buddha Lokesvararaja, of which the eighteenth was the promise that 'when the time comes for me to become a Buddha, I will not enter into full enlightenment unless all beings who believe in me and love me with all their hearts are able to win rebirth in my kingdom if they should wish to do so'.

There is still further to go toward final enlightenment, and they receive training to that end in this Buddha-realm. Entering Sukhavati, the Western Paradise, is final only in a retrospective sense: those who enter it have further to go, but they cannot fall back or be lost from that Paradise. But what is crucial, in order to win that rebirth in Amitabha's realm, is 'that they should wish to do so': there must be devotion to Amitabha or Amida – in Japanese, Nembutsu. It is expressed by Shinran in this way (quoted from Conze, *Thirty Years of Buddhist Studies*, p. 37):

At the very moment the desire to call the Nembutsu is awakened in us in the firm faith that we can attain rebirth in the Pure Land through the saving grace of the Inconceivable Grand Vow, the all-embracing, none-forsaking virtue of Amida is conferred to us. Once belief in Amida's Vow is established, no other virtue is necessary, for there is no goodness that surpasses Nembutsu ... One who strives to accumulate merits through his own efforts is not in accord with Amida's Grand Will, since he lacks absolute, pure faith in its power. But if he re-orients his ego-centred mind and acquiesces in Amida's Grand Will, he will attain rebirth in the True Land of Fulfilment ... To be egoless means leaving good and evil to the natural working of karmic law and surrendering wholeheartedly to the Grand Vow ... For rebirth in the Pure Land, cleverness is not necessary – just complete and unceasing absorption in gratitude to Amida.

Pure Land and devotional Buddhism may seem to be taking us far from the more austere imagination of Theravadins (Theravada Buddhism being the form of Buddhism which is found in Sri Lanka and Southeast Asia, and which restricts the authoritative texts to the Pali Canon). But in fact, even in the Pali Canon, it is clear that karmic continuity can manifest itself, in again-becoming, in many different forms of appearance, and at many different levels of being (including heavens and hells, and in the form of animals, or worse).

Thus the opportunity for the later Mahayana elaborations are already apparent in the cosmology of the Pali Canon, which envisages four planes or levels of reappearance, those of *rupa* and *arupa* (see p. 173), and those of misery and of fortunate or happy sense experience. Those four are then broken down still further. The first is of sixteen grades, which embrace the four *jhanas* (see p. 170), and these in turn necessarily include the heavens of Brahma and of other gods. The level of misery is divided into four (purgatory, animals, the *petas/pretas*, the *asura* demons), and that of happy sense experience into seven (including the heavens of the gods involved in creation).

It follows that the continuity of appearance, in both forms of Buddhism, can be in heaven and in hell. The truth of this can be known, because the Buddha, in his many previous appearances, has been in them all (Dig. N. 1.78). In that sense, there has been a Buddhist 'harrowing of hell', as a Zen Buddhist told me in *Worlds of Faith*:

There's a beautiful Sutra about the Buddha going down into the Seventh Hell, which is the deepest hell of all: it's the hell where it's entirely silent, because everyone is not screaming anymore, because they've given up hope. And the story is that the Buddha goes there and plays. (p. 278)

Obviously, it is not possible to be in hell for ever. The period during which one's form of manifestation is locked into the place of torment may be very long indeed (many, many millions of human years) but it must end eventually, since nothing, not even hell, is permanent. But while it lasts, it is as violent and terrifying, in the Buddhist imagination, as anything that Hindus imagine of the domain of Yama, or Muslims of Jahannam; and much of it is inherited directly from Hinduism (for a graphic description, see Conze, *Thirty Years of Buddhist Studies*, pp. 224ff.). What the Buddhists also retained from Hinduism was a belief that there are *petas*, hungry ghosts who remain very close to the human domain. Their fate is described in the *Petavatthu*, while in contrast the *Vimanavatthu* describes the heavenly mansions. In this passage, the *petas* describe their condition:

We strike each other and drink pus and blood. Although we have drunk much, we are not nourished, we are not satisfied ... Suffering hunger and thirst in another world, the *petas* for a long time lament, since they are in torment. Because they have done deeds of grievous consequence, they receive suffering as their bitter fruits. For momentary are wealth and property; fleeting is the life here on earth: knowing transience from the transient, let the wise man prepare a refuge. (para. II, trans. Horner p. 23)

It therefore becomes an act of virtue and merit (indeed, it becomes an act of obligation) to remember their needs, as the text goes on:

Outside the walls they [the *petas*] stand, at the crossways and outside doors, to their own home returning ... Therefore must those who have pity on their departed kinsfolk make offerings of choice food and drink at seasonable times, saying, 'May this be a gift to our kin: may they be pleased with it.' Then they gather there where the meal is spread, and fail not to return thanks, saying: 'Long live our kinsmen, thanks to whom we have this gift ... For we cannot keep cattle, nor plough fields; there is no trading here, as on earth, nor exchanging of gold. We *petas* who have departed exist on what is given there. Even as water, gathered on high ground, flows down to the marsh, so are offerings given here of service to the *petas*.'

At the opposite extreme, it is possible for the stream of continuity to become manifest in the heavenly realms, or even as a god. There is no denial of God or gods in Buddhism – indeed, there is, both in Theravada and Mahayana, an enthusiastic attention to the gods in prayer and ritual. What is denied is that God is exempt from the process of impermanence and change. Thus the gods in Buddhism are very long-lasting, and can certainly intervene in human affairs to respond to prayers and to help their worshippers. But they cannot last for ever. They too will dissolve and reappear in some other manifestation, unless they attain *nirvana*.

Still, in the interim, it is perfectly possible to reappear in one's next existence in heaven. The Tevijja Sutta even records the Buddha telling an enquirer how to attain union with Brahma, without any suggestion that such an aim is foolish. That is why Spiro has called Buddhism a religion of both proximate and ultimate salvation. The ultimate aim must be *nirvana*. But for virtually all Buddhists alive at any time, that is far too remote and difficult a goal. They set their sights lower, and they aim, more simply, to move up 'the ladder of salvation' into one of the heavenly realms, or even just to improve their condition in a reappearance as a human; 'Typically', Spiro argues, 'instead of renouncing desire (and the world), Buddhists rather aspire to a future worldly existence in which their desires may find satisfaction' (*Buddhism and Society*, p.167).

Although Spiro was commenting mainly on Burmese Buddhism, the same is true – and in some ways, even more dramatically so – of developments in Mahayana. When Buddhism arrived in China, it encountered beliefs about the dead which were still, for many, not unlike those of the other early cultures where the dead have not gone to oblivion, but have only a shadowy existence. It is beyond the scope of this book to describe the early, pre-Buddhist beliefs in China about the status of the dead – there is a good, introductory summary by D.T. Overmyer in F.H. Holck, ed., *Death and Eastern Thought*, pp.198ff. What one can say in summary is that in origin in China, as at the root of other enduring traditions, there was no preoccupation with an elaborate and compensatory life beyond death – with the possible exception of the so-called Immortality Cult, the emergence of which is described by Yü; and here again it is stressed ('Life and Immortality', p.87) that the idea of immortality 'came into existence rather late'. As in India or in Israel, people prayed for long life (*shou*) and for the postponement of death. It was not until the 5th or 4th centuries BCE that some began to pray to become an immortal (*ch'eng-hsien*). They then elaborated a profusion of different techniques to attain that condition, as Yü summarised – by sacrifices, by drugs, by drinking crushed gold and gems, by eating the flowers of the purple boletus, which were believed to make the body light:

There were also people who believed that physical immortality could be achieved by following Lao Tzu's teachings of quietism and dispassionateness, by abstaining from eating cereals, by regulating the breath as well as cultivating nature, or, even more strangely, by metamorphosing the human body into the shape of a bird. (p.110)

Yet even in the Immortality Cult, the condition into which the newly fledged immortals fly is still very imprecisely described. Far more common in early China was a simpler belief that some trace of a dead person remains – and remains for about six or seven generations, still part of the family, or at least in association with it. It was believed that at death the various elements composing an individual were dispersed. There is some variation in what exactly *does* compose an individual, but roughly there are, in addition to the body, two non-corporeal elements, the *p'o* or *kuei*, which activate physical function and remain associated with the body in the grave until the body decays, when it sinks down to the Yellow Springs; this is associated with the Yin principle, the dark and physical side. The Yang side of intelligence and light is the domain of *hun* or *shen*. After death, the *hun* remains in the vicinity of its memorial plate or tablet – a small, often wooden, record of the name of the dead person with perhaps a few further details. Here the *hun* remains for about six or seven generations, in contact with the family, receiving food from descendants, listening to the news and gossip of continuing family affairs. In later formalisation, the *shen* becomes *hun* in its incarnation in a body, and the *p'o* becomes *kuei* similarly. At death they revert to their earlier forms.

But at the level of popular beliefs, not of formality, it was simply believed that the dead were not wholly extinguished but remained in some association with the living. Even if someone had lived so virtuously that his *hun* floated further into heaven, the *hun* would still return to its memorial plaque when needed. Thus the dead could help the living just as much as they needed support *from* the living. If offerings were forgotten, the *hun* becomes an orphan, *ku-hun*, an object certainly to be pitied, and perhaps also to be feared. Undoubtedly to be feared was the vengeful return from the other sphere, the *kuei* associated with the body. The *li-kuei*, the vengeful spirit, would return from someone killed 'out of time' – in war, sickness, murder or accident – or from someone who had been wrongly executed or improperly buried.

All this represents another instance of the widespread and prevalent understanding of death among our early ancestors, that the dead are not wholly extinguished: some trace of them remains. But there was no real sense of elaborate heavens and hells, still less of long-term survival in a compensatory paradise. On this belief-system the arrival of Buddhist missionaries had a devastating effect, as Holmes Welch has described:

The impact of Buddhism upon people with such a belief is easy to imagine. Previously the worst worry had been that one's late parents might be hungry and irritable. Now the possibility arose that they had been condemned to the fires and indignities of hell, or were wandering about the earth as pretas, not merely hungry for offerings, but unable to eat them because their throats were as small as the eye of a needle and everything put in the mouth turned to pus or blood. The thought was almost too horrible to be entertained by a filial child, but what if it were true? Buddhism introduced these fears just as China was falling into the turmoil of the Six Dynasties, when many Chinese must have been wondering whether the troubles of the family and the State were not due to some shortcoming in the service of the ancestors. (*The Practice of Chinese Buddhism*, p. 182)

Once Buddhists had introduced into China the possibility of hell-fire and of extremely long-term punishment (even if it were not to be eternal), the adjustments that were made were neither systematic nor coherent. Thus the *pretas/petas* seemed to resemble the *ku-hun*, hungry and perhaps embittered; but whereas the *pretas* had reached that condition because of their own faults, the *ku-hun* had done so through neglect. Put together, they fused into the *e-kuei*, the hungry ghosts who are in a realm of hell. With equal inconsistency, the Chinese began to accept (c. 4th century CE) the originally Indian belief that it takes forty-nine days for the continuity from a dead person to be allocated its place in one of the four realms (p. 198). Yet they continued to offer food to the *hun* for generations afterwards.

Not surprisingly, Chinese rites in relation to the dead developed into some of the most elaborate and complex (and, needless to say, expensive) yet known. By attaching Buddhism to Chinese tradition, the descendant of a dead person was faced by a wider range of possible outcomes: it might be that the *hun* was still waiting around in traditional style and needed the appropriate attention; but it might be that the proper rites in the forty-nine-day interval would help to achieve a better rebirth; it might be that it was, at worst, *ku-hun* in the traditional sense; but it might be that there had been a rebirth in hell. The only way of being sure of doing the best for one's ancestors was to fulfil *all* the obligations. These eventually came to be sum-marised as *ch'ao-tu wang-hun*, delivering the souls of the dead.

Thus, though Buddhism had brought to the Chinese the terrors of the grave, it did not leave them comfortless. It offered various ways in which a descendant could assist the deliverance of an ancestor from possible harm: by paying monks to perform rituals whereby the good *karma* of the monks and bodhisattvas would be transferred to the dead; by the monks actually teaching *dharma* to the dead; and by mediating to the dead offerings not only of food but of representations of money, gold, cars, or anything else that the continuity from the dead person might need. All at a price: and eventually the operation of the rituals became an important source of support for Buddhist monasteries and monks. Of course it is possible to say, exactly as morticians are inclined to say in America, that they provide a service that has to be paid for. As Holmes Welch concluded his excellent survey of death-related beliefs and practices in China in the period preceding Communist control:

A word of caution is needed, perhaps, at the end of this discussion of rites for the dead as a source of income for Buddhist monks. There is danger of losing sight of the substance of the work in analyzing its financial context – just as there is when discussing medical prac-tice as the source of income for physicians. From a Chinese Buddhist point of view, even the most perfunctory rites, performed by the most commercially minded monks, probably gave some relief to creatures suffering in the lower paths of existence, no less than the physician who is more interested in fees than healing may still heal. Rites for the dead were essentially compassionate, regardless of the money that changed hands in connection with them. Such, at least, was the orthodox, conservative viewpoint. (*The Practice of Chinese Buddhism*, p. 205)

Such, too, is the viewpoint underlying Theravadin funeral rites, though they exhibit in more formal ways the interaction between *bhikkhus* (monks) and lay-people. In Sri Lanka, the monks of the family temple are seated near the house of the deceased, under a canopy of white sheets or cloth. The body is brought out from the house, and those present are invited to join in the thrice-repeated formula of faith. '*Namo tasso*

bhagavata arahato samma sambuddhassa' (Homage be to him
who is *arahat*, the Enlightened One, the Buddha). The Five
Precepts are then repeated (see *Worlds of Faith*, pp. 29f.), followed
by a sermon on the nature of death and transience, and on
the dead person. Cloth and cool drinks are offered to the monks,
followed by the recitation of verses summarising the impermanence of all things. Water is poured into a bowl placed
before the monks and the dead body: as it fills and pours over
the edge, the monks recite: 'As the rains fill the rivers and
overflow into the ocean, so likewise may what is given here
reach the departed.' That leads into a specific transfer of merit
to the departed person, with the prayer, 'May the wealth of
merit acquired by this effort be accepted by all the gods, and
may it result in their welfare in every way.' The coffin is then
closed and removed for either burial or cremation (for a monk,
it is always cremation), and the mourners return for a funeral
meal.

But that is by no means the end of the ritual. On the evening
of the sixth day afterwards, a monk is invited to the house
again, to deliver a further address; and on the seventh day,
a formal giving of alms to the monks (*sanghika-dana*) takes
place, which is again reciprocated by a transfer of merit to
the dead. The same is repeated on the completion of three,
and of six months, and sometimes at the anniversary.

For the Buddhist, therefore, death is transition, only to
cease when the recognition, that nothing is immune from that
transience, is real and absolute. Theravadins and Mahayanists
may differ greatly in what they believe may usefully carry
the transient process, of one whom they have known, through
death. But they agree that 'all component things are impermanent: that which comes into appearance has also its extinction: calming down is happiness'. So, just as Islam exhibits
the development of a religious tradition (the Judaeo-Christian)
in the direction of literalism (so that sacrifice is marginalised
in comparison with a literal description of after-death states,
and of how to attain the good and avoid the evil), Buddhism
exhibits the development of a religious tradition in the direction of
metaphor. Sacrifice remains important at the level of folk-religion.

Otherwise, it is demythologised. Its efficacy is ridiculed by the Buddha in the Jataka (previous birth) stories, and its social function is translated into *dana*, that is, the gift whereby laypeople support the *sangha* and receive merit in return, to help them or their ancestors. In both cases, the category of sacrifice, through which the earliest explorations of the meaning and significance of death were made, is diminished. The question remains to what extent that more original insight has status and importance for us.

III

Conclusion

CHAPTER 7

Conclusion

Even so brief a survey of the ways in which major religious traditions understand death will have made it clear that there cannot be any single or simple generalisation about 'religions and death'. Death has been understood as everything, from defeat and punishment to release and opportunity. Frequently irreconcilable opposites are maintained between traditions, and even in conjunction in the same tradition. But that is not because, as sceptics suppose, the religions are yet again exhibiting their incompetent refusal to face facts, but because the facts of experience demand an attitude of both–and, not an attitude of either–or. In regarding death as both an enemy and a friend, the religions are, as ever, resisting the fallacy of the falsely dichotomous question. The meaning of that, and its importance in understanding religions, is discussed in my *Licensed Insanities*, pp. 101, 109.

But having said that, it remains clear that many of the propositions maintained by the different religions, in relation to human nature and to death, cannot possibly all be true. They may all be false, but they cannot all be true, at least as propositions about putative matters of fact. It is not possible for both a Hindu and a Buddhist to be correct in terms of what they propose about human anthropology (what it is that constitutes human nature and appearance). It is not possible for both a Muslim and a Christian to be correct in terms of what they propose about the death and resurrection of Jesus/Isa (p. 113).

Such differences undoubtedly make a difference. They are not negligible, in the way that a preference for yellow rather than green might be. Thus, Judaism and Islam agree in regarding humans as educable: they can learn from God (through Torah or Quran) what they should do, and receive help from him to do it; they thus have a relatively optimistic anthropology. But Christianity, in contrast, has a radically pessimistic anthropology: the subversions of evil lie at the root (*radix*) of the human enterprise, and we cannot be educated into salvation. The cultural consequences of such differences are obvious.

Yet even on such fundamental issues, it is essential to learn the lessons of this century in understanding more clearly the relations between language and reference, symbol and sign, icon and index. In particular, we now see more clearly that while all our languages, theories and pictures are approximate, provisional, corrigible and frequently wrong, they may nevertheless be wrong (on many occasions of our using them) about something; and that 'something' then sets a limit on language by being what it is, even though we can never describe exactly or exhaustively *what* it is. This is even true of something so relatively obvious as the universe. Truth can therefore be told in fiction as well as in fact, by way of poetry as well as by way of proof.

Those points, about critical realism and phenomenology, have been argued more fully in *Licensed Insanities*. What they imply in relation to religions and death is that the languages and pictures of death, and of what may survive it, may be approximate and mainly wrong as a matter of literal description, but they may be wrong or at least approximate about some fundamental (and universal) demand, arising in or from experience, or human intelligence, emotion and understanding. It is exactly as Simone Weil said of God:

There is a God. There is no God. Where is the problem? I am quite sure that there is a God in the sense that I am sure that my love is no illusion. I am quite sure there is no God in the sense that I am sure there is nothing which resembles what I can conceive when I say that word.

The pictures we use may thus reinforce each other, even though in detail they are incompatible. Issues of truth do not thereby disappear; it is simply that they are not foreclosed. Thus choices certainly remain to be made, far short of immediate verification or falsification, since that, in the nature of this case, cannot be other than eschatological (that is, since so many of the fundamental propositions have to do with the final state, nothing short of finality can verify or falsify what is proposed).

But what is inferred in the meantime about human nature and its destiny is by no means trivial or ill-considered; still less is it only a product of abject wishful thinking, or of cynical exploitation of the credulous. The religious explorations of death, and of the continuities of consequence through death, emerge (both East and West) from very cautious explorations of what belongs to our experience within the boundaries of this body and this life. What is clear from the survey of religions in this book (and here at least a generalisation is possible) is that both major religious traditions, East and West, made exactly comparable extensions of belief and imagination in the two main areas of self and of salvation. Those explorations produced affirmations and concepts which are, in many respects, radically different. But their point of departure in the human experience of itself and its environment is the same; and they resemble each other in affirming through their different imaginations, first, that there is about us that which continues consequentially through the process of time; and second, that even though death may be regarded as an intrusion and perhaps even as a punishment, it is nevertheless also necessary as a means to life. It was, as we have seen, supremely through the category and actions of sacrifice that both traditions originally explored and expressed that truth.

Consequently, the religious affirmation of value *includes* the reality of death, maybe as the last enemy, but also as the necessary condition of life. Attempts to evade death, or to pretend that it is not serious, or to deny its necessary place in the ordering of life, have almost always been regarded by the major religious traditions as false or dangerous or subversive of truth. If such enterprises as spiritualism or the cryogenic treatment of bodies give the impression that death is trivial or unimportant, then they will continue to be regarded by religions as destructive of a truth about ourselves. To the question, in contrast, which is at least as old as Socrates, whether death is so great an evil as many suppose, the religions answer emphatically, No. Through the category of sacrifice, they state dramatically that there are no other terms on which we can live except those of death.

Sacrifice not only articulated that truth, it also made a virtue out of that necessity.

But of what use or credibility is that now? Of all religious categories, surely that of sacrifice is the least viable in a world which has inherited a Frazer-like belief that magic is primitive and poor technology, and that sacrifice is a particularly savage example of magic? Of sacrifice, Frazer observed:

If the test of truth lay in a show of hands or a counting of heads, the system of magic might appeal, with far more reason than the Catholic Church, to the proud motto, 'Quod semper, quod ubique, quod ab omnibus', as the sure and certain credential of its own infallibility. It is not our business here to consider what bearing the permanent existence of such a solid layer of savagery beneath the surface of society, and unaffected by the superficial changes of religion and culture, has upon the future of humanity. The dispassionate observer, whose studies have led him to plumb its depths, can hardly regard it otherwise than as a standing menace to civilisation. (p. 91)

Yet in terms of civilisation, it is exactly at this point of sacrifice that the religious and the secular evaluations of death meet and reinforce each other. In particular, the scientific recognition of the necessity for death is so close to the religious that both in hospital and hospice a shared assertion of the value of death is now possible. If we ask the equivalent question of the sciences (whether it is possible to have life of this carbon-based sort on any other terms than those of death), the answer is an equally emphatic, No.

The reasons why that answer is the same are many and various. But to give three related examples: the first can be apprehended by taking hold of your hand and looking at it. Not so very long ago (at least in the time scale of the universe) most of the atoms in that hand were burning in the depth of some distant star. You are literally a star child, a child of the universe. And you cannot be a child in any other way: to build your body, with its complex molecules, elements much heavier than hydrogen are needed – such elements as carbon, nitrogen, phosphorous, oxygen. Even to build a planet, let alone organic life, elements much heavier than iron are required. But those elements cannot be distributed without the extreme compression of collapsing stars *and* their explosion, because in that way the elements are fused and then scattered so that they become available for new architectures of energy.

This means that we cannot arrive at a planet, let alone at the construction of living organisms, without the death of stars (their compression to form the heavier elements, and their explosion to scatter those elements for new architectures of energy):

> The tides are in our veins, we still mirror the stars,
>   life is your child, but there is in me
> Older and harder than life and more impartial, the eye
>   that watched before there was an ocean.
>
> (Robinson Jeffers)

The second example of why there cannot be life on any other terms than those of death lies also in the palm of your hand – and in every other part of your body as well. Each cell in the body contains in the DNA the same programme, the same genetic information, which, if it could be replicated in the appropriate context, could produce another individual. This is the basis for cloning, which is in effect exact genetic copying; and it was this which led to the flurry of speculation that this perhaps could lead to a kind of provisional immortality, at least of an outward appearance. But despite *The Boys from Brazil* and the sensational claims of David Rorvik, this has not been achieved in the human case. Moreover, it seems likely, where humans are concerned, that it cannot be done (if, as is claimed, adult differentiated cells differ slightly in their DNA and cannot give rise to a viable embryo). Nevertheless, where the gene is concerned, people do talk about 'the immortal gene'. As Macfarlane Burnet put it, pondering the implications of genetics for human life:

For someone still with a capacity for wonder, it can be fascinating to look through a microscope at one of his own white blood cells. He can see the round central nucleus and he knows that in the nucleus are strands of DNA. It is the literal truth that the patterned molecules in that DNA have come down in an immortal, unbroken sequence for 3000 million years from the single micro-organism within which the universal genetic code first took its definitive form. Life in that sense is immortal, and in the early stages, when reproduction was no more than growth and division into two, there was no immediate biological necessity for death. (*The Endurance of Life*, p. 7)

But in fact the word 'immortal' is being used wrongly. In a trivial sense, if all living organisms (built by the genes and replicating genetic information) came to an end, so too would the genes. They have at most only a provisional immortality, of a Vedic kind. But more importantly than that, although the genetic information is extremely stable, there must be some opportunity for changes, since otherwise no advance could be made to different and more complex organisms. It is true that the evolutionary process is immensely conservative – so much so that it led Eigen to observe that what really needs explaining and accounting for in evolution is not change but stability (see, for example, *The Hypercycle*, p. 7). Thus every living organism, from the simplest bacteriophage to human beings, uses an identical set of triplet codons to translate the base sequence of messenger RNA to the amino acid sequence of a polypeptide chain. So, to give an example, a codon AUG universally specifies methionine, and UUU universally specifies phenylananine. Commenting on this, Suso Ohno has argued that the codons are universal, *not* because the triplet coding system represents an ideal solution to the problem, but because the first self-replicating nucleic acid, which was formed those many millions of years ago, was constrained into the coding system because it happened to be able to do the job. Once that had happened, at the very beginning of life, that coding system had to be conserved. As Ohno put it:

Once the coding system was established, at the very beginning of life, there was no choice but to conserve it *in toto* in all the myriad descendants of that first creature. Any subsequent attempt to change the coding system would necessarily have made a mockery of all previous messages that were encoded within the DNA, thus resulting in the immediate extermination of any organism which dared to attempt a change. In this manner, all organisms are bound to the past. As they evolve, their past history becomes an increasing burden which progressively restricts their future evolutionary possibilities. As hard as modern man strives to be free he is a slave chained to the past. ('The Development of Sexual Reproduction', p. 22)

But if evolution is so conservative, how, then, can any advance be made towards more complex organisms? It is possible because, principally, *some* changes or mutations are advantageous: they introduce changes which help an organism to sustain itself better for the replication of its DNA. In this sense, the whole road to human life has been a catalogue of errors. Of course, most mutations are harmful (or at best neutral), so that for every mutation which allows a better hold on the exploration of environments and in the competition for energy or food, there will be many that disadvantage an organism to the extent that it dies prematurely. Already we begin to see that there cannot be life of this complex, evolved kind without death. There is a price to be paid within the disadvantageous mutations.

But there is a further and much stronger sense in which death is necessary. Mutations, to be of any use, require a succession of generations. Mutations and diversity are of no advantage to any except the individuals in which they occur unless they can be transmitted and thus spread into a further population. Death is necessary so that one generation can make space for the next, in which such changes as have occurred can be tested. This means that the process from mosses to mushrooms to me (to paraphrase Samuel Wilberforce) absolutely depends on generations succeeding each other, and that requires death.

So we begin to see the price that has to be paid, in terms of death, if there is to be a universe and if there is to be self-replicating, self-conscious life within it. It is in the succession of generations that the slight mutations in the genetic information occur which allow development and change. There can be no development of life without evolution:

> Children, behold the chimpanzee:
> He sits on the ancestral tree
> From which we sprang in ages gone.
> I'm glad we sprang. Had we held on,
> We might, for aught that I can say,
> Be hairy chimpanzees today.

It follows that there could not be a you, and there could not be a universe, without death, the death of stars and the death of succeeding generations of organic life. If you ask, 'Why is death happening to me (or to anyone)?', the answer is: because the universe is happening to you; you are an event, a happening, of the universe; you are a child of the stars, as well as of your parents, and you could not be a child in any other way. Even while you live, and certainly when you die, the atoms and molecules which are at present locked into your shape and appearance, are being unlocked and scattered into other shapes and forms of construction:

> Dearly beloved brethren,
> Is is not a sin
> To peel the potatoes
> And throw away the skin?
> For the skin feeds the pigs
> And the pigs feed us,
> Dearly beloved brethren,
> Is it not thus?

What that means, in relation to death and why it occurs, becomes very clear: it is not possible to arrive at life except via the route of death. That means, in turn, that the price which has to be paid for any organisation of energy in a universe of this kind is very high indeed. It is not possible to acquire new energy out of nowhere from nothing – as it is equally true that it is not possible to lose energy. What is happening is that available energy is constantly being used and reorganised to build whatever there is – planets or plants, suns or sons. But as energy *is* used, so it is increasingly unavailable to do further work.

All this is taking us into the familiar domain of entropy, which provides one of the most powerful contemporary images of disorder and death. It led Rifkin to propose entropy as 'a new world view' (to quote the sub-title of his book, *Entropy*). It is all the more important, therefore, to be clear that although the Second Law of Thermodynamics (which makes use of the concept of entropy when it is stated as an increase towards maximum disorder in an isolated physical or chemical system) is one of the widest generalisations in physical science, it nevertheless has extremely precise and limited applications, which are certainly not at all as Rifkin supposed. It has had one major application beyond the traditional boundary of physical science, in the development of information theory. Otherwise, its application to society or religion could at best be metaphorical, or perhaps analogical, and it would then have to be handled with great care to ensure the propriety of the candidates for explanation. It would surely be wiser to heed the warning of Hiebert (in his survey, 'The Uses and Abuses of Thermodynamics in Religion') when he wrote:

The laws of thermodynamics demonstrate that no matter how good, how secure, or how elegant a scientific theory is, it is never immune to being used in ways that transgress the limits of credulity to the point of sheer ridiculousness – at least in the eyes of subsequent generations. All kinds of private metaphysics and theology have grown like weeds in the garden of thermodynamics. (p. 1075)

But still, it is important, for the contemporary imagination and evaluation of death, to appreciate, even in the most general terms, what thermodynamics and entropy are affirming. To arrive at a universe of this kind, there have to be what are known as irreversible processes, at least in local regions of the universe. These are such processes as chemical reactions, heat conduction and diffusion. The general flow of available energy in a local region is in the direction of increasing disorder and randomness – that is to say, in the direction of increasing unavailability for further organisation and work. That is what is known as entropy. Entropy is the measure of increasing disorder in an isolated system pointing to a final condition of thermodynamic equilibrium, where particles are still energetic, but no longer able to interact.

But at present, we are in a condition of thermodynamic disequilibrium, in which energy is available to do work. The use of energy in open systems far from equilibrium to build such things as your body or the materials of the house in which you live, is known as negentropy: it is the negation of disorder; it is the use of available energy in the meantime to build order and organisation, even though the overall direction is towards equilibrium – to something like the circumstance described in Genesis as *tohu wabohu*, 'waste and void'; or the non-circumstance known in Buddhism as *nirvana*, where energetic particles (so to speak) *are* but do not any longer interact.

In the end, none of us can escape the claims of entropy, as we know in the aging of our tissues and our body.

> Time doth transfix the flourish set on youth
> And delves the parallels in beauty's brow,
> Feeds on the rarities of nature's truth,
> And nothing stands but for his scythe to mow.
>   (Shakespeare, Sonnet LX)

Courageous Feeble may have owed God a death. We owe a death to entropy. Yet without entropy it would not be possible to have life at all. It would not even be possible to have a universe.

But the two, entropy and negentropy, are, in fact, intimately connected; and it is death, as the necessary condition of both the universe and life, which makes the connection. Conversely, it is because the universe is so precisely tuned to produce life, *but only through the process of death*, that death receives from life the highest possible tribute and value. The earliest religious explorations of death recognised this (in their own way and on their own terms) extremely well. Yet in popular accounts of how death produced religion, exactly the opposite is assumed, as in the accounts summarised or alluded to in chapter 1; or in the even more dubious assertion about the reason for the survival of religion in Cupitt's *The Sea of Faith*:

Religion survives, surely, because the progressive weakening of religious institutions and religious thought does not alter the fact that at the deepest level religious needs and impulses are as great as ever ... We are still prompted to religious dread and longing by the thought of our own death, our own littleness, and the precariousness of human values in the face of Nature's vast indifference. What immense epochs there were before us and will be after us, of which we know nothing and that know nothing of us! (p. 32)

In fact, far from the universe being prodigal or wasteful in its vast immensities of space and time, and in its constant succession of disorder, cessation and death, the universe walks (so to speak) on an extremely narrow tightrope of possibility. That narrow band of possibility is exactly what is required to produce self-directing, self-conscious, organic life. All this is extremely well known and well rehearsed. Bernard Lovell gave many examples in his book, *In The Centre of Immensities*: if the proton–proton interaction had been a few per cent stronger, then 'no galaxies, no stars, no life would have emerged', because the protons, which were the available energy for the building of heavier atoms, would have formed into helium in the first few million years of the universe and would have stayed there; a 1 per cent change in the balance between negative and positive electricity would blow, not your mind, but your head (supposing you could have one), straight out of the solar system; or again, 'if, at that moment [when the universe was one second from the beginning of the expansion] the rate of expansion had been reduced by only one part in a thousand billion, then the Universe would have collapsed after a few million years, near the end of the epoch we now recognise as the radiation era, or the primordial fireball, before the matter and radiation had become decoupled' (pp. 122f.).

A few million years may seem a long time, but it is not long enough to arrive at conscious life, or indeed to arrive at life at all. To fuse the necessary heavier elements requires what the physicist J. A. Wheeler once called 'a cooking time' of several billion years in the nuclear furnace in the interior of a star.

That phrase, 'a cooking time', occurs in his Copernican lecture, in which he asked, Why *does* the universe have to be so immense? The answer is, because, when the time-scale of the universe is calculated from the general theory of relativity, it turns out to be dependently related to the mass. If you try to economise on the size and scale of the universe, you end up with a time-scale too short to produce conscious life. (Supposing, for example, you imagine a Big Bang producing the mass for a galaxy of 10^{11} stars, which in itself would be a large universe, that universe could only last, in our terms, for a single year.) Without the apparent extravagance and indifference of space and time, there would be (as Wheeler put it) 'no opportunity to form new stars, let alone heavy elements, planets and life. The cut-down investment in original matter, far from giving a better return, gives no return at all. From this point of view, any purported extravagance in our universe is far from obvious.'

Wheeler then pressed the argument further and developed what is known as the anthropic principle. But even without that extension (which remains, to say the least, controversial), the basic observations on which it rests are not controversial: they point to the extreme precision that is necessary to produce life, and also to the absolute necessity for death, if there is to be life. Both the scientific and the religious imaginations coinhere at this point, in two ways: first, in rejecting the view that we are trivial and of little worth because the universe is so immense and because its process includes randomness and chance (both observations about the universe are true, but do not lead to the conclusion); and second, in affirming the high value of death as the necessary condition of life. Both, in their different languages, are saying the same thing: it is not possible to have life on any other terms than those of death; but where you *do* have death, there immediately you have the possibility of life.

Death is thus opportunity as well as end. My death, and every death, is necessary if there is to be life at all. Death as sacrifice is far removed from quests for compensation. It is making sacred and recognising the value that lies within the fact of death. But can the virtue and value of death as sacrifice still be affirmed without the brutally dramatic and enacted language through which it used to be expressed? The savage practices of sacrifice, which horrified Frazer, are by no means confined to the past: the sadistic nightmares of William Burroughs, in which boys are successively sodomised and slain, are almost always set in ritual contexts – the Aztec priests in *The Naked Lunch*, the Mayans and the Pyramids in *The Wild Boys*, the Druid and the boy sacrifice in the Sacred Grove of *The Soft Machine*, 'young cruelty and foe child': 'In the city a group of them came to this last bone meal under the hanging tree.'

But here again we are, painfully, in the domain of approximate and corrigible languages. We can reject the way in which a particular language or action attempts to express an important truth or insight, without rejecting the truth which it was attempting to express. No doubt sacrifice also expresses the propensity of human beings for violent cruelty, of which sacrifice is only one example in the long 'martyrdom of man'. But the truth which it defended is that death is necessary, and that it is, paradoxically, constructive. Death is not (in this perspective) a case of life yielding *to* life: it is also a case of life yielding *for* life, life giving way so that other, more complex, life can come into being. The profound intuition, in the human recognition of sacrifice as the key to the meaning of death, is that we cannot have life on any other terms than these: we cannot have life without death, whether it be the death of a star, or of a field-mouse in the talons of a hawk, or of a child before its time. On this, both the religious and the scientific imaginations agree, that we owe both God and entropy a death, if there is to be any life at all. *Of course* that does not make such dying easy, either to experience or to watch. It remains true that the occasions of death are all too often the opportunities of immense evil, and that religious and secular vigilance is deeply necessary if death is not to become an instrument of those who are living beyond morality. But still the fact also remains that we cannot live at all except on the basis of what Charles Williams so penetratingly called, 'the way of exchange', of life yielding to life and for life. For it is that which yields the insight of both religion and science, which in turn gives value to death, that you cannot have life without death: but where you *do* have death, there you have the possibility of life.

So it comes about that every major stage of evolution takes the process of energy over a new threshold of possibility. Pebbles rest, but fish swim; fish swim, but ants crawl; ants crawl, but birds fly; birds fly in an atmosphere, but humans fly in space as well – and rest, and swim, and crawl; and they also understand a little of what they do, and of how they do it.

The religious belief is that the long process of evolution, requiring the good services of death, has brought the organisation of energy in the human case over a new threshold. Just as the emergence of life took the organisation of energy over a new threshold of possibility, so the human architecture of atoms and molecules (organised in such a way that they sustain through body and brain the self which is related to them, but is not identical with them) creates the possibility of a relation with God which will not be destroyed by the death of this particular body.

We already begin to see this, and to experience it, in the way we continue through time, constituted as much (though in a profoundly different sense) by our relationships as by our breakfasts, even while the component parts of our bodies die at every moment. As Richard Baxter was once described, we too are museums of morbid anatomy: 'He was a perpetual invalid: defying the skill of six and thirty doctors, and reducing his attenuated frame to little better than a museum of morbid anatomy, the first wonder is, that amidst the premature old age which they induced, he survived for half-a-century.' What, then, persists through the process of dissolution and living death? For those who, like Buddhists, see us as temporal stages, and who regard John Smith as some man, but who hold that there is no man who he always is, memory is a strong candidate for the self-perceived persistence of identity. Thus Loren Eiseley reflected in *The Immense Journey*:

I suppose that in the forty-five years of my existence every atom, every molecule that composes me has changed its position or danced away and beyond to become part of other things. New molecules have come from the grass and the bodies of animals to be part of me a little while, yet in this spinning, light and airy as a midge swarm in a shaft of sunlight, my memories hold, and a loved face of twenty years ago is before me still. Nor is that face, nor all my years caught cellularly as in some cold precise photographic pattern, some gross mechanical reproduction of the past. My memory holds the past and yet para-doxically knows, at the same time, that the past is gone and will never come again.

Memory is indeed a strong candidate for identity, not in any bleak or abstract sense, but as characterised through experience and time. Stacy Waddy (a missionary and eventually Secretary of the Society for the Propagation of the Gospel) looked back on himself as a schoolboy in exactly that way:

I was a separate self. I remember him: I am the result of him, not altogether him still. There are things he then was that I am 'dead' to. I am interested in him – remember him – hope I have risen above him – don't think I have lost any of his essentials; hope I have shed some of his weaknesses. How interesting!

But while memory may often hold the door (as John Buchan entitled his autobiography), it is not in fact a sufficient, or even a necessary, condition for the human sense of being one's self. You can lose your memory, just as you can lose a leg or weight or your hair or even your reason, and still have the sense of it being your self to whom this has happened. Thus Oliver Sacks, in his book *Awakenings*, reviewed the experience of victims of *encaphalitis lethargica* (sleeping sickness), who had been in a condition of 'zombie-like passivity' for as long as fifty years until they were awakened by the drug laevo-dihydroxyphenylalanine (L-DOPA). On the way in which the awakening was clearly happening to a *person*, and not simply to the dormant machinery in the head, Sacks commented:

It is the function of medication, or surgery, or appropriate physiological procedures, to rectify mechanism – the mechanism, mechanisms, which are so deranged in these patients. It is the function of scientific medicine to rectify the 'It'. It is the function of art, of living contact, of existential medicine, to call upon the latent will, the agent, the 'I', to call out its commanding and coordinating powers, so that it may regain its hegemony and rule once again – for the final rule, the ruler, is not a measuring rod or clock, but the rule and measure of the personal 'I'. These two forms of medicine must be joined, must co-inhere, as body and soul. (p. 251)

That conclusion was reinforced in a later book, *The Man Who Mistook his Wife for a Hat*, which described even more bizarre and tragic malfunctions of the brain in its relation to the world, or to a person's own life and experience, including drastic loss or absence of memory. But still the sense remains of it being one's self to whom this has happened – or, more commonly, of it being one's self in this circumstance:

The patient's essential being is very relevant in the higher reaches of neurology, and in psychology, for here the patient's personhood is essentially involved, and the study of disease and of identity cannot be disjoined. Such disorders, and their depiction and study, indeed entail a new discipline, which we may call the 'neurology of identity', for it deals with the neural foundations of the self, the age-old problem of mind and brain ... Such disorders may be of many kinds – and may arise from excesses, no less than impairments, of function ... But it must be said from the outset that a disease is never a mere loss or excess – that there is always a reaction, on the part of the affected organism or individual, to restore, to replace, to compensate for and to preserve its identity, however strange the means may be. (pp. x,4)

It remains, of course, a matter of dispute what inferences about the nature of the self one is entitled (or required by the evidence) to draw. What at least seems clear is that a crude dualism (of a ghost inhabiting a machine) is clearly false, but so too is a crude materialism (which says that we are our bodies and that 'mind'

is simply a word for particular brain states). In *some* sense, there
is a relation of mind to brain which enables a *person* to be the agent
of its own activity and the subject of its own experience. This is
true, even through the process of death, insofar as the experiences
of those who have been pronounced clinically dead and have then
been resuscitated, give us an indication (for an introductory
bibliography, see Zaleski, *Otherworld Journeys*). Of course, much
stronger claims have been made on the basis of those experiences,
to the effect that 'life after death' has now been demonstrated:
You Cannot Die, to quote the title of one such book, by Ian Currie,
begins:

Few people are aware that death, man's most ancient, mysterious and
relentless adversary, has been studied systematically over the past
century by research scientists working in a variety of fields. Even fewer
are aware that the harvest of this effort has been a host of fascinating
discoveries which lead to four inescapable conclusions: Human beings
do survive physical death; they continue to exist after death at varying
levels of awareness and creativity, in a realm that normal human beings
cannot normally perceive; this realm is periodically left when the
individual takes on a new body, at which time all memory of it, and
of former lives is erased; successive re-embodiments do not occur at
random, but appear to be linked by a mysterious and fascinating law
of causation. These conclusions are stupendous. Their implications are
awesome. And they are solidly based on scientific research. (p.8)

It hardly needs to be said that they are not. They frequently
rely on anecdotes which are open to more sceptical analysis. In
that respect, it is instructive to compare the way in which Ian
Wilson (*The After-Death Experience*) handles exactly the same
'evidence' (see especially chs. 3 and 4). What a more sober
estimate of near-death experience makes clear is that dying can
be one of the good human experiences (this is very extensively
reported), and that in relation to the body and its death, the self
is clearly (i.e., experiences itself as) independent of its body; or,
if that seems too strong a statement, that at least the experience
of being thus independent is so unequivocal and real that no other
language is adequate to describe it.

It is *partly* on this basis (though there have been many other
reasons as well) that religions, including Buddhism, have come to

maintain that there is a persistent identity. All, except Buddhism, have come to believe that this requires and points to a subsistent self which endures the continuing change and eventual death of this body, and for which, therefore, there is no strong reason to suppose that the death of its body entails its own extinction. In Blake's brief statement of the point:

Distinguish therefore States from Individuals in those States.
States Change, but Individual Identities never change nor cease.
You cannot go to Eternal Death in that which can never Die.
(*Complete Writings*, p. 521)

The different religions have then expressed that belief in many different ways, some of which are clearly too literally descriptive of the soul and its destiny to be credible as such. But all our languages are approximate, corrigible and frequently wrong. Yet in this case, as in so many others, it may be that they are approximately wrong about what is nevertheless truly the case. I doubt if it is possible to proceed descriptively much beyond the affirmation of a poet like Andrew Young, whose poem, 'Passing the Graveyard', expresses much more than the conclusion of an argument about mind/body dualism:

> I see you did not try to save
> The bouquet of white flowers I gave;
> So fast they wither on your grave.
>
> Why does it hurt the heart to think
> Of that most bitter abrupt brink
> Where the low-shouldered coffins sink?
>
> These living bodies that we wear
> So change by every seventh year
> That in a new dress we appear;
>
> Limbs, spongy brain and slogging heart,
> No part remains the selfsame part;
> Like streams they stay and still depart.
>
> You slipped slow bodies in the past;
> Then why should we be so aghast
> You flung off the whole flesh at last?
>
> Let him who loves you think instead
> That like a woman who has wed
> You undressed first and went to bed.

It is that basic sense of transformation *and its cost* which led to the religious exploration of the meaning of death through the concept and practice of sacrifice. The virtue of death as the necessary condition of life is recognised equally in the scientific imagination of the process and possibility of a universe of this kind, and of human life within it. Together, both science and religion affirm the high value of death, and it is this which they can take (together) to the dying and to the bereaved – at least as a domain (or background) assumption, informing our attitude, and transforming the way in which we relate to the dying and the bereaved. It certainly does *not* mean that we can impose this perception of death on any in those circumstances, as though it solves their problems or answers their questions. It is wise to bear in mind the protest of Philip Toynbee against what he called 'a much-praised little book', *The Lord of the Dance*, from which he quoted this passage:

Almighty God, Son of God, Lord of the Dance, is thus the principal dancer, and He is at one and the same time perfectly still and perpetually in motion; He abides at the centre of the Dance and is, at the same time, active in every part of it ... The whole creation dances in eternal Joy, and the Ecstasy of Love moves from climax to climax according to the Rhythm of the Dance; and thus it is that this Rhythm finds expression in the cycle of birth, growth, decline and death; and from this death, rebirth again ...

On this, Toynbee commented:

Alas, such rhapsodies are meaningless to me: worse than meaningless – self-indulgent falsifications. For it is not *true* that the whole creation dances in eternal joy: ask the mouse as the owl's talons clutch it; ask the child dying alone after the earthquake; ask my father at any time during the last fourteen months of his life.

There is such a thing, of course, as poetic truth: a truth which deepens and enlivens the literal facts. But if a high flight of words directly contradicts the truths we tell each other in sober prose then it's no sort of truth at all but a dangerous and foolish fancy.

We cannot impose – God forbid – the concept or the fact of sacrifice on others in the moment of their crisis. Still less should we suppose that the truth about death and its necessity can be produced as an argument to make the occasions of death benign.

Death kills. And grief knows it. Even so, it is the stature and miracle of our humanity, in every age and every culture, that we can acquire this sense and this practice of sacrifice for ourselves: we can make it particular and explicit in our own case, by making of our lives a living sacrifice, a positive acceptance and affirmation on behalf of others that there are no other terms on which we can have life and live; and that we must grasp death with gratitude, because without it we cannot grasp anything. 'For greater love hath no one than this, that he lay down his life for his friends.' That is the condition in which we all live or exist, from the furthest signal on the event-horizon of the universe, to the nearest loved one who succumbs to entropy and death. It is a human privilege, just as surely as it is a human suffering, to acquire consciously the necessary condition of death, and to affirm it as sacrifice, as the means through which life is enabled and secured. That, consummately, is what Jesus did on the cross. But it is what countless others have also done through the long centuries of human history.

But still the questions remain, to what end? To what purpose? Why? Is not this sacrifice (this interlocking way of exchange), which unites us with each other and indeed with the whole universe, as pointless as any other sacrifice? Is it not as useless as the blood of goats and bulls against which the Jewish prophets fulminated long ago? 'Will I eat the flesh of bulls or drink the blood of goats?' (Ps. l.13); '"What are your endless sacrifices to me?" says the Lord. "I am sick of burnt offerings of rams and the fat of calves; I take no pleasure in the blood of bulls and lambs and goats"' (Is.i.11). To what purpose, then, this universal sacrifice?

But here, once again, we have to remind ourselves quietly of what we have already seen: the immediate end or consequence is a universe, including our life within it. It is the negentropic organisation of energy which, in the human case, has created us as a kind of castle built by children on the shore to resist the irreversible tide. It is a sand-castle, to be sure: in the end the tide will prevail, and the outward forms of all this, and of all we see, and of all we love, will be carried into a different shape and outcome, far beyond our competence. The sand will be smooth once more.

Yes. But while we *are* here, we know that our resistance to the tide of entropy establishes within us such miracles of relationship and grace and love, that we know already that the fact of death is transcended, at least in a preliminary way. In the formation and transformation of character through time, and in the cognised and appreciated relationships in which we live with each other, we are already at levels of experience which reach through particular death, and which are far beyond those of the stones or the trees or the lilies in all their glory. For some, that is enough; there is no further to go, nor need to do so. But what if we are organised and constructed in such a way that we are capable of entering into relationships of love (and of hate), of acceptance (and of rejection), not only with each other, but also with that responsive and interactive Other, to whom we refer as God? Petru Dumitriu wrote in his novel, *Incognito* (itself wrought out of suffering and death):

A miracle is an everyday event which brings us into direct contact with the meaning of the world, and of God. If we are conscious of the divine nature of every happening and of every fact, then everything is miraculous. But it is so easy to forget. Consciousness flags in its perception of the divinity of the world, and we disregard the miraculous by taking it for granted. For those who worship God, every event is a sign, and there are some signs that cannot be ignored. (p. 445)

That way of living and of being is a true possibility for us all. The different religions, for all the folly, wickedness, sin, malevolence and evil which their histories and present behaviours exhibit, could not have had the long and winnowed histories which they have had (producing a corresponding list of virtues in many lives) unless that were so; nor could the deeply serious reflections on death and the self, which this book describes, have taken place as they have. The religious issue of transcendence is whether this human architecture of energy, the human body which unquestionably owes entropy a death, is the negentropic base from which we climb higher into love – from which, that is, we enter into yet other levels of connection and possibility, in those networks of relationship and love, which are known in Christianity as the communion of saints, and the Triune Life of God: that life which is love, which is connection, which is relation in itself, is understood in Christianity as extending the society of its own being in creation, in redemption and in the making holy of life, so that we who owe God a death are nevertheless enabled to enter into the joy of our Lord.

All that, and the fact that it may be so, is the further end and purpose of sacrifice in this sense, affirming the worth and value of the entire universe which cannot *be* on any other terms than those of death; and affirming that death is the necessary condition of new thresholds and new opportunities of life. That is why we must love the universe as though it is the only thing we have, and yet forsake it, because here we have no abiding city – because 'he is not here: why seek ye the living among the dead?' (Lk. xxiv.5). For Christians, the death and resurrection of Jesus are the singularity (the event and fact) which initiates the new environment, attained through death, in which we are able, now and already, to begin to live. But the crucifixion is a deep statement, enacted in truth, that there cannot be this new life, in a universe like this, without death; and that God, in drawing us freely to himself, has accepted the necessity of death into himself, into his body on a tree. The cross exhibits the cost if there is to be 'newness of life':

> That downbent head raised earth above the stars
> O timeless wonder! Life, because One died.
>
> (Alcuin)

But the resurrection is an equal declaration, enacted in truth, that there is not death without the consequence of life. All the evidence of the universe points in that direction: you cannot have life without death; but where you do have death, there you can have life. In the context of a universe of this kind, the resurrection is not particularly surprising. And this life, this risen life, has clearly led the way to a new limit of possibility. That is why Paul could write with such vigour, 'If our hope in Christ has been for this life only, we are of all people the most pitiable' (1 Cor. xv.19). Then indeed we would be an outcast, as Blake put it, left to the trampling foot and spurning heel:

> I am an outcast –
> I am left to the trampling foot and the spurning heel.
> But I, thy Magdalen, behold thy Spiritual Risen Body.
> Jesus replied, 'I am the Resurrection and the Life.
> I die and pass the limits of possibility as it appears
> To individual perception ...
> Come now with me into the villages, walk thro' all the
>   cities,
> Tho' thou art taken to prison and judgement, starved in the
>   street
> I will command the cloud to give thee food, and the hard
>   rock
> To flow with milk and wine; tho' thou seest me not a season,
> Even a long season ...
> Only believe and trust in me. Lo, I am always with thee!'

We must, therefore, love the universe because it is in us and we in it. But we must love God also, on the base of our mortal body, that we may be in him, and he in us:

> First to be made is a star
>   next to be made is a child.
> First to be made is a flower
>   next to be made is a child.
> First to be made is a dragonfly
>   next to be made is a child.

God made me first like a fragment of star and gave me life, then he designed me like a flower and gave me shape, then he infused awareness into me and made me love.

I believe in the evolution of God's creativity, and I delight in thinking how God takes materials from the rocks to make my body, and designs from the flowers to build up my nerve cells.

But when I think about my awareness, I seek the model in him, in his tri-une life; and he made me in his own image and likeness: communication, freedom, eternal life. (Carretto, *Summoned by Love*, p. 22)

Blessed be you harsh matter, barren soil, stubborn rock: you who yield only to violence, you who force us to work if we would eat.

Blessed be you, perilous matter, violent sea, untameable passion, you who unless we fetter you will devour us ...

Blessed be you, mortal matter, you who will one day undergo the process of dissolution within us and will thereby take us forcibly into the very heart of that which exists ...

You who batter us and then dress our wounds, you who resist us and yield to us, you who wreck and build, you who shackle and liberate, the sap of our souls, the hand of God, the flesh of Christ; it is you, matter, that I bless. (de Chardin, *Hymn of the Universe*, pp. 68f.)

As it is written, For your sake we are killed all the day long; we are accounted as sheep for the slaughter. Yet in all these things we are more than conquerors, through him that loved us. For I am persuaded that neither death, nor life, nor angels, nor principalities, nor powers, nor things present, nor things to come, nor height, nor depth, nor any other creature, shall be able to separate us from the love of God, which is in Christ Jesus our Lord. (Rom. ix.36–9)

Bibliography

alQadi, A. R. b. A., *The Islamic Book of the Dead*, Wood Dalling, Diwan Press, 1977

Anguttara Nikaya: see Woodward

asSufi, A.Q., 'Death, the Beginning of a Journey', in alQadi

Aulén, G., *Christus Victor*, London, SPCK, 1970

Aung, S. Z., *Compendium of Philosophy*, London, Luzac, 1967

Austin, C. R. and Short, R. V., *The Evolution of Reproduction*, Cambridge University Press, 1976

The Authorised Daily Prayer Book, London, Eyre and Spottiswoode, 1957

Barkova, L. L., ed., *Frozen Tombs: The Culture and Art of the Ancient Tribes of Siberia*, London, British Museum, 1978

Beauvoir, S. de, *A Very Easy Death*, London, Weidenfeld, 1966

Beckett, S., *Waiting for Godot*, London, Faber and Faber, 1959

Bendann, E., *Death Customs: An Analytical Study of Burial Rites*, New York, Knopf, 1930

Beyer, S., *The Cult of Tara: Magic and Ritual in Tibet*, Berkeley, University of California Press, 1978

Blake, W., *Complete Writings*, Oxford University Press, 1972

Bloch, M. and Parry, J., eds., *Death and the Regeneration of Life*, Cambridge University Press, 1982

Bowker, J. W., *Problems of Suffering in Religions of the World*, Cambridge University Press, 1970

  Jesus and the Pharisees, Cambridge University Press, 1973

  The Sense of God: Sociological, Anthropological and Psychological Approaches to the Origin of the Sense of God, Oxford University Press, 1973

  The Religious Imagination and the Sense of God, Oxford University Press, 1978

  Worlds of Faith: Religious Belief and Practice in Britain Today, London, Ariel, 1983

  Licensed Insanities: Religions and Belief in God in the Contemporary World, London, DLT, 1987

Brown, J. A., ed., *Approaches to the Social Dimensions of Mortuary Practice*, Memoirs of the Society for American Archeology, 25, 1971

Buddhaghosa, *Visuddimagga*: see Pe Maung Tin; Nyanamoli

Burnaby, J., *Christian Words and Christian Meanings*, London, Hodder and Stoughton, 1957

Burnett, M., *The Endurance of Life: The Implications of Genetics for Human Life*, Cambridge University Press, 1978

Carmichael, C. M., 'On Separating Life and Death: An Explanation of Some Biblical Laws', *Harvard Theological Review*, 29, 1976

Carretto, C., *Summoned by Love*, London, DLT, 1977

Chapman, R., Kinnes, I. and Randsborg, K., eds., *The Archaeology of Death*, Cambridge University Press, 1981

Chardin, T. de, *Hymn of the Universe*, London, Collins, 1965

Conrad, J., *The Heart of Darkness*, New York, W. W. Norton, 1963

Conze, E., *Thirty Years of Buddhist Studies*, Oxford, Cassirer, 1967

Corpus Inscriptionum Iudaicarum, ed. J. B. Frey, Rome, Library of Biblical Studies, 1975

Cupitt, D., *The Sea of Faith: Christianity in Change*, London, BBC, 1984

Currie, I., *You Cannot Die*, London, Hamlyn, 1978

Daly, R. J., *The Origins of the Christian Doctrine of Sacrifice*, London, DLT, 1978

Daniélou, A., *Hindu Polytheism*, London, Routledge and Kegan Paul, 1964

Dietrich, B. C., *Death, Fate and the Gods: The Development of a Religious Idea in Greek Popular Belief and in Homer*, London, University of London Classical Studies, 3, 1965

Digha Nikaya: see T. W. Rhys-Davids and C. A. F. Rhys-Davids

Dresner, S. H. and Siegel, S., *The Jewish Dietary Laws*, New York, Burning Bush, 1959

Dumitriu, P., *Incognito*, London, Collins, 1964

von Durckheim-Montmartin, K. G., *Hara, the Vital Centre*, London, Allen and Unwin, 1962

Eck, D., *Banaras, City of Light*, London, Routledge and Kegan Paul, 1984

Eigen, M. and Schuster, P., *The Hypercycle: A Principle of Natural Self-Organization*, Berlin, Springer-Verlag, 1979

Eiseley, L., *The Immense Journey*, New York, Random House, 1957

Eliach, Y., *Hasidic Tales of the Holocaust*, New York, Avon, 1983

Eliot, T. S., *Collected Poems, 1909–1935*, London, Faber and Faber, 1951

Ettinger, R. C. W., *The Prospect of Immortality*, London, Scientific Book Club, 1965

Evans-Wentz, W. Y., *The Tibetan Book of the Dead*, New York, Galaxy, 1960

Flecker, J. E., *The Golden Journey to Samarkand*, London, 1913

Frazer, J. G., *Magic and Religion*, London, Watts, 1944

Fremantle, F. and Chogyam Trungpa, *The Tibetan Book of the Dead: The Great Liberation Through Hearing in the Bardo*, Berkeley, Shambhala, 1975

Freud, S., 'Our Attitude Towards Death', *Collected Works*, XIV, London, Hogarth, 1964

  Beyond the Pleasure Principle, *Collected Works*, XVIII

  The Ego and the Id, *Collected Works*, XIX

  The Future of an Illusion, London, 1962

Gennep, A. van, *The Rites of Passage*, Chicago University Press, 1960

Giedion, S., *The Eternal Present: The Beginnings of Architecture*, Oxford University Press, 1964

Goff, J. le, *The Birth of Purgatory*, London, Scolar, 1984

Gonda, J., *Vedic Ritual: The Non-Solemn Rites*, Leiden, Brill, 1980

Goulart, P., *Forgotten Kingdom*, London, Readers Union, 1957

Govinda, A., *The Psychological Attitude of Early Buddhist Philosophy*, London, Rider, 1961

Granqvist, H., *Muslim Death and Burial: Arab Customs and Traditions Studied in a Village in Jordan*, Helsinki, 1965

Griffiths, P. J., *On Being Mindless: Buddhist Meditation and the Mind-Body Problem*, La Salle, Open Court, 1987

Harmer, R. M., *The High Cost of Dying*, New York, Collier, 1963

Harris, M., *Raised Immortal: Resurrection and Immortality in the New Testament*, London, Marshall, Morgan and Scott, 1983

Hengel, M., *The Atonement: The Origins of the Doctrine in the New Testament*, London, SCM, 1981

Hertz, R., 'Contribution à une Etude sur la Representation collective de la Mort', *Année Sociologique*, 10, 1907

Hiebert, E. N., 'The Uses and Abuses of Thermodynamics', *Daedalus*, 95, 1966

Hisamatsu, S., *The Vocabulary of Japanese Aesthetics*, Tokyo, Center for E. Asian Cultural Studies, 1963

Hoagland, H., 'Some Biochemical Considerations of Time', in J. T. Fraser, ed., *The Voices of Time*, London, Allen Lane, 1968

Hodges, H. A., *The Pattern of Atonement*, London, SCM, 1955

Holck, F. H., ed., *Death and Eastern Thought*, Nashville, Abingdon, 1974

Horner, I. B., *The Collection of the Middle Length Sayings*, London, Pali Text Society, 1954–9

  Milinda's Questions, London, Pali Text Society, 1963–4

ed. *Vimanavatthu* and *Petavatthu*, in *The Minor Anthologies of the Pali Canon*, IV, London, Pali Text Society, 1974

Hume, B., *To Be a Pilgrim*, London, SPCK, 1984

Humphreys, S.C. and King, H., eds., *Mortality and Immortality: The Anthropology and the Archaeology of Death*, London, Academic Press, 1981

Huntington, R. and Metcalf, P., *Celebrations of Death: The Anthropology of Mortuary Ritual*, Cambridge University Press, 1979

Ishaq, M.b., *The Life of Muhammad*, trans. A. Guillaume, Karachi, Oxford University Press, 1967

Islam, K.M., *The Spectacle of Death, Including Glimpses of Life Beyond the Grave*, Lahore, 1976

Johansson, R., *The Psychology of Nirvana*, London, Allen and Unwin, 1963

Johnston, W., *The Inner Eye of Love*, London, Collins, 1978

Juynboll, G.H.A., *Muslim Tradition: Studies in Chronology, Provenance and Authorship of Early Hadith*, Cambridge University Press, 1983

Kardoff, U. von, *Berliner Aufzeichnungen*, 1942–1945, Munich, 1962

Khrushchev, N.S., *Communism – Peace and Happiness for the Peoples*, I, Moscow, Foreign Languages Publishing House, 1963

Knipe, D.M., 'Sapindikarana: The Hindu Rite of Entry into Heaven', in Reynolds and Waugh

Kurtz, D.C. and Boardman, J., *Greek Burial Customs*, London, Thames and Hudson, 1971

Lauf, D.I., *Secret Doctrines of the Tibetan Books of the Dead*, Boulder, Shambhala, 1975

Lee, J.Y., *Death and Beyond in the Eastern Perspective: A Study Based on the Bardo Thodol and the I Ching*, New York, Gordon and Breach, 1975

Leeuwen, A. van, *Critique of Heaven*, London, Lutterworth, 1972

Lévy-Bruhl, L., *Primitive Mentality*, London, 1923

Lifton, R.J. *et al.*, *Six Lives, Six Deaths: Portraits from Modern Japan*, New Haven, Yale University Press, 1979

Long, J.B., 'Death as a Necessity and a Gift in Hindu Mythology', in Reynolds and Waugh

Lovell, B., *In the Centre of Immensities*, London, Granada, 1980

Maimonides, M., *The Guide for the Perplexed*, London, 1904

Majjhima Nikaya: see Horner, 1954

Malinowski, B.K.: see Needham

Marx, K., 'Contributions to the Critique of Hegel's Philosophy of Right', in Marx and Engels, *On Religion*, Moscow, n.d.

Milindapanha: see Horner, 1963

Mitford, J., *The American Way of Death*, New York, Simon and Schuster, 1963

Miura, D., *The Forgotten Child*, Henley, Ellis, 1983

Narahari, H.G., *Atman in pre-Upanishadic Vedic Literature*, Madras, Adyar Library Series 47, 1944

Needham, J., ed., *Science, Religion and Reality*, London, Sheldon, 1925

Nicolas, A.T. de, *Meditations Through the Rg Veda: Four Dimensional Man*, Boulder, Shambhala, 1978

Nyanamoli, *The Path of Purification*, London, Shambhala, 1956, 1964

O'Flaherty, W.D., *The Origins of Evil in Hindu Mythology*, Berkeley, University of California Press, 1976

 ed., *Karma and Rebirth in Classical Indian Traditions* Berkeley, University of California Press, 1980

 Siva: The Erotic Ascetic, Oxford University Press, 1981

Ohno, S., 'The Development of Sexual Reproduction', in Austin and Short

Organ, T.W., *The Self in Indian Philosophy*, The Hague, Mouton, 1964

Parry, J., 'Sacrificial Death and the Necrophagous Ascetic', in Bloch and Parry

Pe Maung Tin, *The Path of Purity*, London, Pali Text Society, 1923–31

Premack, D., 'Language and Intelligence in Ape and Man', *American Scientist*, 64

Quasem, M.A., *Salvation of the Soul and Islamic Devotions*, London, Routledge and Kegan Paul, 1983

Rabinowicz, H., *A Guide to Life: Jewish Laws and Customs of Mourning*, London, Jewish Chronicle Pub., 1982

Radhakrishnan, S., *The Principal Upanishads*, London, Allen and Unwin, 1968

Reade, W., *The Martyrdom of Man*, London, Pemberton, 1968

Reynolds, E. and Waugh, F.E., *Religious Encounters with Death: Insights from the History and Anthropology of Death*, Pennsylvania State University Press, 1977

Rhys-Davids, T.W. and Rhys-Davids, C.A.F., *Dialogues of the Buddha*, London, Pali Text Society, 1890–1911

Rhys-Davids, C.A.F., and Woodward, F.L., *The Book of Kindred Sayings*, London, Pali Text Society, 1917–30

Rodhe, S., *Deliver Us From Evil: Studies on the Vedic Ideas of Salvation*, Lund, C.W.K. Gleerup, 1946

Rosenblatt, P.C., *et al.*, *Grief and Mourning in Cross-Cultural Perspective*, New York, HRAF Press, 1976

Russell, B., *The Autobiography of Bertrand Russell*, London, Allen and Unwin, 1975

Sacks, O., *Awakenings*, London, Picador, 1982

 The Man Who Mistook his Wife for a Hat, London, Picador, 1985

Samyutta Nikaya: see Rhys-Davids and Woodward

Scholem, G. G., *Kabbalah*, New York (Library of Jewish Knowledge), 1974

Schur, M., *Freud: Living and Dying*, London, IPL, 1972

Shinn, L. D., 'Death and the Puranas', in Holck

Spiro, M. E., *Buddhism and Society*, London, Allen and Unwin, 1971

Suzuki, D., *Zen and Japanese Culture*, London, Routledge

Sykes, C. H., *Troubled Loyalty*, London, Collins, 1968

Toynbee, P., *Part of a Journey*, London, Collins, 1982

Turner, V., *The Forest of Symbols*, New York, Cornell, 1967
  The Ritual Process, Chicago, Aldine, 1969

Ucko, P. J., 'Ethnography and the Archaeological Interpretation of Funerary Remains', *World Archeology*, 1, 1969

Vaihinger, H., *Die Philosophie des Als-Ob*, Berlin, 1914

Wang Ch'ung, *Lun Heng*, trans. A. Forke, New York, 1962

Ward, W., *A View of the History, Literature and Mythology of the Hindoos*, London, 1817–20

Waugh, E., *The Loved One*, New York, Dell, 1948

Weininger, O., *Geschlecht und Charakter: eine prinzipielle Untersuchung*, Vienna, 1903

Weiss, P., *The Persecution and Assassination of Marat*, London, Calder, 1978

Welch, H., *The Practice of Chinese Buddhism, 1890–1950*, Harvard University Press, 1973

What the Cross Means to Me: A Theological Symposium, London, Clarke, 1943

Wilson, I., *The After-Death Experience*, London, Sidgwick and Jackson, 1987

Woodward, F. L. and Hare, R. M., *The Book of Gradual Sayings*, London, Pali Text Society, 1951–5

World Council of Churches, *Baptism, Eucharist and Ministry*, Geneva, 1982

Wright, C. J., in *What the Cross Means to Me*

Young, J. Z., *An Introduction to the Study of Man*, Oxford University Press, 1971

Yü Ying-shih, 'Life and Immortality in the Mind of Han China', *Harvard Journal of Asiatic Studies*, 25, 1964

Zaehner, R. C., *The Bhagavad-Gita*, Oxford University Press, 1969

Zaleski, C., *Otherworld Journeys: Accounts of Near-Death Experience in Medieval and Modern Times*, Oxford University Press, 1987

Zavikukhina, M. P., in Barkova

Index

238